FUTURE OF LAND WARFARE

Beyond the Horizon

FUTURE OF LAND WARFARE

Beyond the Horizon

Editor

Maj Gen (Dr.) P K Chakravorty

Centre for Land Warfare Studies

PENTAGON PRESS LLP

The Centre for Land Warfare Studies (CLAWS), New Delhi, is an autonomous think tank dealing with contemporary issues of national security and conceptual aspects of land warfare, including conventional and sub-conventional conflicts and terrorism. CLAWS conducts research that is futuristic in outlook and policy-oriented in approach.

CLAWS Vision: To establish as a leading Centre of Excellence, Research and Studies on Military Strategy & Doctrine, Land Warfare, Regional & National Security, Military Technology and Human Resource.

Centre for Land Warfare Studies
RPSO Complex, Parade Road, Delhi Cantt, New Delhi-110010
Phone: 011-25691308 • Fax: 011-25692347
email: landwarfare@gmail.com • website: www.claws.in

First Edition 2020

ISBN 978-81-942837-4-4

Published by
PENTAGON PRESS LLP
206, Peacock Lane, Shahpur Jat,
New Delhi-110049
Phones: 011-64706243, 26491568
Telefax: 011-26490600
email: rajan@pentagonpress.in
website: www.pentagon-press.com

Printed at Aegean Offset Printers, Greater Noida, U.P.

DEDICATED TO
ALL THE BOOTS ON GROUND

CONTENTS

FOREWORD

India is a sub-continent with vast land borders, coastline, island territories and exclusive economic zone (EEZ), varied terrains, and operational environments. These conditions require a comprehensive plan to effectively protect India's territorial integrity. Having commanded my regiment in Rajouri (Jammu and Kashmir) and Jodhpur, followed by an infantry brigade in Uri (Baramulla sector), mountain division in Kargil and corps in Leh-Ladakh region, I realised the enormity of the challenges and the tasks involved. It becomes even more complex, as the line of control (LoC), and the actual ground position line (AGPL) in Siachen sector, the line that delineates the de facto border between India and Pakistan, is neither demarcated on the ground nor does it really follow any well-defined geographical features. A near similar situation exists along the line of actual control (LAC) with China, where both countries have different perceptions about the alignment of the LAC on the ground. Thus, the operational environment is unique, both along the LoC cum AGPL and the LAC. During my tenures of command, these unsettled borders remained operationally active, albeit with different intensities. It requires utmost vigil to monitor all activities along and beyond the borders, as also maintain situational awareness up to the appropriate levels. Therefore, given India's unsettled borders with two of its neighbours, Pakistan and China, and the emerging challenges to national security in the Indian Ocean region (IOR), the book is primarily Indian sub-continent centric.

The book looks 'beyond the horizon,' at different geographical areas and terrains, the revolutionary changes in technology, the changes in character of conflicts, employment of myriad forces, threats and challenges to national security, different operational scenarios, and the way forward for the next 10-15 years. It also highlights the significance of air, sea, cyber and space domains in the future conflicts. With the introduction of disruptive technologies, revolution in communications and lethal autonomous weapon systems, and the asymmetric threats, the emerging geo-political and regional security environment has been in a state of flux. Resultantly, with the emerging technologies, the future operating environment would be complex, ambiguous, and uncertain.

Land has been the focus of mankind, be it in the continental landmass, islands or search for habitable lands in outer space. In the book *'Military Strategy: A General Theory of Power Control'*, Rear Admiral Joseph C. Wylie states that despite whatever effort there may be to prevent it, there may be a War. While crystal gazing into the future, we logically inferred that the Centre for Land Warfare Studies (CLAWS) should undertake a seminal research on the "Future of Land Warfare," with primary focus on the Indian subcontinent.

Based on the discussions with the Editor and the Faculty, we decided to include the key areas such as Janapada (territory), challenges to national security, role of emerging technologies and employment of forces in different operational environments. 'Janapada' is a multi-dimensional concept, which has become the prime reason for war and the chief component of state's warfare strategy. Thereafter, the book deals with the national security challenges followed by the application of emerging technologies and information warfare. In addition, it brings forth interesting aspects of manoeuvre warfare, fire power, special forces, airborne operations, transformation of Indian Armed Forces and the impact of theatre commands of the People's Liberation Army of China on India. Logistics remains the most important part of the book, as it provides the edifice for conduct of all operations.

It was felt that each chapter needed an expert, and an editor who could select the authors, and stitch the entire book. Maj Gen (Dr.) PK Chakravorty, the Editor, selected a composite team of professionally competent co-authors. I must say to the credit of the Editor that he held detailed discussions with the Faculty and the co-authors to ensure that important aspects of land warfare are covered comprehensively. Considering the difficulty of crystal gazing the strategic environment far beyond the horizon, it was also decided that the book should aim at the envisaged scenario in the subcontinent upto 2035.

With changing dynamics, both the nature and character of war have been evolving. Given the multiple domain character of war, we remain in a gray zone which keeps the armed forces on its toes with little warning period for mobilisation. Due to the unsettled territorial and boundary disputes with our adversaries for the past seven decades, and the categorical statements by the respective leaders 'regarding no loss of territory', the probability of conventional conflicts, supported by the technological advances and hybrid instruments, will continue to play a predominant role in the Indian subcontinent. In addition, with large-scale intra-state conflicts and humanitarian and relief operations, land warfare will remain the dominant element in the subcontinent.

Although a number of security review committees have been formed, their recommendations have been implemented in parts, which actually tantamount to incremental and cosmetic changes. Having visualised the conflicts of the future, it is important to take proactive steps to transform our armed forces and integrate them, so that all available resources can be applied synergistically during the short window of opportunity in an intense and short duration conflict.

On balance, the main takeaways of the book are: the need to formulate a comprehensive national security strategy (CNSS), and adopt a mission-oriented approach to resolve our ongoing internal armed conflicts. Simultaneously, we should focus on developing Comprehensive National Power (CNP), and progressively transforming our entire defence setup, including defence industrial base, to meet the threats and challenges 'beyond the horizon'. National security should not be held hostage to preservation of turfs or attempting to reach a consensus. Matters like national security require tough calls to be made, and implementation ensured in a time-bound manner, failing which we will be found wanting in the conflicts of the future.

It is a thought-provoking book, which would be useful for the policy makers, practitioners, strategic community, training establishments, the three services and also the civilian and military personnel alike. Finally, I would like to compliment the Editor and his team of authors for the comprehensive compilation of the book.

November 2019

Lt Gen (Dr.) VK Ahluwalia (Retd)
Director, CLAWS
(Former Army Commander, Central Command)
(Former Member, Armed Forces Tribunal)

PREFACE

My interest in Land Warfare started at the National Defence Academy. Khadakvasla, when Mr Bhandari who was the Dean of Social Studies introduced us to the subject of Military History. One was fascinated by the subject and won the Book Prize for the same. Interest grew as one was posted in the North East, Jammu and Kashmir and also along the international borders in Punjab and Rajasthan. However, the inflection points came during a Course in Sweden in 1987 and my posting as the Defence Attaché to Vietnam in 1996 with accreditation to Cambodia, Laos and Vietnam. While in Sweden I learnt of Swedish offensives against Russia in the 18th century, followed by Napoleon's offensive in early 19th century, and the German offensives in both the World Wars during the 20th century. What makes the Russian landmass so attractive? The answer is obvious. Its geostrategic location and its richness in natural resources. Similarly, Vietnam's geostrategic location and its rich countryside have resulted in conflicts with China, France and United States. Currently, Vietnam is disputing Chinese claims in the South China Sea.

It was indeed fortunate that the Director of CLAWS, Lt Gen VK Ahluwalia, gave me the responsibility of becoming the Editor of the book. It was an honour. With his guidance, I selected the chapters and co-authors. Like a good leader, he has written an excellent chapter and jointly contributed to the epilogue. I am grateful to the Director for giving me full freedom in selecting our co-authors. They are Generals Rakesh Sharma, Rakesh Chadha, Balbir Singh, Bhupesh Jain; Colonels Rajeev Kapoor, Puneet Doval, Anuraag Rawat, Ranjan Prabhu, Associate Fellow Amrita Jash and Research Intern Kritika Punia. The authors including the Director were a team of 12, who brainstormed the issues and prepared seminal Chapters. These chapters are worth their weight in gold and point to areas critical for Future Land Warfare.

I must thank Director, CLAWS, for his support, Shreya Das Barman for publishing the book and Raghunandan MC for giving us a nice cover and other staff members of CLAWS. The book is stimulating and crystal gazes logically into the future. I am confident that the book will stir the minds of all readers.

November 2019

Maj Gen (Dr.) P K Chakravorty (Retd)
Editor

PROLOGUE

Major General (Dr.) P K Chakravorty

"Victorious warriors win first and then go to war, while defeated warriors go to war and then seek to win."[1]

– Sun Tzu

Significance of Land

Land has been the most significant component of a human being's life. Existence has resulted in search of Land in the Oceans, across the Oceans and currently in Outer Space. The more powerful the human being the more is his desire to possess land. Power of a nation is determined by its capability to influence large tracts of land all across the Globe. In a protectionist mode, the power is measured in permitting entry to those whom you allow on land. Former President Bill Clinton after reading the Book, "The Social Conquest of Earth", by Edward Wilson stated that human beings and ants were the most cooperative living items in the globe. Both existed on Land and yearned for the same.[2] Land is the most precious possession of humans and provides him life and its vicissitudes.

Land Warfare

Human beings are social animals. Despite the best intentions humans carry animal instincts which are subsumed by social values—Power, Autonomy and Influence are aspects which play an important role with human beings. This has been analysed in detail in a paper by Julie Beck.[3] Often there is a tendency to become powerful to protect oneself from evil designs. The same is applicable to nations. There are issues which exist between nations. Often they are resolved amicably. However, there are occasions when there are disputes which are difficult to resolve. This often leads to conflicts. War is a state of armed conflict between states, governments, societies and non-state actors. Land is an important possession and many wars have been fought for land and its resources. Wars take various forms from conventional to sub-conventional and hybrid. The book primarily focuses on Wars on Land termed as Land Warfare. This includes the combat on land with weapons and surveillance devices being launched from land, sea, under sea, air and outer space. This would also include cyberspace and application of Artificial Intelligence.

Essential Aspects

The book deals with the Future of Land Warfare in the Indian subcontinent. To predict the future is extremely difficult particularly in the field of Warfare. This is due to the fact that wars are impacted by Doctrine, Technology and People. Further the introduction of nuclear weapons has made war less frequent and reduced the duration. There are trends which keep changing with the passage of time. Conflicts in the 21st century are short and swift with a combination of effects. Further aspirations of leaders often point towards different military objectives. In such a scenario we could plan at best for a decade and maybe visualise for about 15 years.

By and large, wars of the future would be, conventional, hybrid and would be interstate or with non-state actors. The causes could be territorial or related to historical differences, ideological biases, economic disparity, security and water distribution. Further issues could exacerbate due to impact of climate change, higher rate of population growth of minorities and sectarian or ethnic extremism.

Initiators

It is necessary to examine what could initiate future conflicts. These are as elucidated below:

- **Demography.** Demography is the study of both quantitative and qualitative aspects of human population. The quantitative aspects include composition, density, distribution, growth, movement, size and structure of the population. Qualitative aspects are the sociological factors such as education, quality, crime, development, diet, nutrition, race, social class, wealth and well-being.[4] As per RAND Corporation current demographic trends will affect the nature and conduct of future armed conflicts by influencing the physical environment of future conflicts and by creating new strategic instruments of conflict. Pertinent aspects are appended below:

- Enhanced urban content of future conflicts.
- Ethnic Diasporas and Renewable resources.
- New Metrics of Combat Effectiveness Quality vis-à-vis Quantity.
- Flow of migrants and refugees across international borders.
- Influence of demography on domestic politics leading to violence.
- Ecological marginalisation which puts pressure on scarce natural resources.[5]

- **Energy.** Energy can be the primary cause and objective in a conflict.[6] Energy was possibly the major reason for the Second Gulf War. It is widely recognised that the presence of some fossil fuels and their routes of transportation can affect the risk of conflicts. Future conflicts could be triggered by Energy. Recent militarization of the South China Sea by China and other South East nations is due to the likelihood of hydrocarbons in the region.
- **Religious Extremism.** Religious violence is undergoing a revival.[7] This could be a major reason for Future Wars. During the last 10 years there has been a stupendous increase in religious intolerance leading to violence. In the Middle East there is a global jihad between the Shias and the Sunnis. In Myanmar the Rohingyas are having insurmountable problems with the Buddhists and between Christians and Muslims in Africa. In 2018 more than a quarter of the globe experienced high incidence of hostilities which was as a result of religious hatred. Religious harmony can only survive once leaders tolerate the views of divergent groups which in the present environment as also in the visualised future would be extremely difficult.
- The United Nations and the International Court of Justice have limited value. Further the United States, China and Russia have been flouting global rules and acting unilaterally.

Characteristics of Wars

The Nature and Character of War will both change. Apart from struggle between hostile, independent and irreconcilable wills, Wars based on Artificial Intelligence, Cyber, Space and Environment would significantly impact the nature of War. The character of land wars would grow even more convoluted from Information Warfare to multi-domain warfares. Non-state actors like Hezbollah, Daesh, Hamas and Al-Qaida would declare hostilities and care less for the nation states lending them support. Artificial Intelligence along with Quantum Communications would enable Robots to participate in combat.

Technology would make issues extremely complex. There would be weapons based on computers which would cause cyclones, earthquakes and volcanic eruptions. These would make wars extremely difficult to fight and win due to large-scale destruction. Analysts have to apply their ingenuity to deal with these aspects in the future.

Future Wars and Battle Space

The Future Wars are likely to follow three types. It could be Overt, Covert and finally Out Sourced. The future battle space as visualised in the next 15 years would have characteristics which would make it non-linear in time and space. Unlike Wars of the past they would be swift and would be based on Speed. Targets would need to be precisely engaged to avoid Collateral Damage. Operations would demand Jointness between the three Services. Further they would be continuous with no pauses. They could be termed as 24x7 operations. In these operations connectivity would play an important part and communications would be available to soldiers, commanders and autonomous weapon systems and vehicles. There would be a need for synergy between Air, Sea, and Outer Space while undertaking Land Warfare. Finally Perception Management becomes extremely important as this alone would lead to an effective reorganisation of people.

Applicability to India

Future Wars in the Indian subcontinent would shift from Conventional to Hybrid Wars. It would be a conflict involving our Northern and Western adversary as also counter insurgency operations in J&K as also North East. The window for conventional operations under a nuclear over hang is extremely small and there is a need for forces with precision weapons which can undertake operations with speed and alacrity. Information Warfare would be extremely important. Further there is a need to develop indigenous technology to manufacture weapons and equipment needed for Land Warfare.

The chapters that follow deal with aspects pertaining to Territory, the Future of Land Warfare, Conflicts, and Security Challenges. The other chapters pertain to the Need to revamp our Forces, Information Warfare, Airborne Operations and the Technological Aspects. There are a few chapters on kinetic aspects dealing with Manoeuvre, Firepower, the Impact of Theatre Commands of People' s Liberation Army and Logistics. Overall the book provides a holistic look at the subtleties of Land Warfare.

NOTES

1 "Sun Tzu Quotes- Brainy Quote", www.brainyquote.com, Accessed on 29 July 2019.

2 Edward Wilson, "The Social Conquest of Earth", Liveright, ISBN-13: 978-0871403636, www.amazon.com. Accessed on 29 July 2019.

3 Julie Beck, "People want power because they want Autonomy", The Atlantic Magazine, www.theatlantic.com, Accessed on 30 July 2019.

4 Business Dictionary, "Demography", www.businessdictionary.com. Accessed on 2 August 2019.

5 Rand Corporation, "The Security Implications of Demographic Factors", www.rand.org, 2014. Accessed on 2 August 2019.

6 Mansson Andre, "Energy, Conflict and War", Lund University, www.portal.research.lu.se, Accessed on 2 August 2019.

7 Robert Muggah, "Religious Violence is on the Rise", www.weforum.org. Accessed on 2 August 2019.

1

Janapada: Territory and its Importance in Indian Warfare

Kritika Punia

ABSTRACT

Janapada = jana (people) + pada (where they put their feet). In simple terms territory or land.

'Janapada' or territory is a multidimensional concept. In the context of India, we see a gradual evolution of territory from a socio-economic entity to a political symbol of state. It evolved from Jana (group of people) to janapadas (people in a defined territory) to the modern Indian state. These economic-sociopolitical values attached to territory made it the prime reason for war and the chief component of state warfare strategy.

Territory has become integral to nationalist discourse for its symbolic role in building national identity. It defines borders, fixes identity and delineates sovereignty.[1]

> *Territory divides. Us from them.*
> *And it unites. By forging bonds of oneness.*

The paper has been divided into the following parts:

- *Territory as a dynamic notion*
- *Importance of Janapada or territory in warfare*
- *Relevance of land warriors or foot soldiers in warfare*

While looking at these three dimensions an attempt has been made to contextualise different facets of warfare and understand their interrelationships. Specific attention has been paid to locate the extent and form in which 'Janapada' and foot soldiers were, and continue to be, essential to Indian warfare. Ideas have been drawn from the work of Kautilya, the Arthashastra, *and have been looked at from the lens of the 21*st *century.*

DYNAMIC WAY OF LOOKING AT TERRITORY

Territorial aspect of the State

The evolution of the idea of the state was a gradual process. Over time it came to acquire the characteristics of a defined set of boundary, citizens that paid taxes and were governed by the law of the land, a political class for governance and a military for its defence.

These characteristics became central to the 17th century Westphalia model of nation state. It considered territory (janapada), in addition to its people (Jana), as an essential defining feature of the modern state. The 19th century era of globalisation introduced certain changes in this understanding. Globalisation diluted the 'territorial aspect of state' by making borders fluid. According to Sasmita Mohanty it pushed the world towards a borderless and de-territorialised world.[2] A significant step in this direction was made by the European states which came together to form the European Union with flexible border regulations.

However it would be wrong to assume that the concept of a 'well-defined and demarcated territorial space' has become irrelevant in the era of Globalisation. Borders still continue to be a defining marker of the modern state. In addition, they should be seen through a new lens. Borders need to be conceptualised as transformative processes. Those that were once perceived as fixed physical lines that divided geographical spaces have evolved (Diener and Hagen, 2009). Borders have become workable.

To illustrate this point we can look at the 2016 and 2019 surgical strike conducted by the Indian Army. These strikes raised several questions. Did India violate Pakistan's sovereignty by crossing the border? Are borders sacrosanct? During the 2016 operation the Indian Army crossed the Line of Control (LoC) and not the International Border (sanctioned by UN conventions). During the 2019 operations, again the LoC was crossed. India defended its decision by calling it a limited strike against terrorist outfits that threatened India's national sovereignty. Internationally it was projected as a response to the attack on India's territorial integrity—the Uri attack and the Pulwama terror attack. Thus borders are not unalterable. They can be worked, fashioned, or manipulated to serve national interest.

Territory in the Psychological Domain

While the territorial borders and an organised army provide a physical form to the state, the psychological form is provided by the emotional connect of the people with their land.

This psychological connect is perfectly captured in the word 'chetana' or shared consciousness. It is a common thread of sentimental values attached to one's 'motherland' that binds the people together. In ancient India such sentimental connections existed with one's village at the micro level and with one's empire at the macro level. In modern times it is reflected in the notion of nationalism, a sense of affinity with fellow citizens and pride in symbols of one's nation. It is a positive reinforcement that is built over time. The evolution of Modern Indian nation as a unified whole was the result of a long-drawn process of assimilation, consolidation and integration spread over centuries. Some of these nation-building processes included political integration under the rule of Mauryas, Guptas, Mughals and colonial rule of the British. This provided territorial and political cohesion. Cultural cohesion was provided by Sufi and Bhakti movements, the socio-religious reform movements and the Indian national movement. The resultant model of nation state with its 'unity in diversity' was different from the imposed linear unity of the Westphalia model of nation state.

The idea of a 'nation' in the psychological domain is fluid. There are pockets of territory and sections of people where reach of state is not absolute. These include the tribes in Andaman and Nicobar islands, insurgency affected regions of North-Eastern India and the red corridor. Thus essence of territory goes beyond the physical or geographical domain to the psychological domain. Mere vertical and horizontal possession of territory is not sufficient. Having influence is equally important.

Sometimes a small piece of land can help a nation expand its sphere of influence. For example, Andaman and Nicobar islands cover a small area of 8,249 square km (Encyclopedia Britannica) but have huge security connotations.[3] It can help India shape the Indian ocean region dynamics in terms of surveillance, maintaining open channels of communication, sustainable resource extraction, etc. Command over the area can help India play an effective role during Humanitarian Assistance and Disaster Relief (HADR), maritime safety and security operations. The naval and air bases on these islands are important from defence perspective. They can help in fulfilment of India's regional aspirations and provide strategic depth to counter increasing Chinese presence.

Beyond the Land Frontier

The word janapada or territory usually invokes the image of land frontier. But today it is possible for a state to target areas across the border without crossing it. This may be done by using drones or surface to air (SAM) missiles etc. An Electro Magnetic Pulse (EMP) weapon can be used to disable enemy aircraft avionics or jam its GPS.

Do these acts violate a nation's sovereign territory? We need to view territory as a multidimensional concept. Today a nation's territory encompasses in addition to land frontiers, the frontiers of air and maritime. It extends to the realm of territorial water, exclusive economic zone and air space. If we look at territory in this dynamic way, violation of space is violation of a nation's territorial sovereignty.

This dynamic way of looking at territory is especially important for India given the emerging threats from the water frontier. Indian Ocean Region has emerged as a theatre for strategic competition. India's coastal security strategy needs to focus on pushing the defensive perimeter further away from the coast into the seas. This can be done by creating national maritime domain awareness (NMDA) grid with sea-based sensors and land based missiles. For situations of escalated confrontation an Anti-Access/Area Denial (A2/AD) strategy needs to be formulated. India's focus should be on development of area-denial weapons that operate on human command. Such systems can be based on combination of either explosives, pre-targeted artillery shelling or smart guns with remote sensing equipment, having some level of Identification, friend or foe (IFF) capability.

However, land remains central to the notion of territory. A nation's air space or territorial waters is determined on the basis of its land border. National air space is the space above one's land; maritime territory is area beyond the mainland/coast.

Territorial Fixation

Threat of possible balkanisation has resulted in 'territory' minded approach in Indian national discourse. This can be attributed to a violent past (Partition 1947) and internal threats posed by separatist forces. Focus on territorial integrity is essential for nation's survival. However one needs to avoid excessive territorial fixation. In the military discourse emphasis remains on 'not losing even an inch of territory'. A limited loss of territory in one sector is considered acceptable if it provides a greater strategic advantage somewhere else.

In the political realm there is a more practical and flexible approach with regard to territory. There have been instances where trading or returning territory helped further national interest. With Shimla Agreement 1972, India returned the territory captured on the western front during 1971 war as a good will gesture. Despite ongoing India-Pakistan border disputes, opening up of Kartarpur corridor provides hope for improved relations. Land boundary agreement (LBA) between India and Bangladesh resulted in exchange of conclaves. In the process India gave more territory than it received. The exchange was undertaken keeping in mind some pragmatic issues such as access to the conclaves, rights of the occupants, administrative convenience. It further helped to foster ties of friendship between the two countries. An overtly emotional way of looking at this deal as 'resulting in loss of territory' was avoided. The 'Jana-chetana' or shared consciousness of the masses was managed and directed. Popular perception was shaped to check hyper nationalist tendencies.

Thus, territorial borders should be seen for their potential to constitute bridges and points of contact as much as they have traditionally constituted barriers to movement and communication (Newman, David).

Changing Attitudes and Solving Indo-China Border Dispute

'Diplomacy is the art of promoting self-interest without the need to resort to conflict.'

Warriors in the past have traded land for personal benefits. Geopolitics is the art of 'giving and taking' based on mutual interest. Janapada is an asset, and like any other asset should be traded if it provides political-economic-strategic mileage. To some we provide access (to territory) while to others we deny.

This flexible way of looking at territory may prove to be an essential step in solving India-China border dispute. We have to consider the possibility of a 'land exchange' deal to settle dispute peacefully based on mutual benefit. Territory is just one limb of the state and thus should not be the only criteria to measure patriotism or loyalty towards one's country.

China has put forward the idea of a land swap several times in the past. In 1960s China proposed swapping of claims. It indicated possible acceptance of the McMahon Line in the east in exchange for India accepting

China's claim on Aksai Chin. In 1980s China demanded Indian concessions in the east, the Tawang tract, for favourable treatment elsewhere.[4] However, India clearly rejected China's land swap proposal concerning Tawang region. India has adopted a firm stand stating that Tawang is an integral part of Arunachal Pradesh.

A land swap initiative cannot move forward without mutual consent of both countries. India and China need to be willing to have an open discussion about each other's expectations and apprehensions. They may start by adopting this model to solve border dispute in minor sectors or small stretches. Continued attempts at confidence building measures (CBMs) can also help in maintaining peace and stability along the line of actual control. Some such initiatives have taken the form of joint efforts at combating arms smuggling and disaster management. Border haats, on lines of Indo-Bangladesh haats, can be effective mechanism for strengthening people to people contact. They can help make Indo-China border more open, connected and flexible. Border Defence Cooperation Agreement (BDCA), another CBM, is an example of sincere efforts by both sides to initiate dialogue. It is based on the principle of mutual and equal security. Under this agreement both sides agreed to exercise maximum self-restraint in case the two sides come to a face-to-face in disputed territory. However, BDCA is yet to provide promising results.

Another important prerequisite for a successful Indo-China land swap agreement is forging *Jana-chetana*. People of both countries need to be willing to accept and actively support such initiatives of settling borders. Jana and jana-chetana are intrinsically tied to janapada. Without their involvement, a land swap agreement or exchange of janapada would be ineffective.

Figure 1.1 shows the major areas of border dispute between India and China. There are around 20 places in the Western, Middle and Eastern sector where their claims overlap. Some of these areas are Trig Heights, Depsang bulge, Pangong Tso, Demchok, Chumur in eastern Ladakh, and Namka Chu, Sumdrong Chu, Long Ju, Dichu in Arunachal Pradesh, and Kaurik, Shipki La, Barahoti in the central sector.[5]

Disputed border continues to remain a core issue between the two countries. There have been several confrontations along the Indo-China border including skirmishes at Depsang (2013), Chumur (2014), Doklam (2017). Such disputes have time and again rendered relationship-building

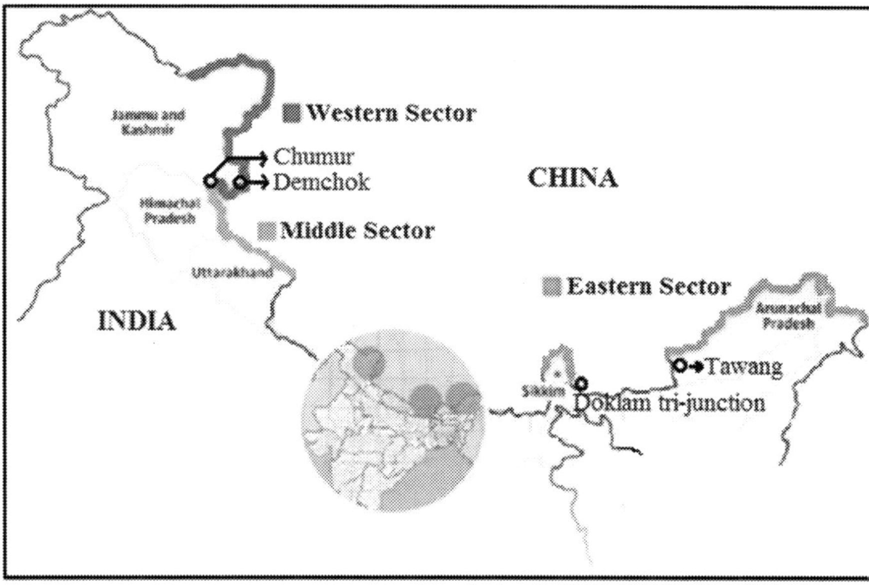

Figure 1.1: Line of Actual Control (LAC) Marking the India-China Border

efforts ineffectual. Solving Indo-China border issue is an essential prerequisite for building good relationship in the future.

IMPORTANCE OF JANAPADA (TERRITORY) IN WARFARE

This section seeks to examine the relevance of territory in India's warfare. Territory constitutes an essential element of India's defence and offence strategy. Some aspects of application of territory to military operations have fundamentally remained the same over centuries. For example, considerations such as controlling the higher ground during war, ensuring uninterrupted supply chain, etc.

Looking at the other side of the coin, one agrees that warfare has changed over time. Factors other than territory have become essential components of today's warfare. With changing domains of war, India needs a dynamic warfare strategy.

War as Fundamental Function of State

Looking at present day international scenario, territory continues to be an important source of conflict and war. This is evident from China's efforts at extending its strategic periphery by building artificial islands.

In fact China's Belt and Road Initiative (BRI) can be viewed as a key part of China's territorial empire building. Further the Kashmir conflict between India and Pakistan is over land and its association with national consciousness. Russia's annexation of Crimea was not only because of economic significance of port of Sevastopol. It was also the psychological aspect of territorial expansion, i.e. building a Russian empire. International borders continue to be redrawn by force. For the state to thrive, territorial expansion continues to be important. War, in all its forms and manifestations, continue to be the instrument for such expansion.

Territory is an integral aspect of India's defence strategy. It was important in the past as well. Kautilya in his work Arthashastra mentions different defensive fortifications.[6] These included water fortification (audaka), forest fortification (vanadurga), mountainous fortification (parvata). Modern-day fortifications and defences include air defence systems, critical infrastructure protection unit, cyber security and so on. Waterway (moat) was used as a defence barrier in the past. Today the Indira Gandhi canal acts as a water boundary and a line of defence on Indo-Pakistan border. Kautilya paid specific attention to the strategic location of the capital city, *sthaniya*. Even today strategic location of the capital continues to remain important, both in terms of connectivity and defence strategy.

The importance of strategic location of a piece of territory and its significance in warfare can be better understood by undertaking the case study of Eastern India.

Eastern India comprises present-day states of West Bengal, Bihar, Jharkhand and Odisha. It extends further east to include the state of Sikkim and the seven sisters (Arunachal Pradesh, Assam, Manipur, Meghalaya, Mizoram, Nagaland and Tripura).

This region provides connectivity with Nepal, Bhutan, Myanmar, Bangladesh and with East Asia through Bay of Bengal. It has provided opportunity for defence cooperation and confidence building through military diplomacy. Combined exercise such as Exercise Sampriti (India and Bangladesh), Exercise Maitree (India and Thailand) and cooperation through regional forums like Bay of Bengal Initiative for Multi-Sectoral Technical and Economic Cooperation (BIMSTEC) are some examples. It has also been a source of several maritime disputes especially between India and Bangladesh. In 2014 the Permanent Court of Arbitration (PCA) ruled in favour of Bangladesh, awarding it a major area of disputed territory in the Bay of Bengal.[7] It resulted in expansion of Bangladesh's territorial sea and exclusive economic zone. India demonstrated its maturity by accepting the ruling.

An important area in this region from military perspective is the Siliguri Corridor. It is also called the chicken's neck of India. This region was central during the Indo-China war of 1962 and Indo-Pakistan war of 1971. This corridor will continue to be militarily significant during Indo-China conflict in the future as well. The rail and road networks passing through this 22 km corridor feed the primary Indian military formations located in the North East. Current Chinese road projects in the Doklam plateau could help China strangle the corridor and cut off the North East from the rest of India during conflict. This would also lead to isolation of crucial military formations, cutting off supplies and reinforcements to them. This shows the continued significance of territory in India's warfare strategy. Land warfare will continue to remain an essential component of defending such strategic sections of territory.

Methodology of Warfare

Kautilya provides the modern military strategist a time-tested model of diplomacy and war.[8] Kautilya's 'Mandala' theory talks about circle of states: *Ari* (Enemies), *Mitra* (Friends), *Madhyama* (Mediators) and *Udasina* (Neutrals). This approach requires an in-depth understanding of the position of the state vis-à-vis its neighbours. Territory is an essential aspect of this understanding. At the same time he understood that no alliance was permanent. Today, the saying in international relations: 'there are no permanent friends or permanent enemies, only permanent interests' reflects this pragmatism. Alliances and counter alliances change with changing national interest and global dynamics.

Based on the complex connections between major players (or nations), Kautilya recommends different courses of action: *Saam* (conciliation/ Treaty), *daam* (reward/exchange for mutual benefit), *dand* (force), *Bhed* (dissension). The path of deterrence or engagement, of alliance or counter alliance to be used when dealing with friends or potential adversaries.

The following table (Table 1.2) displays the possible application of this theory in the 21st century.

Table 1.2: Application of Kautilya's ideas in modern times in India

Saam (Alliance and treaties)	Daam (Exchange of territory)
Treaty of Tashkent 1966 between India and Pakistan. Confidence Building Measures (CBMs), Border Defence Cooperation Agreement (BDCA) between India and China.	2015 Land Boundary Agreement (LBA) between India and Bangladesh which fostered better relations between the two nations.
Dand (War, retaliation)	**Bhed** (Treason, bribery, immoral means)
India-Pakistan war of 1971 resulting in the independence of Bangladesh. Surgical strike (2016 and 2019) conducted by Indian armed forces against militant launch pads across Indo-Pakistan border.	In 1999 Pakistan Army soldiers disguised as local militants captured peaks in Kargil sector, India. Pakistan refused to acknowledge involvement of their army. Low-intensity conflict in the western sector by Pakistan Army. Example: Uri attack (2016), Pulwama attack (2019)

In India's current strategy of war and policy of diplomacy, territory remains relevant. Land-based warfare comprises an essential aspect of conventional war fighting strategy.

However, given the multi-faceted security challenges that India faces today, a linear defence strategy may not suffice. Excessive focus on land warfare may result in neglect of other emerging domains of warfare. While we are looking at territory in a dynamic way we also need to look at its defence in a dynamic way. Attrition based force on force strategies needs to be reconsidered and reworked.

Changing Arena or Battle Field

Outer space is going to be an important battlefield in the future. Defence of this arena would require not only space weapons but also launch pads on earth, moon, manmade rocket launch platforms. Thus, surface warfare will continue to be important. At the same time space assets and weapons would play a crucial role in defence of land and water territory.

For example, recently ISRO launched India's first electronic surveillance satellite—EMISAT. This will add another dimension to current land and aircraft-based electronic intelligence (ELINT). Space-based ELINT is crucial as it will add teeth to situational awareness of armed forces. The EMISAT is capable of providing location and other information about the hostile enemy radars placed at Indian borders.[9]

The reason for future space wars will continue to be land centric. These may include: expanding ones territory or sphere of influence to space, search for new land for settlement or for resource extraction. Man's mission to colonise Mars and the Moon reflects this land centricity. Future wars whether on earth or interplanetary war or space wars would still be fought for territory.

Role of Territory in 21st Century Hybrid War

It is said that in 21st century, territory will have a limited role to play in warfare. War is going to be fought not on front lines but in the domain of cyberspace, information realm and psychological domain. For instance, China is looking at system confrontation and system destruction strategy as the modern mode of warfare. This has led some to argue that China is not going to be specifically focusing on territorial gain or territorial competition. However, China's territorial disputes with its neighbours reveal a territory-centric approach towards projecting state power. For example, China's dispute with Japan and South-East Asian nations over Senkaku/Diaoyu Islands and Spratly islands respectively. Recent skirmishes with India at Doklam and continued Chinese claim over Tawang prove the same.

Any successful warfare strategy focuses on two aspects: capacity and strength of oneself and that of the opponent. In the field of military technology development India is an emerging nation. It has not yet reached the sophisticated level of advanced digital integration achieved by some Western countries. System disruption warfare techniques might not prove to be as successful against India as against technologically advanced developed nations. China's engagement with India in the coming decade is likely to be more platform centric rather than merely network centric.

Nonetheless the importance of such modern techniques of warfare cannot be ignored. Such attacks have the capacity of crippling India's critical energy, banking and financial infrastructure.[10] Quantum of financial loss and damage of national prestige would be unimaginable in such a scenario. India needs to accordingly develop suitable command and control structures and doctrinal concepts.

Ground work has already been laid in this arena. National Critical Information Infrastructure Protection Centre (NCIIPC) was established in 2014 to ensure safe, secure and resilient information infrastructure for critical sector of the nation. In 2018, the Government of India (GOI) decided to set up three new agencies—the Defence Cyber Agency, Defence Space Agency and the Special Operations Division—to address the new-age challenges to national security. Naresh Chandra Committee had gone a step further by recommending creation of separate joint commands to deal with such challenges.[11] Attempts are being made to integrate multiple intelligence models. Some of these include: Human Intelligence (HUMINT), Social Intelligence (SOCINT), Financial Intelligence (FININT), Technical Intelligence (TECHINT), Signals Intelligence (SIGINT), Geospatial Intelligence (GEOINT). This initiative will help provide a comprehensive approach to national security.

IMPORTANCE OF FOOT SOLDIERS

Shaurya (heroism) was and continues to be a greatly valued virtue in Indian culture. In the past hero stones were erected to celebrate valour of the warrior who had the honour of dying on the battlefield.[12] In today's context, India Gate and National War Memorial can be seen as modern hero stones to commemorate the sacrifice of thousands of martyrs.

Declining role of Foot Soldiers

The centricity of foot soldier or infantry in today's military discourse has become an issue of heated debate in the last decade. Weapons of Mass Destruction (WMD) have enabled forces to neutralise target area from a distance. The infantry then walks over and establishes command over the region. This has reduced the quantum of force required to physically capture a territory.

There have been suggestions for rightsising the Indian army, restructuring and streamlining the infantry, reaching an ideal tooth to tail ratio. This will help achieve a cohesive fighting force. In addition structural changes need to be undertaken. This will require development of cross spectrum capability with specific focus on nuclear, cyber, conventional and counter sub-conventional. Shortfalls in core capabilities also need to be eliminated.

While such changes are essential for achieving a cohesive fighting force, the infantry continues to be the building blocks of India's defence and offence capability. They might not be, or remain in the near future, the central component of warfare but they will always be an essential component. This has been elaborated in the following sections.

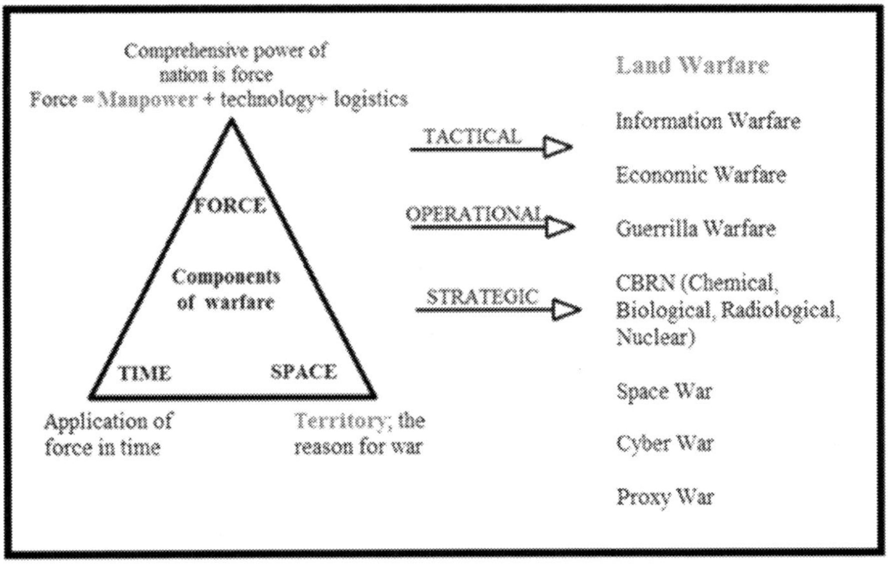

Figure 1.2: Components of Warfare

Figure 1.2 displays three major components of a nations war machinery: space, time and force. Space is the Janapada or territory which is one of the main reasons for war. Timely application of force is crucial to win the space or to defend it. Force is the combination of manpower, technology and logistics. The ultimate aim is destruction of enemy's forces. As long as the force component of the enemy remains, we need our own forces for defence and offence. Foot soldiers are an essential component of this force.

In 2014, India's Prime Minister laid out his vision for the armed forces in his address to a combined commanders' conference. "Full-scale wars may become rare, but force will remain an instrument of deterrence and influencing behavior."[13]

India is Largely a Land-based Power and a Land-based Force

The major bone of contention that India has with Pakistan and China is the border dispute. In the areas of previous conflict and wars, the Northern, North-western, North-eastern sectors, there was limited scope of deployment of air force and navy. The terrain, weather and inter-valley movement capability were the deciding factors. Further, the technicality of 'not crossing the Line of Control (LOC) LOC' limited the role of Air

Force during Indo-China war of 1962. In such situations Air Force played a crucial role in swift attack and large-scale damage but ground troops were needed to block, to attack and capture, and to hold ground.

Today USA is fighting majority of its battles overseas where it has limited land bases. This results in a more robust role for its navy and air force. However, for India, land warfare and foot soldiers will continue to remain essential to its military strategy. For example, Kargil War reinforced the importance of continuous presence of troops to hold post and check infiltration. During the winter months of 1998–99 Pakistani troops infiltrated several kilometer into the Indian territory in Kargil sector of J&K. They were able to do so because Indian troops stationed at the heights had withdrawn during the winter months given the inhospitable climate. In order to recapture the lost territory Air Force played a crucial role. They destroyed Pakistani bunkers and supported the ground troops. However this lost territory was not considered reclaimed till the time it was physically captured by the Indian Army.

It is essential to put ones feet on ground, *one's pada*, to proclaim it as one's territory, *one's janapada.*

Dynamic Way of Looking at Soldiers

Changing concept of warfare demands a fresh perspective of looking at warriors. Today's challenges are multifaceted and India requires specialised forces to deal with non-conventional warfare. Today's soldier needs to be equipped with latest intelligence and weapons, trained in guerrilla tactics and cyber counter-intelligence. This requires a new role for the soldier but the soldier remains important.

India needs a rapid response force backed by latest technology and intelligence to respond to security challenges in a swift manner at short notice. Indian Army is shifting gear to form Integrated Battle Groups (IBGs), changing the way it fights its enemies. IBGs are smaller, self-contained fighting units that can ensure faster mobilisation and provide more flexibility to the Army. These changes are being considered keeping in mind the terrain, threat perception and capability of the enemy.

Man or Machine?

In ancient India weapons based on latest technology were crucial for the defence of territory and for offensive action. These weapons have changed over time but some parallels can be drawn. Catapult and arrows of ancient Indian warfare have been replaced today by missiles and air defence systems. *Rathamusla* (literally mobile clubs) could be considered an early ancestor of today's armoured vehicle.[14] Roots of modern artillery tactics can be traced back to Mughal Emperor Babur who deployed them on a large scale during the First Battle of Panipat.

Today technology plays an indispensable role in warfare. Krishna Rao committee recommended effective utilisation of technological revolution to ensure paradigm changes in war fighting capability. It is critical for ensuring a modern fighting force. However, technology has to aid and not replace the ground troops. Lethal Autonomous Weapons (LAWs) and artificial intelligence are emerging as advanced means of warfare. However, they may not be as central to Indian warfare as to the developed nations of the West, at least not in the coming decades. There are three main reasons for this:

> (1) Level of technological advancement, (2) Fighting capacity and psychology of our adversary, and (3) The terrain.

Firstly, our C4I2SR (Command, Control, Communications, Computers, Information, Intelligence, Surveillance and Reconnaissance) capacity is at the initial stage of development. India needs a national level plan for fully harnessing the national potential in this sphere. Another consideration is the ethical concern for the usage of autonomous weapons. There have been incidents of technical glitches in LAWs resulting in mistaken identification. This is a sensitive issue especially given the possibility of people living near the border who get hurt in the crossfire. Looking ahead there is a possibility of a human-in-the-loop (system requires a human to direct the system to select a target and attack it) or human-on-the-loop (system selects targets and attacks them, albeit with human operator oversight) system but not a human-out-of-loop (human operators out of the decision-making loop completely) system. A scenario where there is a complete shift from 'shooters to sensors' seem to be likely after some time. Thus, man behind the machine remains and will remain important.

Secondly, understanding the terrain is essential. India's borders are diverse and extreme. They encompass high altitude areas, super high altitude snow-bound areas, desert, marshy lands, forests, plains, etc. This brings out the real challenges in guarding and management of borders. Defence strategy needs to take this diversity into account. Technology does not understand diversity, it understands linearity. A standardised autonomous weapon system may not prove to be as effective as ground troops, given mans' capability to adapt to changing circumstances and terrain. That being said, technology can definitely aid in establishing an effective border security mechanism to check unauthorised movement of people and material. India is installing a Comprehensive Integrated Border Management System (CIBMS) with laser fences, CCTV cameras, and quick response team to establish a smart fencing system to detect and counter infiltration attempts. Such electronic surveillance measures can help maintain a constant vigil. They can help reduce the physical deployment of foot soldiers in the field of surveillance and monitoring.

Thirdly, it is important to understand India's two adversarial neighbours. India has to be prepared to conduct military operations in a multi-front scenario, i.e. Pakistan in the West and China in the North and the North East. Achieving a favourable outcome in a 'two front war' scenario would require militarily acceptable force levels. Such force levels have to be adequate to hold one front while taking an offensive approach on another. In addition, sufficient reserve forces, flexible to move between the two fronts would be required. This further reiterates the need for maintaining a sufficient number of foot soldiers.

Pakistan is a low technology adversary in the west. It is involved in Low Intensity Conflict (LIC) with India in the J&K sector. To counter this India requires presence of large number of foot soldiers with specialised training in stealth and guerrilla tactics. Given the mountainous terrain of Kashmir, boots on ground becomes even more important. However, in certain sections of Indo-Pakistan border the dependence on infantry can be reduced. Border areas of Punjab, Rajasthan and Gujarat are plain and desert area with a level topography. Here mechanised forces can help reduce the requirement of men on ground. There is also the possibility of using SAM and Air Force to target anti-national elements across the border. For example, the recent surgical strike (2019) was conducted without using infantry or crossing the border physically.

China is a high-tech adversary with hybrid warfare capacity. To counter China, India needs to enhance its conventional war fighting capacity as well as build on its hybrid and informational war fighting capacity. In addition, China has the advantage of altitude. Tibet provides China the advantage of rapid mobilisation of troops and equipment. This forces India to ensure adequate deterrence by maintaining a minimum force level. Such forces have to be acclimatised to high altitude and stationed permanently in forward position. In addition, a mountain strike corps is being raised as a specialised counter-offensive force. This shows the important role infantry plays at present. Given the challenges of multi-front and multi-dimensional warfare that India faces, infantry will continue to play a crucial role in warfare. It will continue to do so at least in the immediate future as well. Gradually, improved mechanisation and artificial intelligence will change the existing scenario.

In the next few decades there is a possibility of reducing the forces on border during peace time. A step forward in this direction is being taken by building infrastructure in forward zones to reduce time for mobilisation of forces. Projects such as strategic road building, forward military air bases have been undertaken. Attempts are being made to increase the fleet of light combat and Utility helicopters. It will improve the quality of aerial surveillance. It would also enhance capability of moving troops to occupy defensive positions quickly. Such initiatives will provide flexibility in stationing of forces and ensure swiftness in deployment of reserves when needed.

WAY FORWARD: TRANSFORMING INDIA'S ARMED FORCES

Transforming India's Armed Forces into a strong and modern military of appropriate size, structure and capability is a must. It is crucial to deter our foes, defend the country and project India's power. This will help India achieve its regional and global aspirations. Such transformative course of action, especially with respect to Territory and Infantry, may include the following:

- Land Warfare Doctrine 2018 reiterates the importance of land warfare.[15] It acknowledges that defence of national territory and its resources continues to be an important aspect of India's warfare strategies. At the same time it acknowledges that India is facing a multi-domain war today. Articulating a military strategy and a suitable nuclear doctrine in context of these multiple domains is important. Thus, military strategies need to focus on military application of Nano technology, high energy lasers, hypersonic strike technology, and artificial intelligence.
- We need a pro-active approach to border management.

Mr Madhav Godbole, chair of border management task force, recommended a strategy of preemptive reaction. The task force recommended the Central Reserve Police Force to be designated as the primary national level counter-insurgency force. This would enable the other central para-military forces like the BSF and Indo-Tibetan Border Police to return to their primary role of better border management. The border forces must establish closer linkages with the border population to protect them from falling prey to subversive anti-India propaganda.[16]

- Developing self-sufficiency in defence procurement and strengthening indigenous manufacturing capability is of utmost importance. Make in India initiative by the Government is one step in this direction.[17] Such initiative needs to specifically focus on modernising weapons for infantry.
- There is need for Synergy and Integration amongst the Armed Forces and other stake-holders. Some of these stakeholders being Strategic Forces, Central Armed Police Forces, DRDO, space agencies and private defence industry. Joint Forces Doctrine (2017) suggested such synergy to be achieved through joint operational structures, information and intelligence sharing and interlinking capacity.[18] One example of such collaboration is the National Intelligence Grid (NATGRID). It was constituted to ensure seamless information exchange by connecting database of core security agencies of Government of India.

Issues which Merit Importance

- Janapada (territory) and land warriors (foot soldiers) will remain important in warfare strategy due to three reasons: (1) Fighting capacity and psychology of our adversary (2) Diverse and extreme terrain at our borders (3) India is a land-based power and a land-based force. It has not yet reached advanced stage of military technology development. There may be changes as years roll by
- Multidimensional approach of viewing territory. The word territory invokes not only images of land border but extends to the realm of water, air and in future possibly outer space too. Defence of all these dimensions of territory will continue to be an important aspect of India's military strategy.
- With changing domains of war, India needs a dynamic warfare strategy. Land-based warfare comprises an essential aspect of

conventional war fighting strategy. However given the multi-faceted security challenges that India faces today, a linear defence strategy may not suffice. While we are looking at territory in a dynamic way we also need to look at its defence in a dynamic way.

- Territorial integrity is important but one should avoid excessive territorial fixation. Land Boundary Agreement (LBA) between India and Bangladesh was a pragmatic approach to solving land border disputes.
- A flexible way of looking at territory may prove to be an essential step in solving India-China border dispute. Janapada is an asset, and like any other asset should be traded if it provides political-economic-strategic mileage.
- There are three major components of a nation's war machinery—space, time and force. Space is Janapada or territory, the reason for war. Timely application of force is crucial to win the space. Force is combination of manpower, technology and logistics. Foot soldiers are an essential component of this force. The ultimate aim is destruction of enemy's forces. As long as the force component of the enemy remains, we need soldiers. Changing character of war demands a new role for the soldier but the soldier remains important. Foot soldiers are needed to hold ground. It is essential to put ones feet on ground, ones pada, to proclaim it as ones territory, ones janapada.

* The maps and diagrams used in this paper have been created or modified by the author.

NOTES

1 Anon, 2008. Delaney, David (2005); "Territory: a Short Introduction". [Online] Available at: https://www.european-spaces.eu/1-archiv/delaney-david-2005-territory-a-short-introduction/ Accessed on December 11, 2018.

2 Mohanty, S., 2019. Irrelevant Borders: Perspectives of Globalization. [Online] Academia.edu. Available at: https://www.academia.edu/7489092/Irrelevant_Borders_Perspectives_of_Globalization. Accessed on December 11 2018.

3 Lodrick, D.O., 2018. Andaman and Nicobar Islands. [Online] Encyclopedia Britannica. Available at: https://www.britannica.com/place/Andaman-and-Nicobar-Islands. Accessed on January 9, 2019.

4 Joshi, M., 2018. The Wuhan summit and the India–China border dispute. [Online] ORF. Available at: https://www.orfonline.org/research/41880-the-wuhan-summit-and-the-india-china-border-dispute/. Since the early 1980s, both sides have held multiple rounds of talks to draw up a mutually acceptable LAC and

resolve their border dispute. However, even though they have inched towards the goals, they have failed to follow through. Over the decades, China has shifted goalposts at will. Till 1959, it wanted adjustments in Aksai Chin; between 1960 and 1982, it was willing to swap claims, i.e. accept the McMahon Line in the east in exchange for India accepting its claim on Aksai Chin. Since 1985, China has been demanding Indian concessions in the east, specifically the cession of the Tawang tract. Since China now controls Aksai Chin, it denies all disputes there, claiming that the problem relates to only approximately 2,000 km, not 4,000 km as per India's claims. Accessed on January 9, 2019.

5 Joshi, M., 2018. The Wuhan summit and the India–China border dispute. [Online] ORF. Available at: https://www.orfonline.org/research/41880-the-wuhan-summit-and-the-india-china-border-dispute/

6 Kautnalya and Rangarajan, L.N., 1992. *The Arthashastra*. Haryana: Penguin Random House India Pvt. Ltd.

7 Habib, H., 2016. Bangladesh wins maritime dispute with India. [Online] The Hindu. Available at: https://www.thehindu.com/news/national/bangladesh-wins-maritime-dispute-with-india/article6191797.ece. Accessed on December 11, 2018.

8 Sandhu, J.S., 2000. *Military History of Ancient India*. Vision Books.

9 The Hindu (2019). India gets surveillance satellite.[Online] Available at: https://www.thehindu.com/sci-tech/technology/pslv-isro-emisat-launch-from-sriharikota-on-april-1/article26699077.ece Accessed on April 12,2019.

10 Sharma, Rakesh. Reconceptualising Land Warfighting Strategy. *Centre for Land Warfare Studies* (CLAWS), (Summer 2017).

11 Kanwal, Gurmeet. Defence Reforms: Managing Threats and Challenges to National Security. Centre for Land Warfare Studies (CLAWS) Journal Summer 2013. Available at: https://www.claws.in/images/journals_doc/1394685259Gurmeet%20Kanwal%20CJ%20Summer%202013.pdf.

12 Hero stones are memorials commemorating the honourable death of a hero in battle. Erected between the 3rd century BC and the 18th century AD, hero stones are found all over India.

13 Anon, 2014. Indian PM's address at the Combined Commanders Conference. [online] Prime Minister of India PMs address at the Combined Commanders Conference Comments. Available at: https://www.pmindia.gov.in/en/news_updates/pms-address-at-the-combined-commanders-conference/ Accessed on December 20, 2018].

14 Sandhu, J.S., 2000. *Military History of Ancient India*. Vision Books.

15 Indian Army Land Warfare Doctrine, Indian Army, 2018.

16 Kanwal, G., 2011. Border management: Need for reform. [Online] Rediff. Available at: https://www.rediff.com/news/column/border-management-need-for-reform/20110428.htm.

17 Anon, 2019. Defence Manufacturing Sector: Achievement Report. [Online] Defence Manufacturing Sector: Achievement Report - Make in India. Available at: http://www.makeinindia.com/article/-/v/defence-manufacturing-sector-achievement-report. Accessed on December 20, 2018.

18 Joint Doctrine of the Indian Armed Forces 2017.

2

Emanating Land Warfare in the 21st Century

Colonel Rajeev Kapoor

*"I am quite confident that in the foreseeable future
armed conflict will not take the form of a huge land armies
facing each other across extended battle lines
as they did in World War I and World War II or,
for that matter, as they would have
if NATO had faced the Warsaw pact on the field of battle."*

– **Norman Schwarzkopf**

ABSTRACT

It would be ingenuous to think that we can ever get rid of war; it is synonymous with human nature. This chapter identifies how the trends are shaping the land warfare domain and how this anticipated environment would impact the nature and character of future land warfare. The chapter will also discuss the Meta-trends or themes of future fighting environment. Such an examination, however, necessarily avoids any attempt to predict the future but certainly aims to discover current tendencies and draw possibilities, which may bring us closer to possible future realities of land wars. The collage of future land war or land warfare environment can be explicitly built and explained by answering three specific questions: what will it be fought over; how and who will fight; and what are the likely meta-trends or themes of future land war? It is important today to understand the emerging international and regional security environment and the likely trigger and flash points. The current geopolitical flux in the increasingly globalised world is creating new risks and uncertainties; emerging security environment is radically different from what it was even a decade ago and the new security challenges are products, not of conventional inter-state rivalries, but of economic, demographic and societal tensions that are trans-national in nature. Thus, future conflicts are more likely to be a consequence of regional struggles involving a range of actors rather than inter-state tensions or instability. The entry of non-state actors has added a new dimension to low-intensity and intra-state conflicts. Thus, within the contemporary strategic environment the distinction between what is 'conventional' and what is 'unconventional' has surely blurred, and would be a major factor in changing the future character of land warfare.

Exordium

It is certitude that war is an intrinsic part of human history besides being part of life, or in some regions of our World it is life itself. Consequent to this rationale, if we cannot exterminate war, we have to prepare for it. Preparing for war, can we really predict what kind of it will come to us? This challenge has often caused vexation for rulers, soldiers, strategists and theoreticians, who have had the task to prepare troops for the next war. The planners commonly go wrong by preparing to win the last fought war, not the next one.[1]

Warfare eventuated on land. The realm of land warfare, when compared to all the other domains, has the highest ability to create operational friction. It is the deployment of land forces that often marks the transition from coercion to conflict, from threats to action. Although future wars on land would not occur in seclusion, especially given the wholesale contemporary emphasis in many modern armies on joint operations (jointness) and the littoral environment, it nonetheless possesses a kind of centrality and decisiveness that is beyond the preserve of conflict in any other dimension.[2]

Though the current predictions about future warfare still put too much emphasis on new technologies but there is a fundamental shift in how the world now thinks and executes land war. The reposition is to move beyond major land wars, resulting in an increased role for precision weaponry and the employment of a variety of special operations forces.[3] Smaller and more agile forces could make due where larger, ponderous forces had once operated.

This chapter shall deal in identifying how the trends are shaping the land warfare domain and how this anticipated environment would impact the nature and character of future land warfare. The chapter will also discuss the Meta-trends or themes of future fighting environment.

The collage of future land war or land warfare environment can be explicitly built and explained by answering three specific questions; what will it be fought over; how and who will fight; and what are the likely trends or themes of future land war?

Emerging Land Warfare Environment: What Will It Be Fought Over?

"Our modern states are preparing for war, without even knowing the future enemy"

– **Alfred Adler**

It is important today to understand the emerging international and regional security environment and the likely trigger and flash points. The current geopolitical flux in the increasingly globalised world is creating new risks and uncertainties; emerging security environment is radically different from what it was even a decade ago and the new security challenges are products, not of conventional inter-state rivalries, but of economic, demographic and societal tensions that are trans-national in nature. Thus future conflicts are more likely to be a consequence of regional struggles involving a range of actors rather than inter-state tensions or instability. This instability, in turn, is likely to arise as a consequence of the rise of autonomous armed groups and non-state entities and the weakening of governments and state institutions, coupled with population displacement, trafficking—both human and material—and ethno-religious tensions. With virtual absence of direct armed conflict between nations, internal armed conflicts have witnessed and are likely to further see an upward trend. The entry of non-state actors has added a new dimension to low intensity and intra-state conflicts. Thus, within the contemporary strategic environment the distinction between what is 'conventional' and what is 'unconventional' has surely blurred, and would be a major factor in changing the future character of land warfare. The complexities of the wars are ergo changing as intrastate or civil wars which have become relatively numerous, especially in fragile or failing states. The data below, from year 1946 to 2016 further substantiates this belief.

The Uppsala Conflict Data Program (UCDP), the leading provider of statistics on political violence, has identified 285 distinct armed conflicts since 1946. Figure 2.1 displays the number of conflicts around the world by type and year since 1946. Two trends over the long term are immediately detectable. First, interstate conflicts, which accounted for half of all armed conflicts early in the period, have waned. The second trend is the distinct rise in the number of civil or intrastate conflicts, peaking in 1991, followed by a decline. Since 2003, the number of armed conflicts has risen and fallen, ranging between 30 and 52.

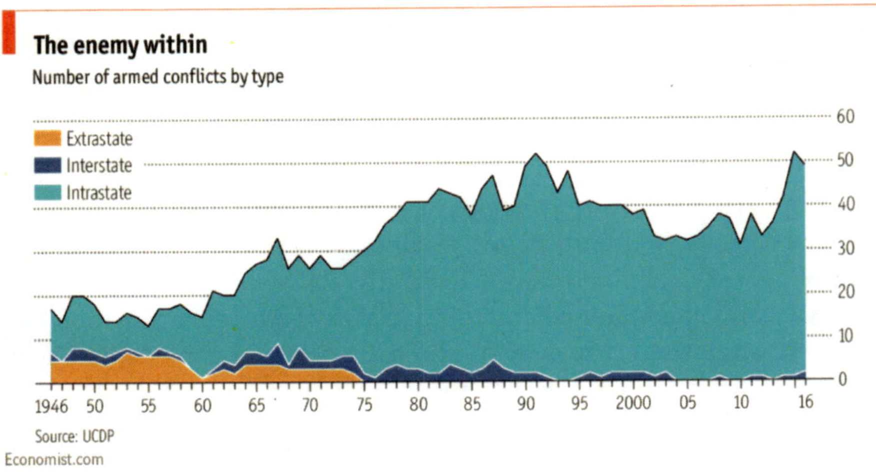

Figure 2.1: Number of Armed Conflicts by Type[4]

Though territorial issues would remain an intrinsic part of land wars, other issues related to historical differences, ideological biases, economic disparity, energy security and water shortage would constitute the prime contributing factors for future conflicts.[5] The rising competition over limited sources of energy, religious intolerance and 'water wars' are unlikely to remain as conjectures in future and would generate new tensions in geo-political relations leading to bitter conflicts.

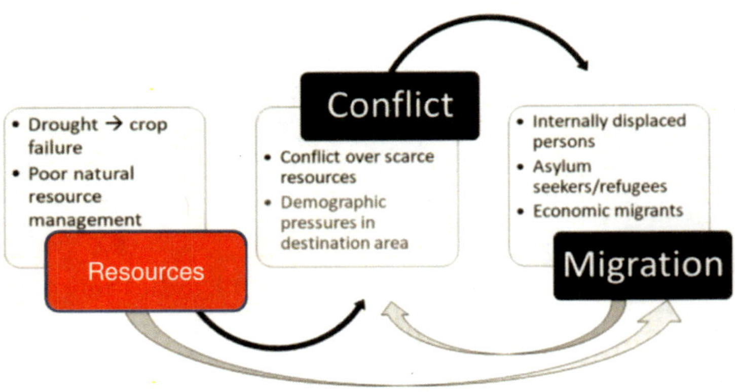

Figure 2.2: Resources-Conflict-Migration Loop (sketch: Authors imagination)

Other pertinent factors like climate change, population growth and sectarian or ethnic extremism are the potential future factors which are anticipated to ensure that such wars will continue. Hence, the nature of military interventions and operations are and would further become inherently unpredictable, making it difficult to define the character of future land warfare. The truth and essence is that, while high-end wars between nations have decreased, war has certainly not gone away, nor is it likely to get any less violent. The prognosis of present security environment in the World will further corroborate and unfold 'On what' the future land wars would occur.

Emerging Land Warfare: How and Who Will Fight?

Given the current tempo of change, it's a fact that the world in the next two decades will be vastly different in appearance and in character to that of today. Nevertheless, the structural and systemic similarities to the contemporary geopolitical, economic and social environments would be retained by the world. In reference to its ever-changing nature, the renowned general and military theorist Carl von Clausewitz (1780–1831) compared warfare to a chameleon. Although this description applies, in different degrees, to warfare; the rate of drastic changes witnessed in warfare; and those expected to be witnessed, makes Clausewitz's phrase seem as if it was written for present times.

In effect, pure conventional operations of the force-on-force methodology, in coming decades, would become constituent of the larger bouquet of options that amalgamate into multi-dominion warfare. These domains may work in concert simultaneously to achieve goals, instead of only operating in or between two domains. Multi domain-specific capabilities can be leveraged to defeat a capable foe in another domain. Along these lines, the foreseeable future of land wars is expected to be drastically different from the warfare of today or the previous century. So, the moot questions which arise here are: what is the anticipated change and 'how' will be the land wars in future and 'who' would be fighting them.

Since, geography is no more a constraint for those who wish to perpetuate violence. Most conflicts would now be internal. Sub-conventional conflicts characterised by intrastate strife would gain ascendency over traditional conflicts, which used to be mostly conventional inter-state wars. The easy availability of cheap, mass-produced small arms, landmines and IEDs has exponentially increased the ability of aggrieved groups to orchestrate violence within societies. The trans-national nature of these threats and the increasing involvement of state actors in using sub-conventional conflicts as "war by other means" have exacerbated their complexity.

The conventional land forces therefore are at crossroads. They alone cannot win tomorrow's wars as the future of land wars is not only about conventional forces or the convergence of regular and irregular forces but also increasingly involve other multiple diverse actors. These are those actors, who would be competing for the allegiances and/or acquiescence of targeted populations. Consequently, the outcome of conflict will be influenced by the perceptions of these populations rather than solely the results of battlefield action. Some war zones in last two decades or so like the Lebanon War (2006), Russia–Georgia Campaign (2008), Sri Lankan Conflict (2009) and the ongoing Operation in Afghanistan clearly indicate this changing trend of wars.

As a matter of fact, countries and their conventional forces, in future would no longer be the only 'party' which would make decisions about waging or announcing wars; there would be other groups or parties, with military power, who would control and contribute in decisions about war and peace. Groups like Hezbollah in Lebanon, Taliban in Afghanistan, Hamas in Gaza, Al Qaeda, and Daesh (the self-proclaimed Islamic State of Iraq and the Levant), are the present-day examples.

Cyberspace along with land will become a battlefield through destroying or hacking into computer systems or sending destructive viruses to enemy electronic systems. An example of this is the Stuxnet virus that hit the Iranian nuclear programme in 2010, causing a major problem. Ralph Langner, a German computer expert, said at the time that the malware set back the Iranian nuclear programme by two years.[6]

Nuclear threat would continue to constitute the future land wars. In the last century, the "haves and have-nots" of the nuclear weapons club membership became the major determinant, and—as seen in the cases of Iran and North Korea today—this continues to be relevant. However, suffice to say that, the scope of conventional conflict in the anticipated conflict narrative has been limited by the destructive potential of nuclear weapons and due to mushrooming of large number of nuclear weapons states.

Thus, the emerging world is expected to be a combination of international rivalries, non-state actors leveraging power asymmetrically, and challenges posed by advances in science and technology. This would entail that the future land wars would be chaotic and in a complex environment of 'Grey Zone'. Grey Zones are spaces between outright war and peace, where diverse types and numbers of actors compete for resources, access, territory, and power within states and across them.[7]

Methods of war would also change from the past, as the world population is increasingly inclining toward urban areas and the numbers are likely to further escalate. Thus, the future land wars would no longer be fought in deserts; rather, they will be in crowded city streets.

Resultantly, the concept of future conflict scenario looks complex and mixed with uncertainties as the dynamics of deterrence and escalatory control are likely to remain relevant only against nation states, while against non-state actors, these capabilities would have little effect. Non-state actors on the other hand would need state support for survival because they are often the expression of social problems and see themselves as representatives of distinct interests and often build on broad support within communities.

Will the Conventional Land Forces Become Irrelevant? No, because contextually, in spite of the advent of so many tangible and intangible factors, territory would remain the clearest expression of sovereignty, and the forces would be the main guarantors for securing territory. Ground forces will remain the dominant asset to assure this guarantee. Hence, what kind of future wars can be anticipated?

Types of Future Wars. Three types of conflicts are likely between now and 2030:[8]

- **Overt War.** Such wars would be similar to the US invasions of Afghanistan and Iraq. Wars in Syria and Yemen are the other types which could be witnessed in the coming decades.
- **Covert War.** Covert operations are there to stay and would expand to more of the globe. Covert wars would include non-contact, Asymmetric, Hybrid wars, etc.
- **Outsourced War.** Outsourced wars have begun in earnest. Estimates of the numbers of outsourced security personnel in Afghanistan vary from 130,000 to 160,000. Private military contracted personnel account for nearly two-thirds of all the

Pentagon's personnel in Afghanistan, the highest ratio in any conflict in the history of the US.[9] This new strategy has pitfalls and military jurists are equally concerned that by ignoring the well-thought out doctrine on civilians' role in warfare, contractors now operate in a legal no man's land, beyond the established boundaries of the military or international law.[10] While all past realities of war remain—the contest of life and death, uncertainty, friction, fog and danger—a number of modern features have emerged. The Pentagon believes that this kind of strategy to fight a war is cost effective and with the least amount of liability and accountability.

Potential Triggers/Reasons of War. It's an established fact that there is rarely one single, clear reason/trigger of conflict and, ultimately, war.

With three types of wars anticipated in future and the looming geo-political uncertainties, what could be the potential triggers?[11] There seem to be **seven** main triggers of war:

- ***Economic.*** An economic motive is always an underlying reason for most wars, even if the war has been triggered due to any other reason. In future, the likely triggers on which the wars would be fought could be oil, minerals, or materials used in manufacturing. The wars could also be fought over current fundamental essentials, such as water and food as with increase in population these basic resources would become scarce.
- ***Territorial.*** This would remain a prime reason for wars due to requirement in future for more land, either for living space, agricultural use or other purposes. Territorial wars could also be undertaken to sort out historical territorial disputes or for creating "buffer zones" between two hostile enemies.
- ***Nationalism.*** In present geo-political dispensation, nationalism would hold primacy and war on the context of nationalism will become a norm to prove that one country is superior to another. Racism can also be linked to nationalism, as was seen when Adolf Hitler went to war with Russia partly because the Russians were seen as an inferior race.[12]
- ***Religion.*** Religious conflicts leading to wars are the most dangerous and likely in coming times. The religious fanatic mind-set could lie dormant for decades, but can resurface in a flash at a later date. Religious wars can be multifaceted and can be coupled

with other reasons, such as nationalism or revenge for a perceived historical slight in the past. Inter and intra religion disharmony (read Shia and Sunni) can also instigate war.

- ***Retribution.*** Wars waging to punish someone as vengeance, seeking to redress a grievance, or simply striking back for a perceived slight can often be a factor.
- ***Civil.*** Fierce or sharp internal disagreement within a country could lead to violent conflict between two or more opposing groups. Such wars can also be sparked by separatist groups who want to form their own, independent country.
- ***Revolutionary.*** These occur when a large section of the population of a country revolts against the individual or group that rules the country. Reasons could be economic hardship or perceived injustices committed by the ruling group. Revolutionary wars can easily descend into civil wars.[13]

The probability of these triggers may not necessarily be in the same order but, all the emerging flash points and scenarios for future conflicts would surely be woven around these seven triggers.

Scenarios and Dangerous Flash points. Having analysed as to 'how' the future wars are likely to unfold, the next obvious step would be to build few scenarios and predict dangerous flash points that could trigger major clashes in the years to come, based on the current geo-political narrative. First is South China Sea (SCS), which has become a tinderbox owing tithe growing trade clash between the United States and China. As of now, conflict is playing out in exchanges of heated rhetoric, tariffs and various other trade sanctions.[14] But, if relations between the two countries deteriorate, either of the two might decide to escalate. Second global flash point could be Ukraine. Given the continuing tensions between Russia and the United States, even a small shift by either of the two could threaten the uneasy balance that has held for the last several years, potentially throwing Eastern Europe into chaos. The third place for likely conflict is the Persian Gulf. The perpetual political and military crisis in the Middle East has settled into an uneasy tedium. Economic pressure on Iran continues to increase; the Saudi war on Yemen is showing no signs of abating; and in Syrian Civil War, both the United States and Russia remain committed to their partners and proxies. Political turmoil in Iran could either push Iran into aggressive posture or make the Islamic Republic a tempting target for its enemies. Given the strategic importance of the region, any such instability could lead to conflict between the United States, Russia or even China. Lastly, it could be Korean peninsula. The situation in this peninsula remains much more dangerous than the most optimistic assessments would suggest. Some other disruptive conflict zones which may emerge could be in the Baltics, in Azerbaijan, in Kashmir, Tibetan plateau or even in Venezuela.

The Nature and Character of Future Land Wars

The foreseeable tectonic shift in future land wars, as discussed above, instinctively raises an inquest, as to how this change in environment would impact the 'Nature' and 'Character' of war in coming decades.

No one argues that warfare is not changing. Where people disagree, however, is whether the nature of warfare, the character of warfare, or both are changing. It is extremely pertinent to understand at the outset of this debate that, 'War' and 'Warfare' are different words with a different meaning, and we should be careful about their use. Warfare, of course, doesn't have an enduring, unchanging phenomenological "nature," as it is merely the way war is made.

The professional military community generally differentiates between an objective nature and a subjective character of war by drawing upon Clausewitz.[15] The former describes what war is, and the latter describes how it is actually fought.

According to Carl Von Clausewitz, war's nature does not change—only its character changes. As per him,

> *"The nature of something is the basic make up of that thing. It is, at core, what that 'thing' is. The character of something is the combination of all the different parts and pieces that make up that thing."*

Gen. Mark Milley, US Army Chief of Staff, at the Association of the US Army Convention, 2017, also echoed the Clausewitzian view and said, *"No one in this room can accurately predict the future, least of all me. The nature of war is never gonna change. But the character of war is changing before our eyes—with the introduction of a lot of technology, a lot of societal changes with urbanization and a wide variety of other factors."*

There has been and would always remain a dichotomy of views between those who say, "It's Clausewitz forever—war will always be the same, across the spectrum," vs. those who straight-line today's concerns to the future and argue, "Its insurgencies that we'll be fighting mostly from now through 2050, including global terror as a form of insurgency, so nature and character of war both would change."

Those who believe that the nature of war is changing argue that, in the coming decades, non-contact and non-interactive wars with enhanced capabilities in robotics and artificial intelligence will change more than just the way warfare is waged and this is also going to change the nature of war. The character of land wars on the other hand is growing ever more convoluted, from pervasive information warfare, to applying multi-functional and multi-dominion military capacities below the threshold of armed conflict or the coupling of economic power with irregular forces.[16]

Trends/Themes of the Future Operating Environment

There are a number of modern-day phenomena that act to shape outward appearance of future land warfare. These are contemporary challenges that, to paraphrase Clausewitz, determine the grammar of land warfare without changing its logic. There are six meta-themes or trends which are likely to influence the future environment of land warfare:

Growing Urban Environment. According to a UN report, the world population is expected to reach 8.5 billion by 2030 and 9.7 billion in 2050, with the overwhelming majority of this increase (95%) concentrated in the developing world.[17] Furthermore, for the first time in history the world is becoming more urban than rural.[18] Today, more people live in cities than rural land by 2030, the current urban population of 3.6 billion will rise to five billion, and 60% of people would live in cities.[19] Figure 2.3 illustrates the projected increase in urban populations by 2030.

Over 33 megacities exist today, with six of these cities home to over 20 million inhabitants.[20] By 2030, Asia alone will have at least 20 megacities, including New Delhi (39 million), Mumbai (33 million), Shanghai (27 million), Karachi (26.5 million), Lahore (12.5 million), Dhaka (26 million), Manila (14.8 million) and Jakarta (25 million).[21] Given the rising importance of cities as political, economic and cultural centres of gravity, armed conflict would increasingly take place in urban settings.

Implications of Urbanised Environment. Power shifts may eventuate between existing authorities and incoming populations having different ethnicities, cultures and values. Unregulated cities with no say of traditional rule of law would emerge, providing a breeding ground for

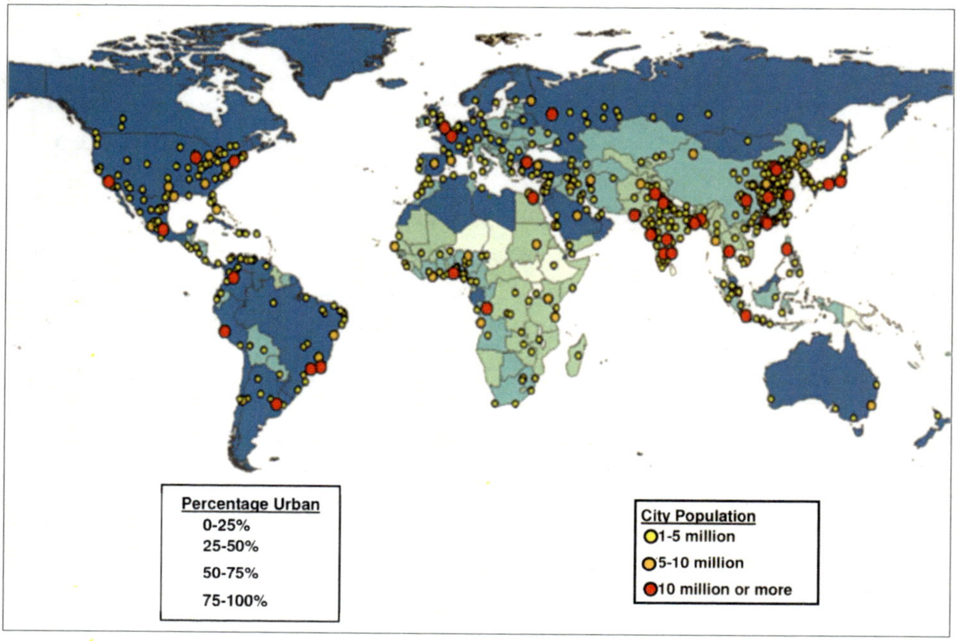

Figure 2.3: Percentage of urban population and concentrations by size, 2030

organised crime, terrorists and insurgents. Based on current trajectories, the Organisation for Economic Cooperation and Development estimates that by 2030 almost half the world's population will live in areas suffering severe water stress. Competition for increasingly scarce resources can lead to both intrastate and transnational conflict.[22] There is also potential for interstate conflict, although wars fought solely over access to scarce resources are uncommon in the contemporary world.

Due to this environment, the land forces operations in high density urban terrain will no longer be a discretionary activity. High density population centres will require the Army to better understand the way cities are designed and how the 'metabolism' of the cities work.[23] This would force armies to enhance their capacity for interoperability and broaden their ability to engage in shared planning with civilian partners. In such environment it would be a prerequisite for the land force to exploit situational awareness from other partners, military and civilian, as well as sources outside the urban battle space. Besides, psychological and intellectual capabilities; ability to negotiate with others; use of interpreters; operate in ambiguous environments; improvise; and understand local cultures would be pertinent for developing in the Army.

Emerging Demographics. Prosperous states will continue to enjoy high standards of living, but will also confront the costs of ageing and sedentary populations with an increasing impact on economic, social and political systems.[24] On the contrary, developing and undeveloped world would face difficulty of 'catching up' to the developed states because of social and economic pressures amplified by increasing populations and strained governance. Greater competition for working-aged populations will drive demand for immigration. Analyst believe that by 2050, global migration will double to 405 million and this would result in employing of future force to intervene in internal conflicts mainly where deep-seated fears of changes in the status quo are fuelling intolerance and conflict.[25]

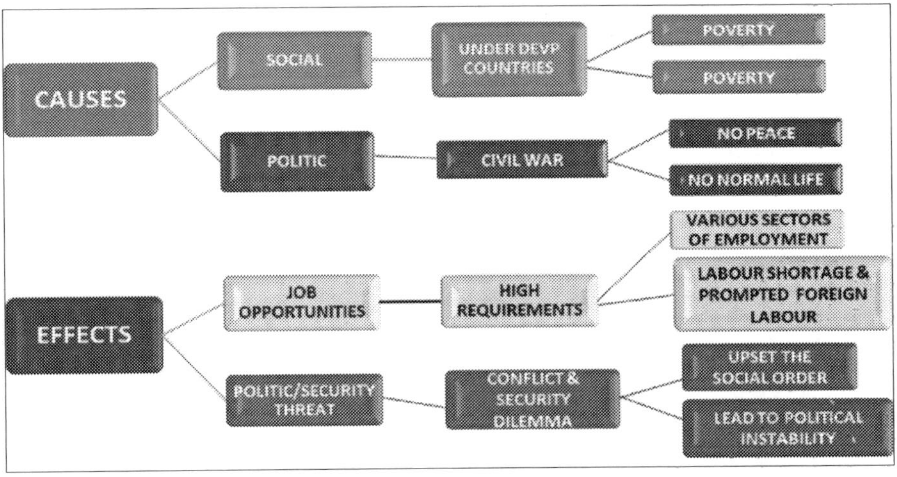

Figure 2.4: Cause and Effect of Migration (sketch: Authors imagination)

With the enhanced global connectivity, there will also be increasing potential for these fears to be fanned externally and for migrant voting blocs to be leveraged by homelands to influence host-lands domestic politics. Russian Federation's use of ethnic Russians in the Ukraine and the Crimea are some recent examples. These pressures will alter the political calculus for homelands, host-lands and when necessary, intervention forces.

Growing Connected and Monitored Environment. Future land operations would be conducted under two aspects of 'Connectivity'. First, enhanced interlinking between global economic, social and communications systems and second, further entwining of land, sea and air domains with the cyber, electromagnetic and space domains. These domains will be the subject of constant competition, with land force operations increasingly enabled (or disabled) by access to digital networks.[26] It would act as a double-edged weapon as it is bound to increase transparency in all domains. Thus, difficulty in achieving operational security and surprise would be the order, plus it will be easier to deliberately doctor, misinterpret or take information out of context. The biggest bane of growing connected environment would be the continued empowering of non-state and semi-state actors by global telecommunications networks besides being supported by state actors either secretly or openly. Resultantly, the future armies need to gear up and build capacities to cope with the demands of a connected environment. Land forces would also need cyber defence capabilities by developing an ability to defend critical networks against cyber-attack, while also being prepared to operate in a degraded network environment. Logistics is expected to transform as automation and robotics within would lead to saving of manpower and also would enhance accuracy and speed of delivery. Similarly, the potential use of additive construction (3D printing, which has already been exploited by the US marines in making 'Nibbler UAVs' and concrete footbridges), and the increased employment of deployable rapid prototyping and development facilities offer the potential to quickly manufacture or modify equipment in theatre. This would dramatically shorten response times and logistic chains and are areas worthy of further investigation.[27]

Growing Lethal Environment. Rapid changes and advancement in technology will continue to drive and shape the conduct of war in coming days. The advances in technology will continue albeit the pace of innovation would outpace it. Technological advances have brought-in improvements to weaponry, sensors and systems that can, in turn, be harnessed by evolutions in tactics and training with the overall outcome of increasing lethality. The British Army's 'Land Environment 2035' study identified 11 areas of technological innovation and growth that were assessed as providing the greatest potential impact on the future land operating environment. These are, Big data; Machine autonomy; AI; Human enhancement and augmentation; Advanced Material and Manufacturing; Synthetic Biology; Nano systems; Quantum Technology; Remote and Autonomous Systems/Drones; Directed Energy and Novel Weapons; Communications; and lastly, Social and Behavioural Sciences. Consequent to likely technological advancements, future land warfare would experience a rapid increase in tempo and periodic intensity which is anticipated to impact three major areas of modern land battle and include, *Information, Weapon systems and Cognitive Science* (Modern armies are becoming increasingly aware of the psychological and counter-psychological aspects and implications of land-based combat).

The brutal truth however is that such capabilities will not be limited to traditional militaries—non-state actors are also increasingly technologically enabled and in some cases they are leading innovation.

Growing Autonomous Environment. The remote and autonomous systems (robotics) will play a far greater role in the future battlefield as they would improve force protection manifold. Since the consequence of destruction or loss of a machine would not be the same as the loss, injury or death of a soldier, such systems thus will be more acceptable and economical in future. Besides, they are likely to be more effective in land wars, than a human, due to greater endurance and far greater levels of concealment. War more likely?

Growing Collective Environment. The rise of non-state actors and growing intrastate conflicts during the last two decades has caused an exponential rise in 'burden-sharing' military deployments. Such deployments have primarily involved a mix of traditional and non-traditional actors. Traditional actors include allied and friendly state military forces and government departments, while Non-traditional parties could include, but are not limited to, non-government organisations, host nation governments, indigenous security forces, sanctioned representatives of corporations and non-state security elements. The flip side of such arrangements is that they add complexity to the force's composition and they require the acceptance of a degree of vulnerability in acceding to the interests of the wider group which has a direct impact on national and military strategic objectives and force structures. The ambit of 'Collective' also includes the joint operations, i.e. relationship between the land forces strategy with maritime and Air strategy, which acts as an important force multiplier.

The Grey Zone Environment. In the coming decades, the land wars are surely to be fought in Grey Zone environment. Adversaries would blend conventional and irregular methods with information and cyber tactics. They would form coalitions of convenience between states, extremists and criminals, create proxies, or employ their special forces to work in the 'grey zone' just below the escalation threshold. Nations would threaten stability by offering states more options in the form of "hybrid" warfare to create plausible deniability and strategic ambiguity. This would bring complexities in the battlefield and the future armies would be required to build capabilities and capacities to be confident in operating in such complex environments. Thus the future land forces must be able to operate on intent-based orders and nuance their responses to match threats and opportunities that might not have been foreseen in doctrine.[28]

The seven trends/themes discussed above showcase the changing character of war and what the future land battlefield would comprise of. They also demonstrate some of the implications that may have on shaping policy. In addition to each trend having characteristics that will affect the future land wars, many of the elements of the trends are mutually reinforcing. This will amplify their effect.[29]

Based on what will be the future land wars fought over; who and how will they fight; and what will be the meta-themes for future, it would be logical and conclusive now to build tenets of the perceived battle space of the future.

Perceived Battle space of the Future

There are **seven aspects** of the future battle space which define it as something beyond traditional conceptions. They are: *non-linearity, integration, connectivity, continuity, synchronisation* and *perception*.[30]

- ***Non-linearity.*** This refers to operations distributed throughout the battle space.
- ***Homogenisation.*** Complete homogenisation within the land force, is the dire need of modern battle space. Besides homogeneity within the land forces, integration between land assets and the joint and/or coalition forces they support is an equal pre-requisite. This aspect would involve need for interoperability, doctrinal/technological compatibility, and cross-cultural understanding between current and future coalition partners. Integration also increasingly implies civil-military cooperation at unprecedented levels. Non-military personnel, governmental and non-governmental agencies also have an unquestionable impact on the modern-day battle space—an impact that will only increase with time.[31]
- ***Speed.*** If future wars are to be won at minimum cost, they must be won quickly.
- ***Continuity.*** In future battles, technology would facilitate

continuity thereby making 24-hour operations both possible and desirable. Technology would also facilitate continuity by moderating the adverse effects of weather and terrain.

- ***Connectivity.*** Connectivity would also ensure continuity and would underpin the linking of sensors to weapons systems to deliver timely effects. Future land warfare will invariably feature an 'information battle', where adversaries compete to protect their own flow of information while disrupting that of their enemy.[32]
- ***Synchronisation.*** In modern battle space for achieving most potent effect there is a need for coordination of activity in space and time. The multidimensional nature of modern land warfare in that it is fought 'in the deep, close and rear battles ... simultaneously and at all levels of intensity, in all dimensions', also demand a high level of synchronisation'. As British Army doctrine asserts, 'the synergistic effect of taking action simultaneously in several different places is far greater than the sum of the individual actions'.
- ***Perception.*** This aspect has gained maximum significance for the future wars. The victory in modern-day land campaign is contingent on this aspect. The media and an increasingly unregulated flow of information to and from the battle space has brought the general public closer than ever before to the face of battle. This disposition makes this aspect a potentially decisive element. All actions of military commanders are under scrutiny as they can't isolate themselves from public audit.
- ***Deception.*** *"All warfare is based on deception. Hence, when we are able to attack, we must seem unable; when using our forces, we must appear inactive; when we are near, we must make the enemy believe we are far away; when far away, we must make him believe we are near."* This quote by Sun Tzu still remains equally relevant. Deception or the 'bluff in warfare' is surely as old as warfare itself. It would not be an understatement to say that, no matter how much the future battles become more expensive and extensive, the more valuable successful deceptions are likely to become. Thus, deception in future land wars would remain a powerful tool for reducing the bloodshed besides having an enormous influence on its outcome. Conversely, it is also pertinent to understand that exact success of any given deception operation is often very difficult to measure and no war has ever been won only on deception.

What is to be done?

Strategic wisdom lies in anticipation of, and preparation for, future wars. The changing nature and character of warfare has rendered the emerging war as ambiguous and irregular.

World thus needs to realise that war of future will be won by whoever best takes advantage of information and connectivity and who uses the full range of the electro-magnetic spectrum to safely operate in multiple domains and is able to blind or distort enemy's perception of the battle. Therefore, future age requires smaller, agile and lean land forces that are flexible and can employ AI-enhanced decision-making tools to further enhance war's rhythm and speed.

The future land force must be capable of surviving and prevailing in an operating space that is crowded, connected, lethal, collective, constrained and converging.

Land forces for future battles should be able to generate a high operational tempo; optimise all elements of combat power; and create confusion in the enemy's mind. To achieve this capability, simultaneity would be the key.

Building joint and combined arms capabilities would be the norm of the future. Integration of resources is imperative for the cyber war, information war, out of area contingencies and hybrid threats which would constitute the basic fabric of future land wars. Nuclear threat on the other hand would be the main reason for big powers to achieve their political objectives short of outright war. We need to realise that nuclear weapons have fundamentally changed the nature of war. The destructive power of nuclear weapons is so great that states understand the awful consequences, thereby resisting from its use. Therefore, countries in future would not hold back their non-nuke and conventional options due to the threat of nuclear overhang. However, such weapons going in hands of non-state actors could become a 'game-changer' in future conflicts. In such a scenario, rogue states like Pakistan and North Korea, using the nukes on adversaries through the non-state armed actors, cannot be ruled out.

Conclusion

If we look back in history, one thing which was common in the first three generations of warfare was that the battle lines were well defined and the enemy was distinguishable. However, chaos and ambiguity has taken over which is likely to continue in coming decades. The nature and character of land warfare would continue to find multiple changes, inducing world's security scenario to be highly dynamic. It will be some mix of state-on-state and ideological/revolution or ethnic conflict.

As geo-economics has become a dominant factor in today's geo-politics, the next decade or so, would see most of the land armies in the world facing budget constraints but would be leaner, "doing more with less".

However, the inability of the international community to generate broader coordinated responses to predictable threats would persist and bother the world's harmony. The United Nations would continue to play a deeply constrained role in international conflict. Regional security pacts and alliances, which proven only marginally effective, would increase in prominence. Flash points, therefore, will remain with us in the future.

The costs of conventional and nuclear war are likely to be staggering therefore, future land conflicts would see a mix of technologically sophisticated offensive cyber capabilities, covert action, information operations coupled with irregular threat. As nuclear weapons cannot be uninvented so their role as a strategic deterrence, in future conflicts, is likely to stay.

Not to forget in the end that, "Everything in war is very simple, but the simplest thing is difficult."

> *"War is still a contest of wills, but technology and geopolitical competition are changing its character"*
>
> – **Matthew Symonds**

NOTES

1 Lt. (Res.) Roland Kiss, "The Future of War, The Wars of the Future" www.honvedelm.hu. Accessed on Oct 30, 2019.

2 Craig Stockings, "The Domain in which we Dwell: The Foundations, Form and Future of Land Warfare", Canberra Australian National University 2007, www.isis.koha.my, Accessed on October 30, 2019.

3 Major Amos C. Fox, "The Re-emergence of the Siege: An Assessment of Trends in Modern Land Warfare", Association of the US Army, www.ausa.org, July 03, 2018. Accessed on October 30, 2019.

4 UCDP, "Number of Armed Conflicts by Type", The Economist, Jan 25, 2018. www.economist.com, Accessed on October 30, 2018.

5 "Changing Nature of Conflict: Trends and Responses", Proceedings of an international seminar hosted jointly by Army HQ and CLAWS, www.mea.gov.in, Accessed on October 30, 2019.

6 Gonsalves, Antone, 'Stuxnet creators defined 21st century warfare', www.csoonline.com/article/2134162/malware-cybercrime-stuxnet-creators-defined-21st-century-warfare.html, Nov 20, 2013.

7 The Gray Zone, CAPT Phillip Kapusta, published by US Special Operations Command, outlines the concept of competition among actors in the space between peace and war. September 2015

8 "The Changing Nature of Warfare", Transcript and Summary of a Conference, at Centre for Strategic Studies, www.apps.dtic.mil, May 25-26, 2004. Accessed on October 30, 2019.

9 Marie-Dominique Charlier, "Afghanistan's Outsourced War", Le Monde Diplomatique, cited in RAWA News, February 9, 2010.

10 Peter W Singer, "Outsourcing the War", The Brookings Institution, April 16, 2004

11 Paul Goodman, "The-Main-Reasons-For-War", https://owlcation.com/social-sciences, February 5, 2019. Accessed on October 31, 2019.

12 ibid.

13 ibid.

14 Dr. Robert Farley, Places Where World War III Could Start in 2019, https://nationalinterest.org, December 22, 2018. Accessed on 31 October 2019.

15 Christopher Mewett, "Understanding War's Enduring Nature alongside Its Changing Character," War on the Rocks, January 21, 2014, http://warontherocks.com/2014/01/understanding-wars-enduring-nature-alongside-its-changing-character/.

16 C. Gray, 'War—Continuity in Change, and Change in Continuity', Parameters, Summer 2010; H. Strachan, 'The Changing Character of War', A Lecture delivered at the Graduate Institute of International Relations, Geneva, 9 November 2006.

17 National Intelligence Council, Global Trends 2030: Alternative Worlds, Office of the Director of National Intelligence (US), 2016, p. iv, http://www.dni.gov/index.php.Accessed on October 31, 2019.

18 Ibid.

19 Population Division of the Department of Economic and Social Affairs of the United Nations, 'World Urbanization Prospects, the 2011 Revision' (2016), http://esa.un.org/unup/Maps/maps_urban_2025.htm, p. 4, 2016.

20 These are: Mumbai, Tokyo, Seoul, New York City, Mexico City and Karachi.

21 Canadian Forces, Chief of Force Development, 'The Future Security Environment 2008-2030', http://www.cfd-cdf.forces.gc.ca/documents/CFD%20FSE/, p. 23.

22 Australian Army (2014). Future Land Warfare Report. Directorate of Future Land Warfare, Australian Army, 2014, Headquarters, Canberra: Australia.

23 See A. Wolman, 'The Metabolism of Cities', Scientific American, Vol. 213 (3), pp. 179–90. On the application of this theory to the conduct of military operations, see D. Kilcullen, Out of the Mountains, the Coming Age of the Urban Guerrilla, Oxford University Press, Melbourne, 2013.

24 Future Land Operating Concept 2035, Integrated Land Missions, NZ Army.www.army.mil.nz., June 26, 2017. Accessed on October 31, 2019.

25 ibid.

26 US Department of Defence, Annual Report to Congress, Military and Security Developments, involving the People's Republic of China 2010, at: http://www.defense.gov, pp. 25–26, 2010.

27 Australian Army. (2014). Future Land Warfare Report. Directorate of Future Land Warfare, Australian Army Headquarters, Canberra: Australia, 2014.

28 Anja Kaspersen, Espen Barth Eide, Philip Shetler-Jones, "10 trends for the future of warfare", World economic Forum, www.weforum.org.

29 Australian Army. (2014). Future Land Warfare Report. Directorate of Future Land Warfare, Australian Army Headquarters, Canberra: Australia, 2014.

30 The Fundamentals of Land Warfare 1, p. 42, www.army.gov.au, 2017, Accessed on October 31, 2019.

31 Craig Stockings, "The Domain in which we Dwell: The Foundations, Form and Future of Land Warfare", www.craigstockings,the domain in which we dwell, 2007. Accessed on October 31, 2019.

32 Ibid.

3

Future Conflicts in the Indian Subcontinent

Colonel Puneet Doval

"If India is to become a great power of the sort that it seeks to become, it also has to become a net provider of regional security, both in the sub-continental and in the extra sub-continental arenas."

– Ashley J Tellis[1]

ABSTRACT

Limited to a 15 years' window, the chapter will endeavour to highlight the perceivable scenarios/triggers/irritants which may manifest into a conflict in the Indian subcontinent in context of India focusing primarily on China and Pakistan, with some of the possible broad conflict/crisis scenarios in the future being:

- (a) *Hybrid Conflict and/or conventional war with China in a nuclear backdrop.*
- (b) *Limited or Conventional Conflict with Pakistan with a nuclear overhang.*
- (c) *Assistance to Indian Ocean Littoral States (pre-emptive or on request).*
- (d) *Terrorism/Insurgency oriented threats in Kashmir, North East and Hinterland, aided and abetted by inimical regional player/s.*
- (e) *Internal unrest due to growth of religious fundamentalism, socio and political inequalities and naxal activities.*
- (f) *Terrorist groups acquiring WMD.*
- (g) *Population/refugee pressures and its impact on security.*
- (h) *The problem of porous skies and waters.*

The way ahead for India lies in the following:

- *Formation of a National Security Strategy.*

- *Strong Military Power.*
- *Broad Doctrinal Pointers:*

(a) *Swap Massive Conventional Response Strategy with Flexible Response Strategy including the Disruptive Domain.*

(b) *Define the punitive deterrence which can be undertaken by ground, air and naval forces.*

(c) *Limited war situation relevant to Pakistan is now equally relevant to China as well.*

(d) *The existing escalation ladders in the sub-conventional domain are largely adhoc.*

(e) *Emphasis on increased Indian aerospace power in a manner that provides a visible asymmetric edge over its likely adversaries.*

(f) *Build Asymmetric Capabilities Against China.*

General

Geo-Politics in Asia is witnessing three tectonic concerns. **Firstly**, the power shift towards Asia can be linked to its phenomenal economic rise, manifesting from the rise of China, Japan and India, in the global economic arena. **Secondly**, the fountainhead of global and regional terrorism also lies in this region, which is a major source of concern for the world community. **Thirdly**, owing to historical baggage, Asia still remains a battle ground for conventional conflicts, worst under a nuclear overhang, in context of a number of adversaries, viz. Pakistan, India, China, Taiwan, Japan, North and South Korea, in various permutations and combinations.

While developments in the fields of economy, information technology and overall consolidation of our comprehensive national power have put India on the growth path, her internal security environment is yet to stabilise and is often exploited by external inimical forces, through asymmetrical, hybrid and grey zone means. Potential rise of India as a global power would require development of all elements of Comprehensive National Power, to secure her interests and enable her to play a more effective role in the regional and global arena.

Drivers Shaping the Global Security Environment

War against Terror. The paradigm shift in the US policy on terrorism brought about after 9/11, saw the US launch its global war against terror. Notwithstanding the limited success, the US intervention in Afghanistan did demonstrate to the world the US resolve to go the extra mile to fight the terrorists and take the war to them. However, has it lessened the threat of terrorism? Will it guarantee the world a tension-free future? Have the terrorists won already? Have the terrorists forced the West to deplete their own precious store of human rights and civil liberties? Are they provoking us to load unnecessary burdens and restrictions on the freedom and profitability of our economic life? Are they tempting us to forget who our friends are and to weaken and split up our most important cooperative institutions, notably at the international level?[2]

All these questions are open to debate. The rise of international terrorism indeed shows that the information age is both an integrating and a dividing force. Terrorism remains the principal challenge to liberal and democratic societies and now occupies centre stage in the international security matrix. The scourge of terrorism, like the Easter Day blasts in Sri Lanka on 21 April 2019, will continue to invite the focus of global attention in the foreseeable future.

Nuclear Terrorism. The efforts of various renegade state and non-state actors to gain access to WMD have highlighted the dangers of proliferation of WMD material and their delivery means, especially if it reaches the hands of terrorists. India remains as concerned on this count as the other global powers. Nuclear weapons have really gained importance. "Until national interests remain secondary to the larger international interests, the role of nuclear weapons in world politics will continue".[3] Another threat is that the terrorist organisations may assemble "dirty bombs" in which high explosives (RDX or TNT) are used to blow up and scatter uranium or other radioactive materials over a large area. Spent nuclear fuel rods that are stolen and radiation waste from large hospitals and laboratories could be used as the "core" in such crude nukes. Although such dirty bombs will not cause horrendous casualties, if exploded in large cities, yet they will create a fear psychosis that will add to the paranoia. "After the 9/11 attacks on the World Trade Centre and the Pentagon, scenarios that were considered alarmist have now assumed nightmarish proportions".[4]

Energy Crisis. Representing 4.3 per cent of the global population, the US claims over 20 per cent of the world's oil use. The upshot is that US dependence on oil has risen from one-third in 1985 to more than half in 2010 and is set to climb to two-thirds by 2020.[5] China has gone to great lengths to ensure their domination over world oil. They have made heavy investments in keeping the immensely oil-rich Persian Gulf region and Africa. They have done so by propping up client regimes with arms and credits, acquiring military bases, overthrowing or marginalising the opposition and trying to influence the routing of oil export pipelines.

Undermining of the UN. In the recent past, we have witnessed increased undermining of the UN in providing the lead role for resolution of conflicts and stabilisation. There is an urgent need to re-structure the UN for it to remain relevant to the emerging realities. The reality is that the five unelected yet permanent members of the Security Council need to share executive authority with new and emerging powers, India being amongst the most prominent.

Radicalisation in the Islamic World. Wars in Iraq and Afghanistan and rising unrest in the West Asia and Middle East are causing an increasing cross-current of disaffection resulting in radicalisation within the Islamic world and isolation of moderate forces. In relative terms a large yet benign Muslim population has added to India's strengths.

Trans National Immigrations/ Refugees. Trans-national migrations from neighbouring countries have become one of the primary resource and security concern for many countries in our World. The data on migration by last residence in India as per Census 2001 shows that the total number of migrants were 314 million. Out of these migrants by last residence, 268 million (85%) have been intra-state migrants, those who migrated from one area of the state to another. Forty-one million (13%) were interstate migrants and 5.1 million (1.6%) migrated from outside of the country.[6]

Environment, Climate Change and Urban Stress. Key global trends leading to insecurity in the world today are climate change, environment degradation and urbanisation which are putting enormous pressure on developing economies. Climate change can reduce the farm output by 20-25 per cent manifesting into distress for communities at large who then try to move out of the farm sector and from rural to urban areas. In India, by about 2050 the urban population is going to exceed rural population, there will be more mega cities. Technology even though has tackled many challenges that the country faces but is available to only a few sections of the society. Therefore, the technology itself becomes a medium of triggering inequality.[7] Climate change stunted India's growth by 31 per cent, according to a study by Stanford researchers published in Proceedings of the National Academy of Science (PNAS), using annual temperatures and GDP data.[8]

Dominance of Outer Space. The testing of the ASAT by India, on 27 March 2019, emphasised on the fact that space-oriented weapon systems are becoming an increasingly important component of military power. Although commercial satellite imagery provides capabilities that are almost trivial compared to those of advanced US systems, these capabilities are revolutionary compared to what was available only a decade ago.[9] There is growing international concern that US and China quest for 'full-spectrum dominance' will give rise to a destabilising arms race in space.

The Indian Subontinent

The complexities in this region include the internal instability and future of domestic and economic fault lines in Pakistan, the effects of the proverbial US withdrawal from Afghanistan in the near future with the return of Taliban and the consequential effect on the internal dynamics and political hierarchy in Pakistan, the North Korean conundrum with its penchant and vulnerability to flare up at any point, the island disputes in the South China Sea, involvement of Japan, Vietnam and Philippines in the island disputes with China. The relations between India and its immediate neighbours retain the potential of manifesting into a confrontation if not handled well.

South East Asian Region. The enhanced economic strength of ASEAN countries and the importance of the region, for transit of global trade and energy, have resulted in India actively pursuing its 'Act East Policy'. We not only share common cultural heritage with the South East Asian nations but also share common concerns on a range of security challenges like terrorism, religious radicalism, gun running, drugs, piracy and illegal immigration.

Growing Security Paradigm with Southeast Asia. The involvement of India with Southeast Asia was never as important as it is now. Southeast Asia is a strategic theatre for India especially in light of its relationship with Japan and South Korea, specifically the economic linkages. Countries like Vietnam, Myanmar, Cambodia and Laos offer immense trade potential and economic linkages and these would thus need to be safeguarded appropriately. Primary concerns emanate from emergence of China as major regional power, given its exorbitant claims in South China Sea and her track record of using military force with impunity. India's EEZ, similarity in environmental concerns, sea lines of communication are major security concerns and require effective engagement with ASEAN countries.

Afghanistan. The outcome of substantial reconstruction efforts in Afghanistan and inevitable withdrawal of US troops will have a profound effect on the global security matrix. India has major security interests in Afghanistan and its stabilisation is in her interest.

China. Its grand strategic aim is to dominate Asia and be counted as a global power. In pursuit of the above, it is slowly but steadily drawing its neighbours into its sphere of influence by economics, trade, infrastructural support and military co-operation with its latest avatar as BRI. Regional players who are seen as potential threats like India are being contained by selective collusive support. China's close defence relationship with Pakistan takes a particular edge in view of the latter's known belligerence and hostility towards India and its acquisition of nuclear assets. "No country has done greater long term damage to India's national security than China".[10]

There are differing perceptions of the role and interests of China and India in South Asia. India's effort is bent on exclusion of foreign involvement and interference in this region. Chinese policies have been designed to establish its major presence in the region.[11] Besides, the very slow progress of the talks on the border issue with India gives rise to misgivings that it probably wants to keep this issue alive till it has totally pacified Tibet to its satisfaction and retain a pressure point with India, which it can exploit should India show reluctance to keep the Tibetan refugees under control. In national security matters, China, unlike India, works on a long-term basis and tries to develop options, which they may need years later should circumstances so warrant.[12]

Pakistan. The single greatest threat to peace and stability in the region is posed by the combination of terrorism nurtured by Pakistan. The obtaining geo-strategic environment is tilting against Pakistan. This is due to the diminishing presence of the US and interest in Pakistan, and its reduced relevance to its policies in Afghanistan and Central Asia, its strategic relevance to China in the subcontinent; concern about radical Islamic and terrorist influences that may move the entire nation towards radicalisation. An important development that has serious security implications is the adoption of nuclear weapons capability as centrepiece of its deterrence philosophy. The "enemy image" of India amongst Pakistanis has much to do with their domestic political patterns and their response to efforts for peace, stability and cooperation in South Asia.[13] The elections have restored a democratic polity, which is hard pressed to restore security and economic stability to the country, in the face of complex challenges like the recent standoff with India. Various contradictions in the Pakistan's social political fabric, power struggles between the various entities, and the fragility of institutions like the judiciary and educational infrastructure are likely to occupy the centre stage in the near future. The biggest challenge faced by the Pakistan government is to moderate the large radicalised sections. Overall the situation in Pakistan remains critical.

India and Its Immediate Neighbourhood. India's immediate neighbourhood includes Nepal, Bhutan, Bangladesh,[14] Myanmar,[15] Sri Lanka, right up to Pakistan and Afghanistan and the Central Asian Republics in the West have distinct security dynamics originating from their respective internal and external dimensions. The Chinese BRI initiatives in these countries cannot be avoided; owing largely to the Chinese trade and huge markets for Chinese goods and resources. Thus, India's relationship with these countries, infused with the spirit of India's Neighbourhoods First Policy, needs to leverage with a mindset of an Elder and not Big Brother.

Indian Ocean Region (IOR). The region is profoundly important from the Indian strategic perspective. It is gaining importance on account of the US presence, increasing Chinese influence and the centrality of sea routes on account of trade and energy requirements. Besides, all future extra regional challenges to India are likely to have specific maritime dimensions. Hence, it is important for India to evolve a comprehensive maritime policy to include foreign, military, economic and technological dimensions.

India's Strategic Frontiers. In the address to the Combined Commanders Conference, Prime Minister Vajpayee on 01 November 2003, stated, "...as we grow in international stature, our defence strategies should naturally reflect our political, economic and security concerns, extending well beyond the geographical confines of South Asia. Our security environment ranges from the Persian Gulf to the Straits of Malacca across the Indian Ocean, includes Central Asia and Afghanistan in the North West, China in the North East and South East Asia. Our strategic thinking has to extend to these horizons".[16] Analytically, this statement can be said to be a definition of India's strategic frontiers.

Implications for India

The world is increasingly witnessing the unleashing of other forms of Warfare over the traditional forms of War. Post the First Iraq War (Op DESERT SHIELD: 1990–91), mankind has not witnessed a Conventional War in true sense but has been suffering from other modes of warfare wherever it faces human induced destruction in our World today, viz. Middle East, South Asia, etc. Hence, India's endeavours to avoid wars can only bear fruit if she is fully prepared for the entire spectrum of Warfare with special emphasis on the grey zone and sub-conventional character of conflict. Infact without being prepared for the latter, India cannot be fully prepared for any form of war given the American experience in Iraq or Afghanistan, wherein, a Comprehensive Victory still eludes the mightiest conventional military of our world. Hence, one may safely assume that the Warfare of tomorrow most certainly will be a hybrid one, with the lines often blurring between one to another form of warfare.

An analysis of recent conflicts reveals the ever-changing nature of hybrid engagements—the blurring lines between conventional and non-conventional warfare, state and non-state actors, regular and irregular conflicts, or conflicts in asymmetric and grey zone domains. While the balance of global power and possession of nuclear weapons by an increasing number of nation states has somewhat reduced the possibility of a total war at the global level, however, at the regional level, its risk remains.[17]

When it comes to the Sub-Conventional Domain, India perhaps is the only Country which has been battling this form of Conflict. India's humane means to conduct operations, with population (Awam) being at its heart, has been the beacon for other armies who conduct such operations with every piece of weaponry and armament in their inventory. Domains like Cyber, Information Warfare, Artificial Intelligence & Robotics and Disruptive Technologies, if not monitored, are potential threats through which, besides inimical nation-states, non-state actors, individual terrorists and even disgruntled elements within a state can cause havoc with a nation's telecom, banking, stock exchanges, power grid, railways and air traffic control, besides military communication and networks. The foremost concern thus becomes security of our communications and the transactions in our economic institutions. Indian security forces will do well to be alive to domains of future conflicts future threats to national security are becoming increasingly difficult to predict due to strategic uncertainty, there is a case in point to study how both the Nature and Character of Conflict will change in the future in the Indian context. Indian Armed Forces have to be prepared for changes in Nature and Character of War. This would demand the highest levels of leadership.

Possible Conflict Scenarios

Limited to a 15 years' window, the perceivable scenarios which may manifest into a conflict in the future would be as under:

(a) Hybrid Conflict and/or conventional war with China in a nuclear backdrop.
(b) Limited or Conventional Conflict with Pakistan under a nuclear overhang.
(c) Assistance to Indian Ocean Littoral States.
(d) Terrorism-oriented threats in Kashmir, North East and Hinterland,
(e) Internal unrest due to growth of religious fundamentalism, socio and political inequalities.
(f) Terrorist groups acquiring WMD.
(g) Population/refugee pressures and its impact on security.
(h) The problem of porous skies and waters.

Way Ahead

National Security Strategy. To begin with, it is time that India laid out its National Security Strategy, exuding her time-bound capability and capacity building goals, as also, dedicated fund allocation towards the same. Wherein, grey zone operations and sub-conventional capability building must be taken as being inherent to its conventional capabilities, coupled with increasing ability to reach out to India's diaspora worldwide during the time of need. Broad nuances of its response options towards various threats must also be outlined to serve as deterrence to her adversaries.[18] Against such a background, India's national aim, in light of its economic trajectory and strategic autonomy, will be best served by the principle avoidance duly supported with credible/assured destruction capabilities. In case a conflict breaks out, its limitation will be a prudent option. At the upper ends of conflict, early conflict termination is highly desirable, lest escalation becomes a fait accompli. Applying the limited war concept makes sense in that it would not deflect India from its economic trajectory overly. Moreover, localised conflicts are easier to terminate, it affords 'quick victory or saving face' options, resources committed are less and prestige is not staked inordinately. Limited war is a concept that has been under discussion in India since 2000, though this has found greater reflection in the India-Pakistan context. Recently, limited war has also gained traction with reference to China and is likely to manifest through an informationalised war.

Military Power. While India's economic and military capabilities have no doubt increased substantially in recent times, with its GDP being third in the world in Purchasing Power Parity (PPP) and its military the second largest in the world. However, India is yet to master the ability "to integrate the creation, deployment and use of military instruments in support of national objectives".[19] In stark contrast to India, China has shown a willingness to use force quite readily in pursuit of its national goals while always insisting that it is defensive in nature, to an extent where defence can even include a pre-emptive strike. While, opportunities for the military leveraging in the statecraft and national interest is only growing, the requisite resources are not always made available, constrained by competing demands from other sectors. Hence, unless India achieves higher rates of economic growth and modernises its military, both quantitatively and qualitatively, and learns to use its military instruments in pursuit of national objectives, its foreign policy will struggle to achieve the results it desires.

Broad Doctrinal Pointers

There is a definitive need to mirror India's military doctrine in tune with the realities and underline the objectives that need to be achieved. It could lie within the domain of a grey zone/limited war under a nuclear overhang and should dwell on the following:

(a) Swap Massive Conventional Response Strategy with Flexible Response Strategy including the Disruptive Domain. Through smart leveraging of military pressure points nations are achieving their strategic and foreign policy objectives often without a shot being fired. South China Sea is a classic example in this case.[20]

(b) Define the punitive deterrence which can be undertaken by ground, air and naval forces. The doctrine must be based on India's capability to deter war and, if so required attempt to fight only on one front and try to manage the other political/ diplomatically through dissuasion. Efforts to upgrade our capability to that of credible conventional deterrence should, however, continue.

(c) Limited war situation relevant to Pakistan is now equally relevant to China as well. The doctrine must lay down means to inflict max punishment within the domain of limited war.

(d) The existing escalation ladders in the sub-conventional domain are largely adhoc. There is a definitive need to legislate rungs that will provide focused and proportionate response options to various scenarios and place the onus of any further escalation entirely upon the adversary. These decision matrices must provide the political leadership with clear options to escalate/de-escalate and facilitate assertion of escalation dominance/escalation control.

(e) Emphasis on increased Indian aerospace power in a manner that provides a visible asymmetric edge over its likely adversaries. Proposal for creation of an Aerospace Command is a step in this direction.

(f) Build Asymmetric Capabilities Against China. This should be executed.

With three broad prongs. ***First,*** capability to leverage existing terrain by triggering an effective insurgency in the areas occupied by Chinese forces and create capabilities in IW domain to target Chinese command and control centres as also through non-contact domain by utilising missiles. The ***Second prong*** is to integrate frontier regions and its people by speeding up and improving communication infrastructure with the mainland. The ***third prong being*** domination of IOR.

Sino-India

From among a menu ranging from compellence, deterrence and defence, India's strategic doctrinal choice is evident. Compellence is ruled out, and to some measure even defence. The choice is restricted to deterrence, with its two variants: offensive deterrence and defensive deterrence. The former involves more expensive offensive capabilities and is predicated on deterrence by punishment (quid pro quo operations). The latter is based on deterrence by denial. Defensive deterrence makes grand strategic sense as articulated by one of the NSA's:

Our goal must be defence, not offence, unless offence is necessary for deterrence or to protect... We must recognise that other countries too could have similar imperatives as ours and their own reasons for what they do. And why create self-fulfilling prophesies of conflict with powerful neighbours like China?[21]

That thought resonated well with the armed forces, with the former Chairman Chiefs of Staff Committee, Admiral Mehta stating, '*On the military front, our strategy to deal with China must include reducing the military gap...The traditional or 'attritionist' approach of matching 'Division for Division' must give way....*'[22] These must be supplemented by 'harnessing modern technology for developing high situational awareness and creating a reliable stand-off deterrent'.

The spectrum of conflict is a conceptual aid to discuss conflict and subsumes along its continuum sub-conventional conflict; conventional war in its limited and total dimensions; and nuclear war in its limited and strategic dimensions. There is a considerable interest among think tanks on a possible conflict with China, and as such, it would be appropriate to first discuss certain probable conflict scenarios in the context of Theatre Commands and China's A2/AD strategy. Various probable scenarios in the conflict spectrum are discussed below.

Sub-conventional Level

At the sub-conventional level are the proxy wars. The Chinese support for rebels in the North East until the late sixties can be subsumed under this. Playing of the proxy war 'card' can be done in peacetime and it can be enhanced in war to keep the communication zone of the adversary unsettled for operational gains. However, the factor of India's own multiple vulnerabilities in this sphere cannot be overlooked. While the foregoing are intelligence operations, military actions can also occur at the sub-conventional level. These include patrol clashes and border skirmishes. For instance Incursions in the Depsang Valley in Eastern Ladakh suggest that patrol clashes can occur inadvertently or by design.[23]

This was the pattern in the run up to the 1962 conflict as part of the 'forward policy' adopted by both states resulting in clashes at the grassroots level.[24] Such occurrences could build up to a border skirmish or be engineered as conflict trigger. The 1967 standoff at Nathu La and the Sumdorong Chu incidents of the late eighties are examples that have the potential to escalate into a lager border conflict.

Conventional Level

The lower end of the conflict at this level could be a Kargil-like situation. China's aim could be to 'teach India a lesson' so as to influence India's rise before its capacity building underway acquires traction. This could be a limited war confined to a specific section of the border or LAC, limited in duration and amenable to a negotiated termination. Though, the conflict could be predominantly land based, PLAAF and Airborne Corps coupled with Special Forces could be employed extensively.

At a higher level it could be a territorial grab by China, for example a bid to take Tawang. At the next rung it could be a more ambitious bid Southwards up to its claim line. Lateral or horizontal expansion of conflict from one theatre to another is the next step, with the conflict engulfing one or more of the four possible theatres: Ladakh (Eastern Ladakh and Sub Sector North), Central Sector, Sikkim and Arunachal Pradesh.[25] A higher end war may spread outwards from the mountains to include extensive use of long range vectors of PLA Rocket Force. The Chinese will resort to employing conventionally armed Short Range Ballistic Missiles (SRBMs) and Cruise Missiles against Indian forces, communication centres, logistic installations and choke points.

Likely Triggers of Conflict. The range of discordant issues between India and China have increased from three initially: Tibet, Border Disputes and Support to Pakistan to many more, viz. Trade Imbalance, Maritime Dominance (especially IOR), Stalling India's bid for UNSC and NSG, Terrorism, aspect of Strategic Encirclement (string of pearls and ring of diamond), Environment (Arunachal Floods of 2000), Space and Cyber, to name a few. Further, if any of the issues mentioned is not managed within limits, it has the potential (individually or collectively) of escalation to any level.

India–Pakistan

With India's strategic doctrinal choice most likely being Punitive Deterrence, the India-Pakistan conflict may be described as enduring rivalry, characterised by long duration, recurrence of armed exchanges and involvement of state and non-state actors. Pak has been waging proxy war against India since the mid-eighties primarily in the states of Punjab and J&K. India's inability to retaliate against the sub conventional challenge prior to 1998 was attributed to lack of decisive conventional edge and the proverbial political resolve. However, a new dimension came into existence in 1998, as the two nations became overt nuclear powers. The cultivated irrationality of Pakistan nuclear threshold in many ways negated India's conventional superiority. Pakistan deemed its nuclear capability as an insurance policy which would dissuade India from escalating the situation and at the same time, provide her a free hand to intensify proxy war in Kashmir.

Nonetheless, a strong Indian conventional response in Kargil in 1999 did bring along a major sobering effect. More recently, after Myanmar raids in 2015, the Pakistan Defence Minister stated on record that similar action, if taken by India against Pakistan, could result in a nuclear war. However, India's surgical strikes post Uri and Balakot air strikes post Pulwama have proven beyond doubt that Pak can no longer play the bogey of low nuclear threshold. This may also point towards the fact that adequate spectrum is available to India to respond to the sub-conventional challenges without tipping the red lines.

Sub-Conventional Level

India is already facing the proxy war aided and abetted by Pakistan since the last four decades. Pakistan's support for terrorists in the J&K and Punjab is well documented along with her attempts to make in-roads with the rebels in the North East through their conduits in Bangladesh and Nepal. Non-state actors thus play a very important role in Pakistan's strategic and executive calculus, given the leverage it accords to Pakistan during the No War No Peace scenario with its Hot War employment in terms of sabotage, blocking of the lines of communication and communication zone upheavals.

Limited War

There may be well be a scenario wherein the exchange of hostilities between India and Pakistan are limited by geographical boundaries, viz. limited only to J&K or limited to an area within J&K {most likely} much like the Kargil Skirmish. It may be Limited to the International Border (IB) Sector or limited to an area within the IB Sector.

All out Conventional Level (With or Without Nuclear Exchange)

As brought out earlier that, while the balance of global power and possession of nuclear weapons by an increasing number of nation states has somewhat reduced the possibility of a total war at the global level, however, at the regional level (especially in India–Pakistan context), its risk remains.[26] Escalation of tensions between the two adversaries' post-Pulwama incident and the resultant Indian Air Strikes at Balakot on 26 February 2019 goes to prove the point that this region remains the Global Hotspot towards an all-out conventional war under a nuclear over hang.

Likely Triggers of Conflict. Ironically the range of discordant issues between India and Pakistan are far too many to be managed by the dispensation in both the countries. Hence, it requires a reconciliatory approach more importantly by the population of both the Nations to avoid a conflict which may escalate across all thresholds. Some of the likely triggers may be: Pakistan's obsession with Kashmir, takeover of Pakistan Occupied Kashmir, proxy war aided and abetted by Pakistan, terrorist incidents in Indian hinterland planned out of Pak territory, threat of use of force by any of the two nations, environmental issues to include Indus Water Treaty, issue of MFN Status, maritime issues (Sir Creek), stalling India's bid for UNSC and NSG, competition in regional Geopolitical/ strategic domain, ideological (Two Nation Theory), pressure tactics and nuclear brinkmanship by Pak.

The Collusive Threat

The 'threat' has been envisaged now due to juxtaposing of infrastructure developments in Tibet coupled with Chinese investment in CPEC.[27] The manifestation of the threat in terms of scenarios could be either Pakistan or China-led. Alternatively, it could be with either state taking advantage of an adverse situation for India brought on by the other state.

A Pakistan-led case is difficult to visualise since China would not like the 'tail to wag the dog'. China could nevertheless participate in such an adventure by providing covert military support in terms of posturing in the garb of military exercises in Tibet as also opposite Eastern Ladakh, besides critical military equipment/deficiencies would be made available.[28] A 'hyena act' by Pakistan is easier to visualise than one by China, since China is more likely to be able to place India at a military disadvantage than Pakistan. In such a case, with India militarily distracted in an engagement with China, Pakistan could try and gain psychological ascendancy, remove vulnerabilities through military action or recreate proxy war conditions.

Way Ahead

National Security Strategy. To begin with, it is time that India laid out its National Security Strategy exuding her time-bound capability and capacity building goals, as also, dedicated fund allocation towards the same. Broad nuances of its response options towards various threats must also be outlined to serve as deterrence to her adversaries.[29] Against such a background, India's national aim will be best served by the principle of avoidance duly supported with credible destruction capabilities. In case a conflict breaks out, its limitation will be a prudent option. At the upper ends of conflict, early conflict termination is highly desirable, lest escalation becomes a fait accompli. Applying the limited war concept makes sense in that it would not deflect India from its economic trajectory overly. Moreover, localised conflicts are easier to terminate, it affords 'quick victory or saving face' options, resources committed are less and prestige is not staked inordinately. Limited war has recently gained traction against both adversaries.

Military Power. India is yet to master the ability "to integrate the creation, deployment and use of military instruments in support of national objectives".[30] In stark contrast to India, China has shown a willingness to use force quite readily in pursuit of its national goals while always insisting that it is defensive in nature. While, opportunities for the military leveraging in the statecraft and national interest is only growing, the requisite resources are not always made available, constrained by demands from other sectors. Hence, unless India achieves higher rates of economic growth and modernises its military, both quantitatively and qualitatively, and learns to use its military instruments in pursuit of national objectives, its foreign policy will struggle to achieve the results it desires.

Broad Doctrinal Pointers

There is a definitive need to mirror India's military doctrine in tune with the realities and should dwell on the following aspects:

(a) Swap Massive Conventional Response Strategy with Flexible Response Strategy including the Disruptive Domain. Through smart leveraging of military pressure points nations are achieving their strategic and foreign policy objectives often without a shot being fired. South China Sea is a classic example in this case.[31]

(b) Define the punitive deterrence which can be undertaken by ground, air and naval forces. The doctrine must be based on India's capability to deter war and, if so required attempt to fight only on one front and try to manage the other political/ diplomatically through dissuasion.

(c) The doctrine must lay down means to inflict max punishment within the domain of limited war which may be limited in dimensions of time-frame, area and damage caused to the military and economic potential of the adversary.

(d) The existing escalation ladders in the sub-conventional domain are largely adhoc. There is a definitive need to legislate rungs that will provide just, focused and proportionate response options to various scenarios and place the onus of any further escalation entirely upon the adversary. These decision matrices must provide the political leadership with clear options to escalate/de-escalate and facilitate assertion of escalation dominance/escalation control.

(e) Emphasis on increased Indian aerospace power in a manner that provides a visible asymmetric edge over its likely adversaries.

(f) Build Asymmetric Capabilities Against China

Pakistan

Amicable relations with Pakistan are mired with historical baggage, deep-rooted animosity and strategic miscalculations. Having fought three wars and Kargil conflict in 1999; India still suffers from a perpetual proxy war abetted by Pakistan, manifesting perhaps from an ever increasing support from China and American ambivalence. This course under taken by Pakistan has two grave ramifications. **Firstly**, its own survival being at stake from the forces of radicalisation and economic downturn and **secondly**, the possibility of a conflict with India.

The current policy of bleeding India suits Pakistan. Accordingly, India should be prepared for adopting the hard option if all else fails. The conflict initiation is more likely to be by India and should be prepared for this eventuality over the next five to ten years. At the same time the stage should be set diplomatically and economically. A number of contingencies must be worked out and refined in the form of a limited conflict to an all-out conflict with varying terminal objectives. Further, India's plan must exploit technology in the cyberspace and develop capabilities in the domains of conventional missiles, armed UAVs, precision fires so that even its non-contact kinetic options become more viable. The Indian Air Force and Indian Navy will have to play a major role in the next conflict. With increasing foreign presence around the waters of Pakistan, the Indian navy will have to relook at its strategy. Lastly, as far as Pakistan is concerned her nuclear bluff has to be called out and for this India should seek the support of the US and Russia and may be even China.[32]

China

As far as India's northern front is concerned, there are issues of convergence as also divergence. Despite the fact that there has not been a single shot fired between border guarding forces of both the countries since Nathu-La engagement and positive progress in Indo-China relations since the visit of PM Rajiv Gandhi to China, unsolved border claims and mutual distrust still remains. However, what cannot be ignored by India is the massive development of dual use infrastructure in Tibet Autonomous Region and the related rapid deployment capabilities acquired by the PLA, coupled with organisational and doctrinal upgradation, viz. the theatre commands. China, therefore, remains the long-term challenge to India's national aspirations—not a threat but a challenge. Accordingly, as part of its holistic strategy towards China, India should engage China on multiple levels such as trade, commerce, cultural and political engagement, people-to-people contacts. All this should be done from a position of strength both in terms of infrastructure along the borders and military capability development for our Northern borders.[33]

NOTES

1 Ashley, J Tellis, Senior Associate, Carnegie Endowment for International Peace, Washington. "Future Fire: Challenges Facing Indian Defence Policy in The New Century". *The India Today* Conclave, New Delhi. 13 March 2004.
2 Alyson, JK, Bailes, Director SIPRI. "Have the Terrorists Won Already". Scanbus Conference, Riga. 14 September 2004.
3 Rajpal, Budania. India in the Post War Uncertainties: A Security Perspective, in "Security and Foreign Policy in South Asia. Jaipur: Mukesh Kumar Kayathwal, 1999, p. 133.
4 Gurmeet, Kanwal. Nuclear Terrorism: New Threat Posed By Briefcase Bombs".

Bharat Rakshak Monitor. Volume 6. March 2004.
5 Michael, Renner. "Fueling Conflict". Vital Signs, World Watch Institute.
6 Office of the Registrar General & Census Commissioner, MHA, Government of India.
7 Lt Gen DS Hooda (Retd), Director CLAWS - Annual Army Seminar, Manekshaw Centre, New Delhi, 14 February 2019.
8 Hindustan times Article, dated 24 April 2019.
9 John, Spike. "The Military Uses of Outer Space". Chapter 11: SIPRI Yearbook 2002.
10 G Parthasarathy. "The Foreign Policy Challenges Ahead". The Hindu Business Line, 22 May 2004.
11 Iqbal, Khanam. Indo-China Relations in Security and Foreign Policy in South Asia. Mukesh Kumar Kayathwal. Jaipur: Pointer, 1999.
12 B Raman. National Security Doctrine (An analysis). Institute for Topical Studies, Chennai.
13 Moonis, Ahmar. Pakistan's Democracy and Co-operative Security Arrangements in South Asia, in "Security and Foreign Policy in South Asia", Mukesh Kumar Kayathwal. Jaipur: Pointer, 1999, p. 109.
14 Baylis, 2008, op. cit., pp. 7-9.
15 Ibid, pp. 190–95.
16 Prime Minister A.B. Vajpayee. Combined Commanders Conference. 01 November 2003." India Defines her strategic Frontiers", South Asia Analysis Group, Paper No 823, 04 November 2003, www.southasiaanalysis.org, Accessed on 31 October 2019.
17 Gen Bipin Rawat, COAS - Annual Army Seminar, Manekshaw Centre, New Delhi, 14 February 2019.
18 Puneet Doval, "Pulwama 2019: Introspection and Way Ahead, CLAWS Issue Brief No 174, March 2019, p. 4.
19 Ashley J Tellis, "Future Fire: Challenges Facing Indian Defence Policy in the New Century", Lecture delivered at India Today Conclave, New Delhi, March 2004.
20 Lt Gen Raj Shukla - Annual Army Seminar, Manekshaw Centre, New Delhi, 14 February 2019.
21 Shiv Shankar Menon, 'Our Ability to change India in a globalised world' *Tribune*, 14 August 2011.
22 Admiral Suresh Mehta, India's National Security Challenges; An Armed Forces Overview Address at India Habitat Centre – 10 August 09.
23 India-China Territorial Dispute: Way Ahead, CLAWS Article 1933, 25 August 2011.
24 Srinath Raghavan, War and Peace in Modern India, 2010, pp. 270–87.
25 Ali Ahmed, A Consideration of Sino-Indian Conflict, IDSA Issue Brief, 24 October 2011.
26 Gen Bipin Rawat, COAS - Annual Army Seminar, Manekshaw Centre, New Delhi– 14 February 2019.
27 Shreyas Deshmukh, "Strategic Framework for Understanding OBOR & CPEC, CLAWS Issue Brief No 87, 16 October, p. 2.
28 Ali Ahmed, "A consideration of Sino-Indian conflict", IDSA Issue Brief, 24 October

2011, p. 5.

29 Puneet Doval, "Pulwama 2019: Introspection and Way Ahead, CLAWS Issue Brief No 174, March 2019, p. 4.

30 Ashley J Tellis, "Future Fire: Challenges Facing Indian Defence Policy in the New Century", Lecture delivered at India Today Conclave, New Delhi, March 2004.

31 Lt Gen Raj Shukla - Annual Army Seminar, Manekshaw Centre, New Delhi–14 February 2019.

32 Ibid.

33 Ibid.

4

Security Challenges and Land Warfare

Lieutenant General (Dr.) VK Ahluwalia

"On balance, it is hard to escape the conclusion that South Asia contains major potential for large scale operations by ground forces, whether in the context of interstate conflict, severe internal violence, or complex humanitarian catastrophe in which the effects of natural disaster are compounded by weak governance and political instability."[1]

– Michael E. O'Hanlon

ABSTRACT

India is a subcontinent with vast land borders, coastline, island territories and exclusive economic zones (EEZ) which require a comprehensive plan to manage them effectively. Given the emerging world order and changes in the security matrix, India must take a hard look at the emerging threats and challenges to our national security, in the backdrop of prevalent nuclear powers in the region. With the changes in geopolitical environment and the emerging technologies, the future operating environment would be complex, ambiguous and uncertain. Technology will play a critical role in all future conflicts. In a multi-domain environment, tri-services integration is vital to inspire confidence among all ranks to undertake bold operational missions, in the short window of opportunity. It is important for strategic leaders to comprehend the emerging politico-economic-social scenario and analyse its impact on the strategic scenario in a multi domain warfare environment. It is also expected of our strategic leaders to keep abreast with the application of the 4th Industrial Revolution—the fusion of technologies—as it affects national security. With the latest technologies in place, employment of unmanned aerial and ground vehicles, precision guided munitions, space-based intelligence gathering systems and reconnaissance by stealth will play a predominant role in support of land operations. The Chapter covers significant aspects of security challenges as applicable to land warfare faced by India and the possible solutions.

Introduction

To mark the 70th anniversary of the People's Republic of China on 1 October 2019, China showed its military muscle power, and sent out a clear message, towards an information-based war-fighting capability by including an information battle group. A stream of early warning radars, electronic warfare equipment and the rocket force showcased China's investment in capabilities integral to high-precision strike capabilities.[2] The display of Rocket Force section included the DF-41 road-mobile intercontinental ballistic missile (ICBM), the DF-17 hypersonic glide vehicle/medium-range ballistic missile combination, and the supersonic CJ-100 cruise missile. Though some of these may be symbolic at present, these potent systems are /or would soon be part of the PLA's inventory.[3] General Joe Dunford, Chairman of the US Joint Chiefs of Staff, 2017, was justified in saying, *"The character of war in the 21st century has changed, and if we fail to keep pace with the speed of war, we will lose the ability to compete"*.[4] In fact, we have to keep abreast with the 'speed of change' in a multi-domain environment, in the larger interest of our national security.

Looking back, there has been a progressive increase in the intra-state conflicts the world over since 1946. Since early 1960s, there was a sharp rise in the insurgencies, which peaked around 1994 when the genocide took place in Rwanda. Since the turn of the millennium, there has been a significant deterioration in the global security environment due to prolonged conflicts in the Middle East and North Africa (MENA), South Asia and Africa. MENA continues to remain the most unstable and violent region of the world, closely followed by South Asia. In 2017 alone, besides several flash points for potential armed conflicts, there were seven active armed conflicts each in MENA, and in Sub Saharan Africa.[5] Both Middle East and South Asia rank among the lowest in peacefulness out of the nine regions evaluated. Image 1 below shows that Asia leads the world in various types of conflicts, which are predominantly land based. Presence of nuclear powers in the South Asian region and neighbourhood add a critical dimension to security considerations.

South Asia comprises eight nation states, with 3.5 percent of the world's land surface, and about one-fourth of the world's population (1.908 billion).[6] Despite geographical, historical, cultural, ethnic and linguistic linkages, South Asia is one of the most violent and unstable regions of the world. Former US President Bill Clinton had called South Asia as the *"World's most dangerous place"*.[7] It is beset with many interstate disputes, and, more importantly, intrastate conflicts with hybrid adversaries playing their role. Interestingly, due to the colonial legacy and mindset, the armed forces of all the South Asian countries are organised primarily for conventional operations, which, with the present capabilities, cannot address the applications of disruptive technologies, information warfare and the emerging hybrid threats. India continues to remain affected by boundary disputes, and is subjected to proxy war cum cross-border terrorism from Pakistan, primary reason being anti-India stance and the Kashmir dispute. India ranks rather low (141st) in its peacefulness in comparison to 163 countries that were evaluated.[8] India is situated in one of the most volatile, fragile and conflict-prone regions of the world.

National Security and Land Warfare

National Security, as a concept, aims to safeguard and promote the core values and interests of the nation state, and its people, against covert or overt nature of conflicts. The traditional and non-traditional forms of

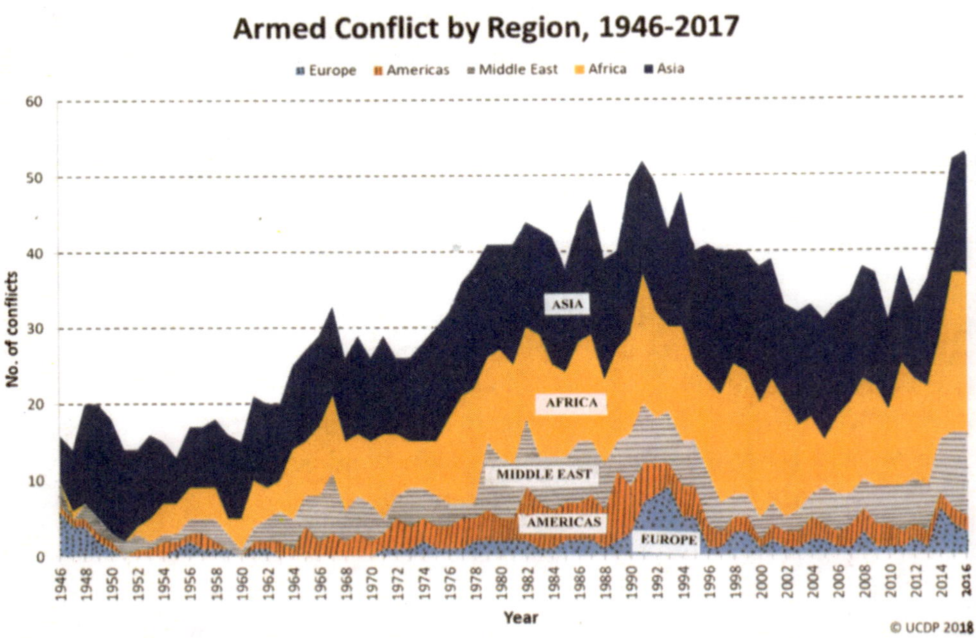

Figure 4.1:Armed Conflict by Region

Source: UCDP, 2018 (annotated by the author).

security threats also must be addressed. Since the human beings live on the land and operate and support all their systems into the seas, air, space and cyber domains, land bases would have to be secured to promote the interests of the nation state and its people. India shares major land borders with China (4056 kms), Pakistan (3074 kms), Bangladesh (4095 kms), Myanmar (1643 kms), Nepal (1751 kms) and Bhutan (690 kms). The LoC (Line of Control) and Actual Ground Position Line (AGPL), the borders with Pakistan in Jammu and Kashmir are 772 kms and 121 kms long respectively. Along the entire stretch of the boundary with China, the Line of Actual Control (LAC), there are many areas of differing perceptions, which often result in transgressions by either side and avoidable standoffs between the two countries. In addition, India also has a long coastline along the mainland and the island groups Andaman and Nicobar, and Lakshadweep. Due to large stretches of land borders, along with territorial disputes both with China and Pakistan, India has remained focused primarily on land-based operations and force. A few illustrations would suggest whether this thought process requires a change.

- Several lessons were learnt from the Gulf War (1990–91) and the conflict that resulted in the breakup of Yugoslavia (1992–93), due to the employment of new technologies in support of land operations. These included employments of airborne forces conducting surgical strikes, Special Forces (SF), stealth technologies, use of Patriot missiles to bring down Scud missiles, precision guided munitions (PGM), space-based intelligence gathering systems and the enhanced intelligence, surveillance and reconnaissance (ISR) capabilities. It was then considered that these have revolutionised the concept of land warfare. However, with the increasing use of unmanned systems in support of land war fighting, such as unattended ground sensors, small unmanned aerial vehicles (UAVs), swarm drones, fire-and-forget missiles and robotic vehicles, we are seeing virtual networked systems that would dominate the warfare of the future.
- Despite employment of advanced technologies, a close look at the course of wars/conflicts since 1990s, such as Gulf Wars (1991 and 2003), Kosovo Conflict (1998-2000), Kargil Conflict (1999), Lebanon War (2006), Russia's invasion of Georgia (2008), Sri Lanka—Liberation Tigers of Tamil Eelam (LTTE) Conflict (2009), Russia-Ukraine conflict (2014), Battles of Mosul, Aleppo and

Raqqa against the ISIS in West Asia (2016-18), would suggest that major component was land warfare with a fair measure of air power, information and hybrid elements thrown in.

- In the 34-day Israel–Hezbollah war of 2006, the Israel's Army, one of the most technologically advanced militaries of the world, were pitted against the fundamentalist Muslim organisation Hezbollah in southern Lebanon. Hezbollah was armed with high-tech weaponry and other disruptive technologies, such as PGMs, anti-tank missiles and unmanned aerial vehicles (UAVs) that are traditionally used by the regular forces of a country. The group's guerrillas operated in a decentralised manner at the tactical levels, both from their urban and mountain bases, and shocked the Israeli Defence Forces (IDF) with their conventional-cum-unconventional forms of warfare. Israel accepted that it committed mistakes in not adequately preparing for a 'hybrid' conflict with Hezbollah.[9]
- ISIS had spread to a few towns in Iraq and Syria, where it controlled a very large portion of the territory. To clear the ISIS from towns like Mosul, Aleppo, and Raqqa in 2016-18, it was finally the land forces (regulars and irregulars), suitably backed by the air and most modern weapon systems, which achieved success. Success came after a prolonged period of fighting by the ground forces, both in rural and urban areas.
- While discussing the role of US Air Force (USAF) against the Taliban in Afghanistan, Col Wilkinson, USAF, and Dr Hill have argued that 15 years of overmatch has so far contributed to nothing more than a stalemate, and suggests that, ***'superb high-end strike capability is an incomplete solution in a low-end conflict'.*** After more than a decade of air dominance, 'use of air blast bombs',[10] they further reiterated that the security situation in Afghanistan is deteriorating.[11] It is true that in a low-intensity conflict in a terrain as obtaining in Afghanistan, even with the availability of an overwhelming air power and strike capability, it is virtually impossible to achieve success against motivated insurgents unless there are adequate 'Boots on the Ground'. Even during the attack on Iraq in 2003, the US had to finally change their strategy, to increase the boots on the ground to achieve victory. With the increase in low-end conflicts, this is likely to be the scenario in the future as well.

Fundamental Questions on National Security and Land Warfare

The pace of changes in the geopolitical environment and revolution in technologies give rise to several questions with reference to the Indian subcontinent:

- What would be the objective(s) of conflicts in the future?
- Would the future wars/conflicts be based on ideology, geopolitics, identity, territorial disputes, ethnic and religious intolerance, religious fundamentalism, economy, water or environment issues, or a combination of a few such factors?
- Although technology would be the driver of change in the 21st century, how would it impact land warfare and at what levels: strategic, operational or tactical levels?
- How is the multi-domain warfare likely to unfold in the Indian subcontinent? How are the hybrid threats likely to impact our national security in the foreseeable future?
- Are we prepared to operate with the joint services, inter-agency elements, particularly in the disputed areas in the mountains and the complex urban terrain environments?

Flash Points and Areas of Concern

West Asia has remained unstable due to the rivalry for regional dominance, intra-regional armed conflicts, civil wars, sectarian and ethnic conflicts, religious fundamentalism, criminal networks and drug trafficking. According to SIPRI Fact Sheet 2019, Iran, Qatar, Saudi Arabia and the United Arab Emirates (UAE) had high levels of military expenditure as a share of their GDP in 1994–2018. Saudi Arabia was the third-largest military spender globally ($67.6 billion) and the largest military spender in the Gulf region in 2018. Expenditure on military is also a good indicator of the prevailing apprehensions, fears and tensions in the region. Thus, the region has several flash points.

President Xi Jinping's statement, 'China will not lose an inch of territory' is an indication that it maintains a territory centric focus when dealing with territorial disputes with its neighbours. Cases in point are India-China standoff at Doklam, and disputes with its South-East Asian nations as also Japan over island territories in South China Sea and East China Sea respectively. These identified flash points are likely to witness conflicts in the future; thus, causing turbulence and instability in the geopolitical environment.[12]

Important security issues that concern India are the strategic encirclement of India by China; the territorial and boundary disputes; repeated transgressions that take place on the LAC; and the China-Pakistan Economic Corridor (CPEC). While developing CPEC project of US$ 62 billion through Pakistan-occupied Jammu and Kashmir (PoJK), China has increased its presence by positioning its security personnel in Gilgit and Baltistan, and other regions in the hinterland. It has high geostrategic cum economic stakes in the region due to its projects. The situation could get further compounded by the China-Pakistan collusion, which has serious challenges to India's security.

Religious fundamentalism will continue to pose a serious threat to both regional and global peace. ISIS, although defeated in Syria and Iraq, its virulent ideas, identity and motivation to achieve its aims and objectives still continues to remain vibrant and active. According to a UN Report, Al-Qaeda is also reviving itself to spread its influence in other parts like Sahel region, South East Asia and South Asia.[13] Drones are much sought after by terror groups against ground targets because of the out of proportion results, and of being smaller, cheaper, noiseless, non-detectable in comparison to large conventional weapons. A case in point is the deadly attack by a swarm of drones on the two major oil plants of Saudi Arabia (Aramco), and the resultant losses suffered, on 14 September 2019. Actions by drones and non-state actors (NSA) are closely intertwined with ground operations. Such UCAVs can be employed effectively in support of ground operations in all types of terrains, including urban areas.

CHALLENGES TO NATIONAL SECURITY

> *...a new type of war that would become increasingly common in the future will be "a hybrid of irregular warfare and conventional warfare."*[14]
>
> **– Gen. George W. Casey, Army Chief**

External Challenges

Two neighbours of India—China and Pakistan—are not just the principal source of her external security threats but are also nuclear-armed states. China and Pakistan share a deep friendship 'stronger than steel' and 'sweeter than honey' . With the ongoing sensitive CPEC projects, we must also factor the aspect of collusion between the two for actions against India. The territorial dispute lies at the core of long-standing conflict between India and its two adversaries, which is the result of its unique geostrategic location, its neighbourhood, its history and legacy of the Partition. India has fought four wars with Pakistan, one with China, and a few border clashes/stand-offs with both separately, over the years. Twenty rounds of talks between the special representatives have not resolved the boundary dispute. In fact, Chinese actions are aimed at 'salami slicing'[15] of the disputed territory without provoking a robust response from India. With this backdrop, as the idea of territorial integrity and sovereignty weighs heavy on the minds of Pakistan, China and India, land warfare would continue to play a predominant role.

Besides the five integrated theatre commands (ITCs), PLA Army (PLAA) has two military commands: Xinjiang military command and Tibet military command (TMC). As observed, in May 2016, TMC was elevated by one level compared to other provincial-level military districts and placed under the PLA Army (PLAA).[16] It was reported that the TMC will be responsible for operations against India, at least in the Arunachal Pradesh area, training forces for specialised high-altitude mountain warfare and long-range mobility for such a contingency.[17] Further, PLAA intends building 'a new type of strong and modernised land force',[18] to win wars. China's military has been restructured into ITCs to face specific threats that it may face in the future. For instance, Western Theatre Command, with the TMC, is responsible for combating extremism and terrorism in Tibet and addressing the Indian border dispute contingency.[19] India, on the contrary, has yet to move beyond its single-service operational practices.[20] After implementing a few of Xi Jinping's 2015 military reforms, the PLA has developed a potent non-kinetic capability in its new Strategic Support Force (SSF), which comprises space, cyber, information (psychological) and varied other dimensions. It can paralyse adversaries' command, control, communications, computers, information, intelligence, surveillance and reconnaissance (C4I2SR) systems.

Putting these two aspects together, it is evident that the PLA draws its strength from its advancements in fusion of technology for defence systems that it produces, and jointness cum integration of capabilities of both kinetic and non-kinetic forms of threats. It has its hard power lined up in its army, air force and navy's arsenal. In addition, it continues to develop unmanned systems, like the drones, for surveillance, reconnaissance, target acquisitions, terminally guided munition systems, and post-strike damage assessment (PSDA). To minimise the human interface, PLA is looking at variety of AI, big data and robotic systems for operations in a multi domain environment. We certainly have a hi-tech adversary in the North.

The security situation in the Indo-Pacific region in general, and the Indian Ocean in particular, are of great concern to India. Therefore, the security of India's long and porous coastline, offshore islands, Exclusive Economic Zones (EEZs) and sea lanes of communications (SLOCs) in the Indian Ocean merits attention. Undoubtedly, India faces complex strategic challenges, over a wide spectrum of conventional, sub-conventional and hybrid wars.

Internal Challenges

On internal security front, India continues to face several complex security challenges since its independence. It is indeed strange that India continued to witness new insurgencies erupt in each decade, commencing with the Naga insurgency of 1956. Similarly, Naxalbari uprising, Manipur and Mizoram insurgencies commenced in 1960s, turbulence took the centre stage in Assam in late 1970s, militancy in Punjab and other insurgencies in the North East region in 1980s, and proxy war cum insurgency shook the state of J&K from 1989 onwards. Therefore, the country faces multiple insurgencies in the North East region, Left Wing Extremism (LWE) in a few parts of India, proxy war cum cross border terrorism in J&K, and the societal violence in general. LWE was at its peak in 2009 and 2010, as it covered about 223 districts in 20 states of the country; and now it has progressively shrunk to less than 90.

According to Barry Buzan, Emeritus Professor of International Relations at the London School of Economics, *"India is a country of several nations"*.[21] Given India's size, its population base and the scope of the security arena, internal security challenges are truly complex. There is huge diversity in geographical regions, ethnicity, religions, and languages. This coupled with social discrimination, inequality in human development indices (HDI), lack of inclusive growth, polarisation of population, and mass unemployment among the youth, makes India vulnerable to internal armed conflicts. The aim of the armed conflicts in India is primarily to achieve one or more of the following: capture political power, or seek separation or secession or greater autonomy.

The major turning point of the insurgency in the Kashmir Valley was in July 2016, when HM militant Burhan Wani was killed in South Kashmir by the SF. Since then, Pakistan has made concerted efforts to destabilise J&K: to indigenise the insurgency in J&K by indoctrinating and radicalising the youth; to provide huge monetary incentives to promote the culture of homegrown terrorists; and insist on making terrorist bases in built up areas or in the urban centres for certain obvious advantages to the terrorists. Moeed Yusuf argues that warfare within South Asian states has been far more prevalent, with far more conflict related casualties, than war between states.[22] Our external and internal security challenges are closely interconnected. As the lines distinguishing them are rather blurred, hybrid of conventional and unconventional is here to stay in the foreseeable future. Operations on the LoC, AGPL, LAC and against insurgents/terrorists are intrinsically manpower intensive, and require boots on the ground to achieve success.

Hyper-urbanisation and Non-Traditional Challenges: Threats in Being

Looking back in history, cities and urban areas—hub of communication centres—have played a prominent role in the campaigns of World War II and thereafter. Post the Cold War, several unique land-based operations in urban environments—both with successes and failures—have taken place which should be studied to draw lessons for the future. A few of these operations are: US and other UN military forces in Mogadishu (1993), Russians in Grozny (1994–96, 1999–2000), US and allied troops in Baghdad (2003) and Sadr City (2008), and US, Iraqi and British troops in the second Battle of Fallujah (2004). In recent times (2016–19), intense operations against the ISIS in urban terrain in Mosul, Aleppo, Raqqa are a few examples of fighting against a blend of conventional and unconventional form of warfare. Mosul was finally captured after nine months of intense land and air operations against the ISIS.

Given the increasing trend of urbanisation, particularly in Asia and Africa in the 21st century, the urban centres are not only the communication centres but also the hub of political, governance, economic, social and cultural importance. While insurgencies continue to sustain in the least developed and developing countries due to several reasons, they are likely to further enhance their spread to urban areas in the future. India is certainly witnessing accelerated urbanisation, including along most of our borders. According to Census of India 2011, India's urban population increased from 217 million in 1991 to 377 million (31.2 percent of the total population) in 2011, a phenomenal increase by 77 percent. Further, it is expected to increase to 590 million by 2031, an increase of 57 percent.[23] It is also true of other South Asian countries. Therefore, the armed forces should be prepared to fight in the complex built-up areas (BUAs), in a conventional and low intensity conflict (LIC) environment, or in a combination of both in the future. The future battlefield will also be fought in a dense urban terrain,[24] which is the toughest form of combat. It has huge implications to land forces on collection of intelligence, manoeuvre and firepower, use of vehicles and weapons, security of logistics and follow on echelons, both in conventional and LIC environment.

In the future, non-traditional threats to human security—food, water, environment, pollution, energy, financial, information, cyber, natural disasters, survival needs—may become the basis of conflicts, both within and outside the states. Fight for fast diminishing mineral resources would continue to be a source of conflict. Most of these threats pertain to employment of land resources.

Analysis

An analysis of the global scan, the pace of rapid changes in technology and the geopolitical scenario, the ongoing trends, the threats and challenges to national security, suggests the following:

- Considering the global geostrategic environment and 'the mutually destructive power of nuclear weapons, international legal constraints and the declining appetite for violence of relatively prosperous societies',[25] the probability of all-out wars between the global powers is very low. However, the probability of sub-conventional conflicts or limited conflicts in different regions, have the potential to spill over into a major conflict with hybrid threats.
- Given the challenges of the intra-state conflicts, state-sponsored terrorism, unsettled borders with our adversaries, and obsession

among all the stake holders 'not to lose an inch of territory', land warfare is likely to dominate the multi-domain battlefield in the foreseeable future. Even under the shadow of nuclear overhang, land warfare is here to stay.

- It is visualised that India, in another 10-15 years, may face an ultra-high technology adversary in the North, with hybrid warfare as the key feature, or a low to medium technology adversary in the West with greater focus on the sub-conventional threats including proxy war, cross-border terrorism and information warfare/propaganda; or a combination of both against a nuclear backdrop. Much of these conflicts would be in covert domains, along with a combination of hybrid threats. Considering our current technological threshold, our conflict with China would still be predominantly platform centric rather than network centric. This would change progressively towards network centricity. Therefore, spectrum of conflicts will be seen between the nation states (interstate) and proxy-cum-internal armed conflicts. India is facing both.
- For the next one decade, major complement of the war or the conflict would predominantly be based in multi-domain operational environment'. This will progressively increase the fighting in dense urban terrains. Also, the conflicts would progressively transcend beyond conventional domains into the world of Information and Artificial Intelligence (AI).
- With the increased focus on Asia, the Indian Ocean and the Indo-Pacific region and their strategic significance, maritime security would also require extra attention. We require a high level of surveillance, situational awareness, rapid response capability, and synergy between all enforcement agencies to provide effective maritime and air space security.
- In addition, the frequency and intensity of natural disasters and complex humanitarian-cum-relief related activities on the Indian subcontinent, and beyond, would also suggest a predominant role of land forces in the foreseeable future.
- Both from the threat and capability point of view, we require a force-structure that would not only combat conventional forces, hybrid threats with cyber, information and space-based assets, but more importantly, the intrastate conflicts involving insurgents, terrorists and Violent Non State Actors (VNSAs). Light and agile

force structures, backed by technology-enabled systems, should be able to operate with other services as homogeneous teams.

THE WAY FORWARD: NATIONAL OUTLOOK FOR NATIONAL SECURITY

'...Hybrid threats incorporate a full range of modes of warfare, including conventional capabilities, irregular tactics and formations, terrorist acts that include indiscriminate violence and coercion, and criminal disorder'.[26]

– Frank G Hoffman, a Marine Corps officer

A strong economy is one of the most powerful weapons in the emerging world order. It would be challenging times for all countries, especially when the International Monetary Fund (IMF) has projected that global growth would be 3.3%, down from 3.6% in 2018.[27]

Regional and Global Level

Given the emerging strategic environment in Asia, the Indian Ocean region (IOR) and the Indo-Pacific region, and in keeping with India's enhanced political, economic and military status, India needs to enhance its role to improve cooperation and strengthen the regional organisations like SAARC and BIMSTEC; thus, reducing the prevailing interstate tensions. India has strategic interests in the IOR, and vital interests in the areas east of the Malacca Strait. It should, therefore, progressively increase its involvement in the Indian Ocean and fragile Indo-Pacific regions, in that order. It would be imperative to develop defence cooperation and build cooperative partnership at strategic levels with leading global powers and strategically located countries. Also, India must maintain the tempo of military exercises with the neighbouring and other friendly countries, with multiple aims. Indian Armed Forces must operate in a multi-domain operational environment.

4th Industrial Revolution (4th IR) and Security Challenges

The 4th IR is a major industrial revolution that has built itself on 'electronics and IT' of the third revolution. It is different because it is the 'fusion of technologies', which has resulted in blurring the lines between the physical, digital and biological spheres,[28] collectively referred to as 'cyber-physical systems'. As soldiers in uniform and civilians alike, we must take a note of the new technologies like: internet of things (IoT), cyber security, simulation, lethal autonomous weapon systems (LAWS), artificial intelligence (AI), big data, augmented reality, cloud computing, addictive manufacturing, 3D printing, etc. Digital connectivity remains one of the prime requirements to exploit the full potential of these technologies and their application on warfare of the future. These technologies would enable development of devices with minimum human interference. It would also provide the architectural support for hybrid threats and challenges to security. These should be examined and exploited by us for compilation and analysis of surfeit data, and predictive analysis to our advantage.

Cyber weapons are the new weapons of mass destruction and disruption, where the 'mass' is made up of information and critical assets. There are many networks in the civil domain like the financial, banking, railways, transportation, education, medical services, which, if attacked (even a single network like banking or transportation services), can paralyse the entire nation. Severe form of such attacks can also lead to open conflicts. Similarly, the armed forces have widely networked systems like command and control, communications, fire control, air defence, intelligence, surveillance, logistics, and information systems. These are also highly vulnerable and would adversely affect land operations at all levels. While looking at the offensive aspects of cyber warfare, it is important to first take actions to protect our networks from cyber-attacks. Militarisation of space is yet another dimension that needs to be explored for military purposes. Due to competition among the leading powers to dominate strategic space, cyber and outer space, information warfare has moved ahead at a rather fast pace. The Government's decision to raise cyber, space and Special Forces (SF) organisations at the national level is a positive step, as these would facilitate and complement operations in a multi-domain operational environment. These must be integrated with the national security apparatus.

With rapid developments in AI, land forces would also feel the impact of its practical applications in the future. AI is a branch of computer science concerned with the simulation of the intelligent behaviour of human beings. In simple terms, it is the capability of a machine to take decisions that are normally taken by a human being, and at a much faster pace, handling much larger data. AI technology has tremendous applications in social, economic, medicine, transportation, mining and military fields. AI has the potential to change both the nature and character of future wars. USA and China are far ahead in their research on AI and its application, especially in the military domain. The Chinese have been refining the autonomous systems to develop miniaturised UAVs (for swarm attacks), unmanned loitering missiles or sea launched weapon systems. AI and information warfare should form a critical element of our National Security Strategy (NSS), with clear milestones laid down. On balance, with the AI and the latest technologies in place, employment of unmanned aerial and ground vehicles, precision guided munitions, space-based intelligence gathering systems and reconnaissance by stealth will play a predominant role in support of land operations.

Intelligence Architecture and Intelligence Surveillance Reconnaissance (ISR): Real Challenge

The attack by the JeM' terrorist at Pulwama on the convoy of CRPF personnel on 14 February 2019, is yet another example of inadequacies in the intelligence architecture of our country. It is a major challenge to our security. The recommendations by various security committees aside, the ineffectiveness of our intelligence agencies has been debated after various operations/conflicts and terrorist attacks (the 1999 Kargil Conflict, the December 2001 attack on our Parliament, the November 2008 Mumbai attack, attacks in Gurdaspur, Pathankot, Uri, Nagrota). To further improve the performance of the intelligence architecture at the national level, we must focus on capacity building, integration and coordination, timely dissemination, and oversight to monitor and provide resources to evaluate their performance.

As regards ISR, acquisition of accurate and timely intelligence at the tactical and operational levels has been one of our major weaknesses. Path-breaking innovations in the field of information technology, artificial intelligence, big data computing, communications, data storage and data processing have enhanced the ISR capabilities. Drones have revolutionised the concept of ISR deep in the adversary's territory. PLA's UAVs like the DF-17 and CJ-100, have long-range reconnaissance collection and dissemination capabilities.[29] With imported systems, we run the risk of embedded platforms, which can compromise our security system at crucial moments. We need to indigenously develop ISR capabilities for ground, aerial, sea (above and below surface) and space-based systems to improve our response mechanism. This would also quicken our Observe-Orient-Decide-Act (OODA) loop. In fact, the aim should also be to enhance the situational awareness of soldiers on the ground, who will be operating on a wide front, in a decentralised manner.

Do we require a strong military and strategic capability?

In consonance with China's White Paper (2015) statement, "*Without a strong military, a country can neither be safe nor strong,*" China has provided adequate budgetary support to modernise its military.

If India is unlikely to fight a conventional war, then why should there be so much focus on building conventional capabilities? First, given our territorial disputes and seven decades of hostile attitude of Pakistan, the probability of war with our adversaries continues to remain high. Given Pakistan's indulgence in state-sponsored terrorism, the probability of a sub-conventional conflict or a limited conflict on land, with elements of information warfare, converting into a full blown conventional one remains high. Further, our adversaries should understand that India will react with full force if provoked by Kargil or Uri or Pulwama-like incidents and that India will not hesitate to escalate because of the nuclear weapons status of the adversary. Second, if India does not maintain its superior/ credible conventional capabilities, it will be kept engaged by our adversaries in sub-conventional and hybrid war at multiple levels, with impunity. They would take full advantage of our weaknesses. Hence, rather than being reactive, India should seize the initiative and become proactive. This can happen only if we have the requisite capabilities.

What does 'military deterrence' mean? It means that a country has the capability that is qualitatively and quantitatively, in that order, far superior to that of its adversary, and that it would take a timely decision and action(s) to deal with a situation. Therefore, effective military deterrence can only be achieved by improving our military capabilities in both conventional and non-conventional war-fighting mechanisms, soft power and demonstrated power. Military deterrence would be credible if it is backed by comprehensive national power (CNP): political will, strong economy, social cohesion, vibrant industrial base, integrated logistics system, supportive public information system, and a strong technology and innovation culture. Thus, India needs to progressively build capabilities of hard military power, soft power and demonstrated power that can deter threats to its stability and territorial integrity from potential adversaries. Besides taking actions to build a strong economy, we need to understand that political clarity and political will are required to achieve Military Deterrence.

Politico-military synergy is essential to ensure a seamless defence planning in consonance with our national objectives. It is time to have adequate civilian staff that, along with the armed forces officers, forms a good team of specialists to holistically examine all issues pertaining to changing nature and character of warfare, latest technology in defence industry, weapons and equipment, ammunition, trials at different levels, ISR platforms, and the defence procurement procedures. They should also examine the transformation of our higher defence organisation, defence industrial base, i.e. review of the complete structures, organisations, processes and procedures. Along with increase in defence budget, there should be meaningful discussions on national security issues, including our defence preparedness, our deficiencies and the defence budget in our Parliament.

India promulgated its nuclear doctrine in January 2003, which is defensive in nature, but with a sound deterrence capability. With two nuclear armed states as our neighbours, with whom we have unresolved border disputes, reservations have been expressed at different forums on whether our nuclear doctrine, being 15 years old, needs a review. Credible minimum deterrence (CMD) capability should be based on Triad (precision delivery means), survivability and second-strike capability, and a sound command and control system. With changes in the security environment, it would be correct to review our doctrine periodically. While it may not necessarily result in any change, a review allows us to take stock of the situation in the emerging strategic environment. Also, there is a need for 'threat perception and scenario building exercises' to be held periodically with the concerned stakeholders, to make them aware of the threats and capabilities, and to take timely decision during various contingencies that may arise.

Army Doctrine, Organisation, Operations and Training

Patrick Cullen and Eric Reichborn were emphatic to state, *"Hybrid warfare is designed to exploit national vulnerabilities across the political, military, economic, social, informational and infrastructure (PMESII) spectrum.... This process should direct comprehensive cross-government efforts to understand, detect and respond to hybrid threats."*[30] Hybrid threats would certainly be a part of the future conflicts. It, therefore, requires a national level response to prepare for conflicts of the future, and not the armed forces alone.

Considering our envisaged operational environment for the next one to two decades, as discussed, do we have a responsive and robust doctrine, strategy, organisations, war fighting concepts, training philosophy and equipment profile? As we have territorial and boundary disputes with two of our neighbours, there is a great emphasis on not losing even an inch of ground of one's territory. To reduce the boots on the ground, we must indigenously develop effective ISR capabilities to achieve battlefield transparency, communication structures and situational awareness. Looking at the future, the aim should be to have light, agile formations and units, which can operate in joint services environment, and be capable of rapid insertions at short notice. With an agile command and control structure, and quick decision being taken, the force should be capable of delivering a mass effect at the point of decision.

We have to achieve a position of advantage in a short window of opportunity against an enemy in varied operational environments, with a nuclear overhang. We should focus on manoeuvre, firepower, technology enabled devices, air power, light integrated battle groups (IBG), ISR, psychological operations, Special Forces (SF), and operational-oriented organisational structures. In addition, an agile command and control system, directive style of command, robust infrastructure, and effective logistics would prove to be battle winning factors. It is also a fact that Pakistan-based terrorists continue to infiltrate across the LoC, taking advantage of the extremely difficult nature of terrain. With our operational commitments along the LC, LAC, Siachen Glacier, and deployments in management of internal security, our soldiers remain most vulnerable. Our troops, both in the front line and hinterland, deserve to get the best weapon systems, night vision devices, equipment, communication systems, training, medical, and logistics facilities. As a nation, we must address this issue with great seriousness, to provide state-of-the-art weapon systems and equipment that facilitate the requisite agility, mobility, lethality, protection, battlefield transparency and situational awareness at different levels.

Border Management, and Impact of Infrastructure and Environment

Land warfare, in the Indian context, is synonymous with the ongoing territorial and boundary disputes, among other internal threats. The aim of border management strategy should be to effectively maintain the territorial integrity of the borders, and to take care of the multifaceted threats and challenges along each border. Besides utilising technology to manage borders (smart management), there is a need to have clarity in responsibility, command and control, authority and accountability for each border, more importantly the borders under dispute. Deployment of multiple forces on the same border has often led to problems of command and control, responsiveness, sharing of intelligence and accountability. In addition, while a large segment of the land borders is not demarcated on the ground, the maritime boundaries are also not clearly defined.

In the case of China, they have a border-guarding police force, the People's Armed Police Force (PAPF), which operates under the People's Liberation Army (PLA), along with the PLA border regiments. Recently, PAPF has also been placed under the PLA through the CMC. In India, a plethora of armed police forces has continued to guard our borders (BSF, ITBP, SSB & Assam Rifles). As each border has unique threats and challenges, "One Border One Force" was recommended by various committees, which has not happened, particularly along the LAC.

Development of infrastructure, particularly close to the borders, has enormous implications for the land forces, their operations and logistics. The pace of infrastructural work, especially close to the border areas, has been rather slow due to several constraints. Generally, these result in delay in completion of the project along with cost overruns. More importantly, it has an adverse impact on operational preparedness, of which logistics are a vital part. We need to improve our work output towards development of infrastructure along the borders in terms of roads, helipads, airfields, telecommunications, power facilities, infrastructure for logistic nodes in critical areas. Roads and infrastructure of strategic importance should be prioritised and completed with a sense of urgency.

Environmental degradation occurs due to land degradation (deforestation, desertification, and salinisation), atmospheric degradation (climate change, greenhouse effect, and ozone depletion), water degradation, biodiversity degradation, and pollution. Given the tasks of the armed forces, the army in particular, we have to understand that environmental degradation has huge implications on our security at strategic, operational and tactical levels. There is a need to analyse the impact on the operations, infrastructure, human health, habitat; and requirements of force structures, infrastructures and training. To analyse the long-term impact, a study be conducted on environmental degradation on the Indian subcontinent and its effects on two important aspects: one, the security and operations at various levels; two, vulnerable areas that may require humanitarian assistance and disaster relief (HADR), and aid to civil authority.

Manoeuvres and Firepower

India has huge geographical diversity in terms of varied terrains, climatic conditions, and operational environments. Invariably, each terrain and operational environment lends itself to manoeuvre, by almost all elements of combat power. The essence of manoeuvre in combat is to acquire a position of advantage, destroy the enemy, and break his will to fight, while firepower aims at destroying his capabilities by multiple firepower means like guns, mortars, rockets, missiles. Genghis Khan, who lived about 800 years ago, is considered to be a legend in practitioner of manoeuvre. More often, his forces were outnumbered by his enemies; he still attained unmatched degree of operational and tactical mobility, to achieve speed, surprise, shock, disruption and dislocation of enemy forces. His contribution to manoeuvre theory includes the concept of force (F) equals {mass (M is the total force level on horses) times acceleration (A is the rate of change of velocity), F = MA}; and the technique of achieving of speed, surprise, dislocation and disruption.[31] There is a need to examine its application in the digital age, unmanned combat aerial vehicles (UCAV) like swarms of drones armed with missiles, to achieve an advantage over the adversary, and break his will to fight or to continue with the insurgency campaign.

In the future, manoeuvre will be characterised by more simultaneous actions than sequential and widespread over larger areas. Therefore, faster, lighter, and lethal forces with relatively lesser logistics would be more successful. With effective surveillance, target acquisition, and real-time information and response mechanism, firepower can be manoeuvred over long ranges and on the adversary's rear areas, concentration areas, logistics, and key assets. To achieve optimum results, the broad concept of operational art must be understood; it refers to war fighting concept that bears a direct relationship between firepower and manoeuvre. Manoeuvre and firepower are complimentary terms, applicable to all combat elements; and must therefore part of the overall operational plan. On balance, if our troops are light, agile, networked, and well led, well trained and well equipped, they would be able to manoeuvre, as also adapt to the 'non-appreciated' operational environment. It is, indeed, difficult to predict the future courses of action of the enemy with any certainty.

INTEGRATION & JOINTNESS: NEED OF FUTURE CONFLICTS

> *"Success no longer goes to the country that develops a new fighting technology first, but rather to the one that better integrates it and adapts its way of fighting...."*[32]
>
> **– US National Defense Strategy**

Over the next two decades, the future conflicts would be rather short, intense, non-linear, multi-dimensional and hybrid in nature. We could expect them to straddle land, sea, air, space, cyber and information domains. In order to remain below the threshold of an all-out war and yet achieve its objectives, these conflicts would be orchestrated to remain in the grey zone. We, on our subcontinent, have an extraordinary responsibility towards territorial integrity, as loss of any territory is not acceptable under any circumstances. Therefore, in a short and intense nature of conflict, we will not have the luxury of delayed decision-making, delayed mobilisation and delayed application of forces. While addressing the Combined Commanders Conference 2015, Narendra Modi, Prime Minister of India said, *"...we should promote jointness across every level of our armed forces. We wear different colours, but we serve the same cause and bear the same flags. Jointness at the top is a need that is long overdue"*.

One of our main fault lines has been that we do not have jointness at both strategic and operational levels. Along with other contributory reasons, 'lack of desired tri-service integration' is one of the reasons for exercising restraint in India's operational actions. Tri-services integration should actually inspire confidence amongst the rank and file to undertake bold and offensive missions. Timely and synergistic application of forces can only take place if we have unity of command, which would further ensure unity of effort. To achieve synergy, we need to integrate ourselves at all levels. To begin with, we must certainly ensure integration of the MoD with the armed forces, and jointness in cyber, special operations, intelligence, information warfare, training and logistics among the services. Concurrently, the concept of integrated theatre command (ITC)—geographical or functional theatre command or a balanced mix of both—should be considered and a decision taken.

A brief examination of the rationale for introduction of theaterised command system in the US and China merits a mention. It was re-structured by an act in 1986 due to two main reasons: one, gross inadequacies observed in the operational effectiveness during the Vietnam War; two, the catastrophic failure during the Iranian hostage-rescue mission in 1980. Similarly, based on operational requirements of the future, China has carried out major transformations in their defence set up. These involved affecting changes in the cognitive domains, organisational structures, streamlining the command and control systems, bringing in jointness and integration among the three services, and introduction and absorption of new technologies.[33] The bottom line is that we should be effective operationally, with the ability to ensure synergistic application of all available resources for that operation in the very limited window of opportunity. Matters like national security require tough calls to be made, based on the principle of 'national outlook for national security'.

Conclusion

Due to the unsettled territorial and boundary disputes with our adversaries for the past seven decades, and the categorical statements by the respective leaders' regarding no loss of territory', the probability of conventional conflicts supported by the technological advances and hybrid tools will continue to play a predominant role in the Indian subcontinent. In addition, with a large-scale intra-state conflicts and humanitarian and relief operations, it means that we must not lose our focus from the land warfare, as the dominant means of warfare.

Having visualised the conflicts of the future, it is important to take proactive steps to transform our armed forces and integrate them, so that all available resources can be applied synergistically during the short window of opportunity in an intense and short duration conflict. On balance, the main takeaways of the paper are: the need to formulate a comprehensive national security strategy (CNSS), to improve our internal security. Further, a mission-oriented approach is required to resolve the ongoing conflicts. As a country we should focus on developing our CNP, and finally we need to progressively transform our entire defence setup, including defence industrial base. India has to use all instruments of its national power—political, economic, diplomatic, military, social, technological, psychological, cultural—in a coordinated manner to address its security concerns. CNSS is perhaps the first step to place everyone on the same page. National security should not be held hostage to preservation of turfs or attempting to reach consensus. Matters like national security, which have been well debated and deliberated, require tough calls to be made, and implementation ensured in a time-bound manner, failing which we will be found wanting in the conflicts of the future.

> *'Maintaining territorial integrity and preserving national sovereignty continues to remain a major strategic challenge for India.'*[34]
>
> – **Joint Doctrine of India Armed Forces – 2017**

NOTES

1 Michael E. O'Hanlon, The Future of Land Warfare, Brookings Institution Press, Washington DC, p. 57

2 Henry Boyd, Meia Nouwens, China's PLA: New Weapons, New Approaches, IISS, *Military Balance Blog*, 3 October, 2019. Dong Feng DF-41: the missile can carry 10 independently targeted nuclear warheads, with a range of 15000 km. DF-17, DF-100 and DF-41 made a debut at the National Parade on 1st October 2019.

3 Ibid.

4 Robert Kozloski, Commentary 'War on the Rocks, The Path to Prototype Warfare', 17 July 2017

5 Economic Value of Peace 2019.PDF. Sydney: The Institute For Economics and Peace, October 2018, available at http://economicsandpeace.org/wpcontent/uploads/2018/11/Economic-Value-of-Peace-2018.pdf

6 Southern Asia Population 2019, World Meters, accessed on 9 April 2019, http://www.worldometers.info/world-population/southern-asia-population/

7 Moeed Yusuf, Insurgency and Counterinsurgency in South Asia, Through a peace building lens, United States Institute of Peace Press, ISN+BN 978-1-60127-191-4, p. 2

8 Global Peace Index 2019, Institute for Economics and Peace, Sydney,

9 Samuel C Rajeev (2018), "Israel and the Challenges of Hybrid Warfare", in Vikrant Deshpande (ed.) (2018), *Hybrid Warfare: The Changing Character of Conflict*, (IDSA/Pentagon Press: New Delhi), pp.122–23.

10 The US had dropped a most powerful non-nuclear bomb, called the GBU-43/B Massive Ordnance Air Blast on 13 April 2017 heavy air blast bomb on the ISIS operating in the Archin District in Afghanistan.

11 Col John C. Wilkinson, USAF, Dr. Andrew Hill Airpower against the Taliban Systems of Denial, *Air and Space Power Journal*, pp. 2 & 50

12 VK Ahluwalia, Rajeev Kapoor, 'Strategy, Surprise and 'Vijay', 20 Years of Kargil and Beyond, Pentagon Publisher, 2019

13 "United Nations Official Document." United Nations. Accessed 17 September 2018.Available at http://www.un.org/en/ga/search/view_doc.asp?symbol=S/2018/14.

14 Greg Grant (2008), "Hybrid Wars: What if the battles of the future are neither conventional nor irregular, but a combination of both?", *Government Executive*, 1 May, available at: https://www.govexec.com/magazine/features/2008/05/hybrid-wars/26799/ Accessed on 6 September 2019.

15 HV Pant and K Bommakanti, India's National Security, International Affairs, p. 844.
16 Ibid.
17 McCauley, no. 14. To note, most provincial-level military districts are under the National Defense Mobilization Department of the CMC with responsibility for reserves, militia and conscription. The Xinjiang Military District is also under PLAA command.
18 China's National Defence in the New Era, July 2019, Printed in the People's Republic of China
19 Ministry of National Defence of the PRC, " Theatre Commands," https://en./Theater_commands_of_the_People%27s_Liberation_Army
20 HV Pant and K Bommakanti, India's National Security, International Affairs, p. 845.
21 Barry Buzan, People States and Fear: The National Security Problems in International Relations, Trans Asia Publishers, 1987, p. 45.
22 Moeed Yusuf, Insurgency and Counterinsurgency in South Asia, Through a peace building lens, United States Institute of Peace Press, ISN+BN 978-1-60127-191-4, p. 1.
23 Census of India 2011, and http://www.census.gov/population/www/popclockus.html,
24 Matthew Symonds, The new battlegrounds, The future of war, Special report, 25 January 2018, p. 41.
25 Ibid.
26 Frank G. Hoffman (2009), "Hybrid Warfare and Challenges", *Small War Journal*, Issue 52, 1st quarter 2009 / JFQ, p.39, Available at: https://smallwarsjournal.com/documents/jfqhoffman.pdf, Accessed on 7 September 2019.
27 Sriram Lakshman, IMF forecasts dip in global growth in 2019, *The Hindu*, 10 April 2019, p. 12,
28 World Economic Forum, Fourth Industrial Revolution, Accessed on September 5, 2019 https://www.weforum.org/focus/fourth-industrial-revolution
29 Henry Boyd, Meia Nouwens, China's PLA: New Weapons, New Approaches, IISS, *Military Balance Blog*, 3 October, 2019
30 Patrick J. Cullen, Erik Reichborn- Kjennerud (2017), "MCDC Countering Hybrid Warfare Project: Understanding Hybrid Warfare A Multinational Capability Development Campaign Project",.
31 Robert Leonhard, The Art of Manoeuvre, The English Book Depot, Dehradun, p. 35.
32 Deploying Prototype Warfare, US National Defence Strategy, Qinetiq,
33 China's National Defence in the New Era, July 2019, Printed in the People's Republic of China, (In specific terms, it refers to large scale mechanisation, to prepare to fight under conditions of informationisation, to streamline the higher defence organisation, and to carry out theaterisation of their military regions).
34 Joint Doctrine of India Armed Forces – 2017.

5

Land Warfare and Emerging Technologies

Colonel Ranjan Prabhu

"A nation's ability to fight a modern war is as good as its technological ability"

– Frank Whittle

ABSTRACT

Land warfare in the future will not only be fought from the ground on which forces are deployed but will encompass multiple domains of air, space and cyberspace from where land warfare will be influenced. There are three main pillars of warfare, viz. organisational structures, doctrines and technology. These three pillars are interdependent and have driven warfare through the ages. The future belongs to technology. The world today is driven by technology and various niche technologies whether matured or being developed have the ability to play a disruptive role in warfare. Technology is and will drive changes in organisations and doctrines in order to allow for a nation to adapt its armed forces to be able to optimally utilise technology to gain asymmetric advantages on the battlefield. The aim of this chapter will be to identify and discuss the dominant technological trends that will influence future land warfare covering historical perspective of land warfare, emerging and dominant technological trends in future warfare, current challenges in adoption of niche technologies and way ahead for the Indian Army.

Introduction

Air Cmde Sir Frank Whittle was the inventor of the turbojet engine. What he professed in the early 1930s about the importance of technology in modern warfare has stood the test of time. The efficacy and effects of technology in modern warfare was amply demonstrated to the world in the year 1991 by the Coalition forces lead by the United States military during the First Gulf War. The visuals of Stealth fighters carrying out precision bombing, Patriot missiles bring down Scud missiles, Apache helicopters taking down Iraqi armoured units with ease and individual soldiers equipped with high-end night vision goggles and GPS navigation units brought about the realisation as to how technology had revolutionised warfare. Though the impact of technology was not lost on exponents of modern warfare, the actual effect was seen during the two Gulf Wars. The early thoughts on warfare and technology grew from Soviet writing of the 1970s and 1980s, particularly a series of papers by Marshal N.V. Ogarkov analysing the revolutionary potential of new military technologies.[1] The Soviets at that time called the theory Military Technological Revolution (MTR) a term which has now metamorphosed into Revolution in Military Affairs or RMA. At the time of the initial development of MTR, the Soviets anticipated that certain technologies, including energy weapons and robots, would be in use by 2015 at the latest. They believed that the use of large ground forces would be minimised. In place of some ground forces, these new technologies would be implemented in order to establish dominance on the battlefield. However, over the period of time it has been seen that though technology is the driving force behind evolution of modern warfare techniques, it alone cannot drive the RMA. RMA therefore encompasses the complete gamut of doctrine, technology, tactics and organisations, their interplay and effect on modern warfare. Technology, however, remains the cornerstone of the theory as it is the technological evolution in weapons systems which has and which will drive the application of doctrine, tactics and organisations in the modern battlefield. The evolution of warfare has been in synchronisation with the development of technology through the ages. Every emerging technology has had a deep impact on warfare and therefore the future land warfare will also certainly be impacted by emerging technologies.

Historical Perspective of Technology in Land Warfare

The various landmark inventions of tools of warfare driven by improvements and developments in technology have resulted in creation of newer generations of warfare. The First Generation of War began with the Peace of Westphalia in 1648, the treaty that ended the Thirty Years'

War. With the Treaty of Westphalia, the state established a monopoly on war. Previously, many different entities had fought wars—families, tribes, religions, cities, business enterprises—using many different means, not just armies and navies. The First Generation of Modern War runs roughly from 1648 to 1860. This was war of line and column tactics, where battles were formal and the battlefield was orderly. The relevance of the First Generation springs from the fact that the battlefield of order created a military culture of order. Most of the things that distinguish "military" from "civilian"—uniforms, saluting, careful gradations or rank—were products of the First Generation and were intended to reinforce the culture of order.[2] The invention of the rifled musket and breech loading weapons ushered in the second generation of warfare forcing a revolutionary change in tactics and organisations of armies of those times.[3] The line and column tactics became obsolete and suicidal thereby demanding change in method of warfare. This change was driven by the development of Artillery and its application in massed indirect firepower. This concept is relevant even today though it has been massively refined and improved through immense developments in target acquisition, lethality of fire, precision delivery and Post Strike Damage Assessment (PSDA).

Massed firepower could however be defeated by digging in the defences. This type of trench warfare led to large number of stalemates in battles amply demonstrated in the battles of World War I. The development of the tank, armoured personnel carriers and fighter aircraft which allowed for greater speed and manoeuverability of forces on the battlefield ushered in the third generation of warfare which overcame the stalemate of trench warfare and linear defences. The new weapon systems allowed the attacking armies to get into the enemy's rear and collapse him, instead of seeking to close in and destroy. Defending forces could now draw the enemy to close in and then manoeuvre to cut him off. The relevance of this concept is valid till date though the dimensions (land, air, water, cyber and space) in which manoeuvre can be undertaken have increased due to the technological ability present in the world today.

Nation states fighting conventional wars and having huge and competent armies with similar doctrines and weapon systems capable of delivering lethal firepower and causing mass casualties could only be defeated through creation of asymmetric capabilities. This gave birth to the basic concept behind the fourth generation of warfare where the lines between war and politics, combatants and civilians have become blurred.

The asymmetry is gained by utilisation of non-state entities that use tactics of education/propaganda, movement-building, secrecy, terror, and/or confusion to overcome the technological gap. The adversary is forced to capitulate economically and psychologically by wearing him out through creation of chaos and disorder. There are numerous examples of large and powerful armies finding it difficult to sustain such forms of warfare, i.e. British Army in Falklands, the Russians and subsequently the Americans in Afghanistan and the US forces in Iraq. India of course has been subjected to this kind of warfare since its independence. The first war of 1948 fought between India and Pakistan consisted of the tribal non-state element. Even till date, the Indian Army while facing the conventional Pakistani Army on the Line of Control (LoC) regularly has to contend with skirmishes with terror elements that do not form part of the regular army but are surreptitiously supported by the Pakistani establishment.

While the fourth generation of warfare is more about conflict over ideas than about conflict over land and resources, Fifth Generation of Warfare will be a vortex of violence, a free-for-all of surprise destruction motivated more by frustration than by any coherent plans for the future when the world's disaffected direct their desperation at the most obvious symbol of everything they lack.[4] The obvious question then is whether such warfare can be defeated by technology alone? While it may be true that the disaffected may have to be won over through economic and social development, however prevention of such acts of violence will still require technology for intelligence agencies to be able to sift through billions of bytes of multi-domain, multi-source disparate datasets to arrive at the right and timely information and carry out preventive measures. At the same time the acts of violence cannot be done without the tools for perpetrating high degree of destruction. Such tools can only be made available through nation states which support such non-state actors in a discrete manner. Thus, ultimately nation states may be drawn into the battlefield though initiation may have been by a non-state actor (funded and supported by one of the nation state) whose aim would not have been a full-blown war. Therefore, whichever form of warfare we may talk about especially of future wars, technology will be the driving force behind the power of the spear.

While the first generation warfare was limited to a small area with armies facing each other akin to a sports field, advancements in weapons which could fire at longer ranges starting from rifles to artillery cannons forced the armies to disperse over larger areas and also dig in to protect themselves. With larger dispersion came the need of knowing where the adversary has dispersed his forces and also the problem of command and control of not only the dispersed forces but also of the attacking forces which needed to attack the dispersed forces at multiple places in order to win the battle. With increasing ranges of weapons and greater lethality, forces had to be further dispersed and have better protection. Intelligence gathering, surveillance and reconnaissance means thus needed greater range and sophistication to give information about the adversary's forces. Highly lethal and precision targeting became the need of the hour as engagement of dispersed targets by dumb munitions was neither economical nor decisive. With greater dispersion of both the defender and the attacker, command and control of forces became a complex issue especially in a highly lethal and fast changing environment. Thus, was born the requirement of networked forces. The human cost of war became extremely high due to the highly lethal weapons now in use. Thus, was born the concept of use of robotics to ensure better human survivability. Greater computing power, high degree of networking, precision strike capability and higher mobility platforms, the tempo of warfare has increased manifold. In such a scenario the speed of decision became a major battle winning factor.

Technology has therefore been harnessed in all these spheres to provide an edge to whosoever can field better systems which can support the needs of the future battlefields. A networked grid of multi-domain sensors which can pass on data to an Artificial Intelligence (AI) based decision support system, which in turn can allow precision targeting of the adversaries war waging machinery in any domain be it land, air, water, space or cyber, while at the same time allow for effective management of the adversarial public perception as per our narrative will be the battle winning combination in any future war. Given this requirement, it is clear that kinetic elements of war like the artillery, tanks, rockets, missiles and small arms will continue to be relevant in the future. However, they will be smarter, highly networked and more capable with greater reliance on higher endurance longer range Intelligence Surveillance and Recce (ISR) for precise target acquisition than ever before. Decision support systems will become smarter and thus will allow commanders orientation and decision making process faster and more informed at all levels, thus outwitting the adversary's OODA loop in time and space.

Dominant Technological Trends and Utility in Land Warfare

While there are umpteen numbers of technologies being researched around the world they may be broadly classified under eight major pillars on which systems in future warfare will be engineered to take on modern conflicts. These pillars are ISR, networking, reduction in human effort, lethality, precision and volume of fire, invisibility, increased survivability and detectability. The first three, i.e. ISR, networking and reduction in human effort can be co-related to the Observe, Orient and Decide elements of the OODA loop. A networked environment will not only have military elements but will also consists of the entire gamut of a nations machinery which will work in tandem to achieve the political aim putting into action all types of resources many of which may not have ever been used in traditional forms of warfare before, for example social media for spreading propaganda and disinformation campaigns, financial networks to stress and break the economic backbone of the adversary, irrigation networks to flood land of the adversary to prevent him in utilising land forces and also cause unimaginable damage to the civilian population, etc. Many of these efforts would be directed at an adversary much before the actual military means are employed thus leaving the doors wide open for employment of every means available at a nation's disposal to force an adversary to capitulate even before he plans to employ his military assets. Thus, technology which may be utilised in future land warfare may not be ones which are restricted to military systems alone. Technologies being utilised today in civilian domain may be utilised to disrupt an adversary's strategic networks and decision-making process early in a conflict scenario. Large number of cutting-edge technologies being utilised in the world today are capable of dual use and if properly identified, catered for and utilised can have a devastating effect on an adversary. It is possible for own civilian mobile towers along the border with our adversary to be tuned to a frequency which is utilised by civilian networks across the border thereby spoofing and disrupting them. Advanced Data Analytics being utilised by various business conglomerates to shape consumer opinion and preferences through predictive analysis and consequent targeted ads can be re-programmed through addition of pre-planned modules which can then be used to sway and shape public opinion of an adversary. Resources of 3D Printing technology being used extensively in civilian domain can be diverted for printing critical components and spare parts of military equipment which are in short supply when war clouds are looming. The "Nibbler" mini UAV deployed by the US Marines is an apt example of how this technology can be employed in the field.[5]

While there are numerous emerging technologies which can be considered to have a disruptive effect on the battlefield of the future, some of these technologies have matured considerably over the last couple of years to rise from the realms of science fiction to reality. Much of these technologies are being deployed in the civilian domain primarily because the civilian domain lends itself more flexible to change and absorbs technology faster. Technologies like AI and robotics are now a buzzword both in the corporate world and also in the military though developments in the corporate world are more visible and faster. Moore predicted that the numbers of discrete elements on a square-inch silicon integrated circuit will double every two years. While it's not exactly a direct relationship, you can interpret that to mean that computers will double in processing power every two years. However, the silicon chip is slowly reaching the limits of its performance and may only dominate the chip market until 2040s.[6] In this context the advent of compound semiconductors is a game-changer that has the potential to be as transformational as the internet has been for communications. Compound semiconductors have the potential to be as much as 100 times faster than silicon. This vast increase in computational power can easily fuel the applications like AI, Robotics and intelligent sensors in military weapon systems. Ethical concerns about application of these technologies notwithstanding, these two between them, when fully mature and applied in military systems will be able to drastically reduce the human effort and human cost of war.

While the innovations in high energy explosives paved the way for higher degree of lethality at the target end by weapons which carried them, they are susceptible to detection due to the production of sound and light during launch/firing and are also prone to errors of trajectory as they are bound by gravitational and other forces since they are carried in casings of heavy materials towards their targets. Directed Energy Weapons (DEW) overcome these limitations as they can remain outside the visible spectrum, make no sound, reach the target at the speed of light and have a precise flat trajectory towards a target not affected by gravity or other disruptive forces of nature. Such weapons can thus counter ballistic missiles, hypersonic cruise missiles, and hypersonic glide vehicles.[7] Laser weapons currently deployed by US (**AN/SEQ-3 Laser Weapon System** on board the USS Ponce) are designed to be used against low end asymmetric threats and are still in developmental stage with low ranges and kill power. However, their high precision and low cost of operation has raised hopes of developing weapons of greater ranges. Hence countries like the US, Russia and China have not stopped research into such weapon systems. China's progress in DEWs must be of greater concern for us due to our ongoing territorial conflict with it.[8]

Nano Technology is another emerging technology which holds strong promises for use in the defence industry. Current thinking is that nanotechnology can be used in two main ways by soldiers. The first is miniaturisation of existing equipment to allow it to be not only smaller, but lighter, use less energy and be more readily concealable. The second is to develop and adapt new materials for military purposes which can make military equipment lighter and stronger at the same time thus increasing survivability. Advances in material technologies especially in the field of advanced composites have allowed for combat systems to be made light weight, better resistant to corrosion and have better survivability against attacks. Such composites have also allowed combat systems to become more fuel efficient due to lighter weight and also capable of being adaptable to electric powering which will make them quieter in the future thus further enhancing their stealth characteristics and thereby ensuring a higher degree of survivability. Such advanced composites are more mouldable and therefore adaptable to stealthy designs which allow for lower RCS thus rendering them invisible to most radar systems. Lighter weight armour made out of such composites have increased the personal protection of an individual soldier without tying down his mobility due to higher weight of older personal armour.

Another area where technology has moved miles in so far as military applications are concerned is the use of drones for reconnaissance, surveillance, target acquisition and precision targeting. Long-range, multi-spectral and armed drones have brought in a revolution in the capabilities of land forces to assess the moves and location of the adversary and engage him with precision deep into his territory. Persistent eye in the sky type of High Altitude drones running on solar energy can provide 24x7 surveillance over large swath of area while being cheaper to operate and launch as compared to a satellite. Such type of drones will perfectly complement space based sensors mounted on satellites which can provide coverage over wide swath of adversaries land. Such resources are more secure from enemy offensive actions and hence better on survivability count as compared to other type of drones which can be detected and brought down by even slow moving armed helicopters.

Huge advances in Information Technologies now allow for highly secure and rapid transmission of data and voice over broadband networks capable of handling higher amounts of transmission than ever before. Millimeter-wave and optical communication links to satellites, as well as fibre optics networks, offer long distance as well as local information distribution on a secure high bandwidth network. Spread-spectrum electromagnetic and miniaturised broadband links allow remotely operated air and ground vehicles to interface between each other which enable the intelligence of humans and smart machines to be merged for many applications, including reconnaissance and targeting. 5G communication networks being trial tested this year will herald in a new revolution into Internet of Things (IoT) and will allow devices to talk to each other paving the way for truly autonomous systems. This type of revolution in communication technologies will link each individual soldier on a network of sensors, weapon systems and smart devices thereby ensuring battlefield transparency and effortless and better control by commanders at each level.

Electric propulsion technology has also come of age with massive developments in the civilian vehicle domain led by Tesla. Electric vehicles have huge advantages over conventional fossil fuel based vehicles as electric drive enables fundamental changes in vehicle configuration as the engine and transmission do not have to be connected mechanically enabling increased flexibility in the choice of power sources and their location, facilitating easy introduction of fuel cells and advanced battery/ energy storage technologies. Such systems offers improved acceleration, agility, fuel efficiency and maintainability as opposed to the systems currently used on other combat vehicles and enables exceptional force protection and mobility in a lower weight vehicle. Fast moving advances in electrical energy storage devices will result in more powerful, lightweight and extreme long-life battery packs, which can sustain long duration combat missions which are the only limitation of electric drive vehicles as on date.

While the above listed technological trends and arenas support the eight pillars of future warfare, they are by no means the only ones. A large number of more such trends exist but broadly put together the shape of things are being led by the technological trends discussed till now. The need of the hour is to correctly identify thrust areas of R&D while taking into account the geopolitical situation which is likely to emerge in the next decade or so, terrain in which future land warfare will be fought, our current technological thresholds, absorption capabilities, national fiscal concerns and consequent priorities. While every armed force dreams to possess the very best in cutting-edge technology, a very fine balance has to be drawn between the wish and the need.

Challenges in Adoption of Niche Technologies and Way Ahead for Indian Army

India's Land Warfare Doctrine released in 2018 clearly enunciates that the Indian Army needs to be prepared for a two-front and a half-threat scenario. It is unlikely that it will face a weak adversary on either front in the future not counting the high chances of collusive threat from both in event of a conflict. Accordingly it is imperative that as a nation it invests in the right direction in developing its military might to ensure that its economic and social development climate is secure from types of existential threats. However, given the burden of a burgeoning population much of which is below the poverty line, the Human Development Index (HDI) rank of India is 130 out of 189 nations.[9] With such a social and economic development index, it is not surprising that the focus of the nation must be to alleviate the issues plaguing its development. This threat has always been overshadowing the thrust for social and economic development as both its adversaries have been using all means at their disposal to bleed India whether it is through supporting terror networks or utilising strategic encirclement to strangulate it geopolitically. The butter vs guns dilemma has therefore always been a matter with which policy makers at the highest levels of the security establishment have been struggling. In spite of a reasonable GDP growth, India has consistently remained at the bottom of the HDI charts. It is thus natural that fiscal prudence demands expenditure on human development to be higher than on national security related expenditure. In such a scenario, funds will never be enough to fulfil the dreams but will just about make up for the bare needs. Almost all of these equipment will be found wanting in any future war where they would be pitted against weapon systems possessing the latest technology. Equipping a military force has long gestation periods especially when limited defence industrial base is available in the country. Procurement processes are lengthy and time consuming and therefore sustained focus on equipping the armed forces with the right equipment over the years would have distributed the fiscal burden evenly. Neglect of the need of the armed forces over the years has now led to a situation resulting in a paradox where there is an emergent need to procure new generation equipment with capability of the government of the day to dedicate only limited financial resources for defence capital procurement. Though India's defence spending is quite high in global terms and is the world's fourth largest defence budget,[10] however most of its budget goes in paying for salaries and allowances of its currently manpower intensive military and therefore very little remains for capital procurements and investments in defence R&D. In the interim budget of 2019, presented in the parliament by Finance Minister Piyush Goyal on 01 Feb 19 which have been widely applauded for its very versatile policy initiatives there has been very little change in the defence outlays.

The budget looks healthier but it is unlikely to meet the vast modernisation requirements of the armed forces. This is more so given that the previous allocation was not even sufficient to meet the committed liabilities (CL) or to pay for signed contracts. With such fiscal allocations it is clear that the Indian Defence forces particularly the Army cannot hope to incubate adopt and induct all niche technologies which are being touted as revolutionary in the field of future land warfare. While the army can hope to induct a few sophisticated weapon systems procured from technologically advanced nations which would have a force multiplier effect, however it may not serve the purpose of indigenisation in the field of military technology R&D and manufacturing which is a must if it hopes to gain asymmetry against its adversaries in the region. Therefore, it is important to analyse and recommend the technology that needs to be prioritised for development and induction within the Army over a 15-year horizon which will give an asymmetric advantage to the forces against not only China which is its superior adversary but also against Pakistan which is capable of throwing up new and innovative challenges on the sub-conventional front.

The eight pillars of future warfare on which systems would be engineered should be an important guideline for development of technology by the Indian Army in the next decade. In order to reconcile competing interests and allocate resources in a coherent manner, it would be useful to consider investments in domains which would have spin-offs for the civilian world too. The demands of the Armed Forces must therefore be aligned and projected in a manner so as to have acceptable political resonance.

Cyber Weapons

The interconnected world of today lends itself to huge payoffs. The huge advantages of better command and control, battlefield transparency and situational awareness at all levels provided by networked forces have made Network Centric platforms the choice of all modern military forces. The proliferation of cyber networks in the civilian domains is even more widespread because of the economic advantages of interconnectivity. Therefore, successful targeting of these networks can bring an adversary's financial services, transportation systems, electrical grids, irrigation networks and critical communication networks to a grinding halt thereby lending a severe blow his ability to wage a war. Developing full spectrum of cyber power in the armed forces which would comprise cyber-crime investigation, including cyber forensic, counter cyber terror operations, cyber espionage, and in-depth cyber defence with particular emphasis on platforms, cyber offensive, cyber deception, cyber-enabled operations and cyber war either by itself, or in conjunction with EW and kinetic means would lend itself to asymmetric advantage against an adversary in any future conflict.[11] India has a large pool of talented and skilled workforce in the software and cyber domain which if cultivated with a strategic focus and adequate investments can be moulded and developed to produce cutting edge offensive and defensive cyber weapons. Such systems, especially defensive systems, would be of interest to civilian industries as well because of their potential to provide a high degree of cyber security to their networks as well. Hence, dovetailing of civilian R&D effort in this field in concert with military efforts is highly possible and should be exploited to have credible cyber offensive and defensive capabilities by the next decade.[12]

Military Grade 5G Communication Network

Seamless and responsive communication forms the backbone of any Tactical Command Control, Communication and Information (Tac C3I) Networks. Fielding of such networks will be non-negotiable in any future conflict to be able to beat the adversary's OODA loop. However, such net-centric systems require a communication backbone which is secure, reliable, fast, mobile and seamless. The present tactical communication systems in the Army are unsuitable for net-centric operations as they do not possess the capacity to support high speed data and voice transmissions. Though the civilian sector has seen a tremendous revolution in high speed mobile communication networks hardly any progress has been made within the Army to introduce such vital communication technologies which will form the backbone of any future net-centric Tac C3I. The technological capability of the supporting tactical communication infrastructure is below par. It is therefore imperative that in order to fully exploit such net-centric systems which will be fielded in due course of time, the Army must look at investing in the future. While it may be argued that a 5G military network for the Army is a distant dream as even a 4G enabled tactical communication system is not yet in place, it is worthwhile to consider that all the clamour for development of AI based systems and robotics for the army will be futile without having a 5G technology in place as it forms the backbone of such systems. Therefore, the investment in such a technology will be needed. With enough expertise available in the country in establishing and running 4G networks and trials of 5G starting in 2019[13] such a project is feasible if the decision makers have clear focus with policy initiatives which encourages the industry to participate with due vigour and support of the Armed forces.

TAC C3I Systems

In a swift and fast paced future war, the need for net centricity of both the soldier and the weapons and sensor platforms is non-negotiable. The only way to beat the adversaries OODA loop is to be able to orient and decide faster that he can. Such a capability can only be developed in a networked environment, where automated decision support systems are able to generate options based on inputs from various net centric sensor fused systems. A robust Tac C3I system can give an asymmetric advantage to any force possessing it. Higher computing power, availability of robust and seamless communication technologies in the present era allow for ease of developing and deploying a highly advanced Tac C3I system. The thrust must therefore be to deploy these systems at the earliest lest the army remains in a catching up mode with its adversaries especially when modern communication and information technology available in the world today allows for easy development of such systems.

ISR Sensors and Platforms

The Indian Army will continue to lead operations against sub-conventional threats and therefore it would be prudent to invest in technologies which give the forces a definite edge in ISR domain (strategic operational and tactical) which would not only be useful in detection and subsequent elimination of sub-conventional threats but could also easily adapt to conventional warfare. While ISRO has been carrying out commendable and path-breaking work on military surveillance satellites for the defence forces, construction and launch of satellites is a costly affair which is therefore a hindrance for a country like India which has to balance national resources for nation building. It would therefore be prudent to develop Stratospheric Persistent Remotely Piloted Aircraft Systems (RPAS) with multi-spectral sensor payloads which can provide the capability of a satellite with a flexibility of a drone. In addition to this there must be an all-out effort to develop and induct mini-RPAS which can be used on the tactical battlefield to provide information in real time to the infantry soldier on the ground. Such types of RPAS when inducted will also be hugely useful in sub-conventional role where confirmatory recce and close surveillance post detection and target acquisition of threat by larger systems can be carried out by the soldier deployed on the ground thus allowing for rapid actions by small teams to eliminate the threat.

Precision Munitions

While it is in possession of highly accurate missile system like the BrahMos, however the use of such a missile is not only costly but restricted to high value targets. Thus, there is a void in precision engagement of targets which are comparatively of lower value whose engagement decision can be taken at a much lower level. Revolution in military technology has not only enabled guidance technology on munitions to become smart but also cheaper. While there are versions of smart ammunition which are highly precise but costly, there are some versions which through strap on fuze based guidance kits, e.g. the M1156 Precision Guidance Kit (PGK) can provide reasonable accuracy at a much lower cost. Such ammunitions provide a wide range of flexibility for usage with a high degree of accuracy as compared to dumb bombs, thus economising on effort and quantity where expenditure far outweighs the expected results. Coupled with mini RPAS such munitions will be able to provide the power of precision targeting to the lowest tactical level commander on ground. The army must therefore, look at acquiring such technology within the next decade.

Advanced Composites

Advanced composites-based ground combat vehicles offer better protection with lighter weight thus making for economical operation. Advanced composite technology has been mastered by the HAL in its quest to build the LCA Tejas[14] and by the DRDO while developing the Kanchan Armour for the Arjun tank. Ultra-Modern Lightweight Thermoplastic composite based armour may well be a breakthrough that can provide the Army with a much-needed cheaper and lighter personal protection vest something that has been lacking in the inventory of the Indian soldier.[15] Such composite technology will ensure a greater degree of survivability for the soldier in the highly lethal environment of future battlefield. It will also protect the soldiers against IED attacks and encounters with terror elements during operations in sub-conventional conflicts.

Advanced Analytics

In this age of social media and information explosion, any future conflict will be preceded by a huge information campaign to shape perceptions of not only own or the adversary's population but also the global public and media which can twist narratives to suit own diplomatic initiatives. The ability to use accurate information while distorting its meaning and removing its context with accurate timing to push a factually accurate narrative in particularly crisis-prone periods to distort the public narrative in own favour will be a game changer for any diplomatic war preceding kinetic operations. Russia's success with social media narratives in Turkish crisis and the annexation of Crimea is an apt example of the power of information in today's interconnected world where public opinion can be shaped to own advantage[16]. Such information campaigns can be run concurrently with predictive analytics of likely turn of events to shape a narrative which can prevent conflicts altogether or control escalation. Availability of WMDs with India, Pakistan and China makes for a high-risk environment where conflicts can escalate to dangerous proportions. Such a situation can lead to catastrophic actions in self-defence by any one of the nation's leading to mass destruction events. Conflict prevention is therefore in the interest of stability in the region. Big Data Analytics Technology can therefore be employed to carry out predictive analytics of events through analysis of humongous data flowing throw the social media channels. Such predictions then would allow a nation to control the narrative to prevent conflict escalation by shaping global opinions. India must invest in projects similar to Global Database of Events, Language, and Tone (GDELT) project[17] and Integrated Conflict Early Warning System (ICEWS) in order to predict events[18] for escalation control.

Drone Killers

Drones are the ISR and weapons platforms of the future. There are numerous examples of use of drones in both ISR & offensive operations both by advanced armies and also by militant outfits like ISIS. Advances in communication technologies will be a harbinger for drones and its employment across the complete spectrum of warfare. China has already taken a large leap in development of large varieties of drones including armed versions. Their collusive relation with Pakistan has ensured that Pakistan has and will continue to have access to such technology and platforms from China. Drones are difficult to be brought down by conventional Anti Air Defence systems due to its very small RCS. It is therefore imperative that we develop anti-drone capability in terms of both kinetic & soft kill (EW) options. We have to induct Swarms and develop effective counter to such technology.

Conclusion

Lack of adequate funds will always be a reality in a nation like India where social and economic development is still to reach the poorest of the poor. Resources thus will always be at premium and correct prioritisation with good foresight of relevant technologies which can be inducted is the need of the hour. Arming without aiming will neither benefit the Army nor the nation. There are definite solutions to the problem which we are facing. The need of the hour is for a focused approach at the national level to direct efforts at building capabilities in the defence manufacturing, R&D, academic studies & procurement.

- **Defence Manufacturing**—This field has been the exclusive preserve of the Defence PSUs since independence. However, poor management, strategic lethargy associated with no competition and captive armed forces as customer base, poor work ethos and unionism & no investments in R&D have made these DPSUs non-performing white elephants which have produced substandard warlike stores and equipment for the armed forces. Over the years the DPSUs have only manufactured equipment from semi-knocked down kits without absorption of any technology. Thus, it is time that in a world where technology is changing at a rate faster than one can adapt to it; DPSUs are faced with private sector to ensure innovation and competitiveness. It is a known fact that competition drives innovation, competitive costing and higher investments in R&D. The "Make in India" project is therefore a shot in the arm for the private defence manufacturing industry wherein they can partner with major foreign players in this domain to manufacture high-tech land warfare platforms and offer them to the Indian armed forces. Such an arrangement will lead to technology absorption, creation of sustainable and profitable MSME ecosystem for supply of minor parts for major equipment being manufactured by larger defence manufacturing companies and higher share of investments in R&D in this sector to stay ahead of the competition. The need however is to ensure a level playing field for the private sector with equitable access to the defence market without which no corporate entity will be willing to invest funds in a domain which is known for high cost of investments and long gestation periods for profitability.

- **Defence R&D**—This domain has since independence been an exclusive turf of the DRDO which is a government establishment. Like all government institutions, it too has been plagued with a large number of issues leading to low quality of research output, numerous time delays in completion of projects and research in large number of unwanted and uneconomical fields. The field of Defence R&D also needs a fresh impetus with R&D being funded by private conglomerates as part of their strategy to remain competitive through innovative application of emerging technologies. Institutes of higher learning both private and government aided may be allowed to be brought on board by such private entities to fund cutting-edge research and academic studies which will go a long way in establishing an ecosystem of cutting-edge R&D.
- **Procurement System**—The present procurement system is at best archaic and not in sync with modern-day realities of technology requirements, trials and testing, standardisation, life cycle concepts, costing and contracting. The procurement is handled by generalists who have no expertise in negotiations and procurement concepts. The General Staff Qualitative Requirements

(GSQRs) are drawn up by individuals whose expertise in the field are suspect and procurements are processed in a disjointed manner by individual services and arms in a compartmentalised manner leading to non-standardisation of equipment being procured though many a times the requirements are similar. It is therefore imperative that we learn from the procurement models followed by France, USA and UK wherein specialised organisations have been created which are staffed by experts who have specialised in the field of procurement, technology, life cycle concepts, costing, contracting and price negotiations. These organisations look after the procurement processes of all the three services in a joint environment right from drafting GSQRs to contract negotiation.

NOTES

1 Steven Metz, James Kievit, "Strategy and the Revolution in Military Affairs: From Theory to Policy", 27 June 1995

2 Lind, William S, "Understanding Fourth Generation of Warfare", https://original.antiwar.com/lind/2004/01/15/understanding-fourth-generation-war/ accessed on 19 April 2019.

3 Lind, William S., Nightengale, Keith; Schmitt, John F.; Sutton, Joseph W.; Wilson, Gary I. (October 1989), "The Changing Face of War: Into the Fourth Generation", *Marine Corps Gazette*, pp. 22–26

4 Axe David, "How to Win Fifth Generation Warfare", https://www.wired.com/2009/01/how-to-win-a-fi/ accessed on 19 April 2019.

5 Sandra Erwin, "Marines take 3D Printing from the Lab to the Field", https://defensesystems.com/articles/2017/05/08/marinecorpprint.aspx, accessed on 17 June 2019.

6 Carter Jamie, "Silicon Chips are Reaching their Limits: Here's the Future", https://www.techradar.com/news/silicon-chips-are-reaching-their-limit-heres-the-future, accessed on 30 April 2019.

7 Amy Butler, "Thaad-ER In Search Of A Mission" – Aviationweek.com, 20 January 2015.

8 Richard D. Fisher, Jr. Senior Fellow, International Assessment and Strategy Center —China's Progress with Directed Energy Weapons, Testimony before the U.S.-China Economic and Security Review Commission hearing, "China's Advanced Weapons", Washington, DC, 23 February 2017

9 UNDP Human Development Report, HDI Ranking 2018

10 Defence Spending by Country, https://www.globalfirepower.com/defense-spending-budget.asp accessed on 7 May 2019.

11 Vivekananda International Foundation Task Force Report, "Credible Cyber Deterrence in Armed Forces of India", p. 25.

12 Sukumar Arun M, "Upgrading India's Cyber Security Architecture", https://

www.thehindu.com/opinion/columns/upgrading-indias-cyber-security-architecture/article8327987.ece accessed on 8 May 2019.

13 IANS, "5G spectrum trial to begin from next month in India", https://www.livemint.com/industry/telecom/5g-spectrum-trial-to-begin-from-next-month-in-india-1557296615019.html accessed on 9 May 2019.

14 Dreger, Paul (February 2004), "SE Asia Indigenous Fighter Programmes", *Military Technology,* Vol. 28 no. 2. Bonne pp. 28–30

15 India Today Webdesk, "In a first, Indian Army to get Indian bullet-proof vests designed by Kolkata professor", https://www.indiatoday.in/education-today/gk-current-affairs/story/made-in-india-bullet-proof-vest-982280-2017-06-12 accessed on 11 May 2019.

16 Unver Aakin H, "Russia Has Won the Information War in Turkey", https://foreignpolicy.com/2019/04/21/russia-has-won-the-information-war-in-turkey-rt-sputnik-putin-erdogan-disinformation/, accessed on 11 May 2019.

17 Global Database of Events, Language, and Tone (GDELT) https://en.wikipedia.org/wiki/Global_Database_of_Events,_Language,_and_Tone, accessed on 11 May 2019.

18 Integrated Conflict Early Warning System (ICEWS), https://en.wikipedia.org/wiki/Integrated_Conflict_Early_Warning_System, accessed on 11 May 2019.

6

Emerging Role of Information Warfare in Indian Subcontinent

Lieutenant General RC Chadha

ABSTRACT

Information Warfare is a highly complex and evolving warfare. The role of Information Warfare is gaining prominence. The human resource development is important to minimise its effects.

Defence Information Assurance and Research Agency (DIARA) and the Defence Intelligence Agency (DIA), the two tri-services information warfare assets which function under Headquarters Integrated Defence Services (IDS). Additional Directorate General Military Operations (Information Warfare) functions under Military Operations Directorate, Integrated Headquarters of Ministry of Defence (Army) and Additional Directorate General Public Information are ad hoc organisations to handle Army's Public Affairs functions. In addition, Directorate of Information Warfare in the Indian Air Force performs the required functions.

Future conflicts may not be geographically localised. The likely international reactions would have to be weighed. Global reach of media and advances in communications technology have added new dimensions. Wars are also required to be fought in the minds.

"Emerging Role of Information Warfare in The Indian Subcontinent" would cover the following aspects:

(a) An Overview of the 'Indian Subcontinent'.
(b) An Insight into the 'Future Battlefield'.
(c) Capabilities Employed for the 'Desired Effect'.
(d) Effects of 'Information Warfare Weapons'.
(e) Existing Set Ups.
(f) The Way Forward.

Introduction

The growth of information has changed the world and the way people connect socially, communicate, entertain, recreate, exchange information, remain abreast with the latest happenings all over the globe, attend to professional work, shop, and even deal with the community in entirely newer ways, not imaginable till a few years back. The internet as a digital infrastructure, which has assumed significance as much as our daily needs. There are more than four million articles of information available on internet for everyone to access and billions of social media users are actively engaged in communicating round the clock. The people are connecting to the internet through devices like laptops, personal computers, mobile phone, and using the same for communications, information, education, data storage, e-commerce and a host of other digital activities. This rise in the number of users and the variety of ways in which the internet is getting exploited makes a much larger arena of activities vulnerable to disruptions. The cyber security too assumes significance as we become increasingly dependent on digital processes and systems.

The social media is also being exploited to minimise the impact of the magnitude of issues affecting common citizens and for misinformation about followers of a particular ideology. Immediate denials or corrections using the internet, to a message, published news or an article has made it possible to keep in the check the ill effects of misinformation. Thus, perception management is being done in real time, of all thinkable aspects of an activity concerning common users. Social media is increasingly being used for public discourse, to influence group opinions or for achieving political goals by disseminating propaganda or misinformation about various events. The public reaction can be now controlled/altered through publicity of certain messages and themes and their distribution through the internet.

At least 12 of the world's 15 largest military powers were reported to be engaged in building cyber warfare programs, suggesting a cyber-cold war already in progress. Cyber-attacks threaten Government's everyday affairs in view of web intrusions and web defacements reported after Pokhran-II (1998) nuclear weapons tests.

As per Vivekananda International Foundation Task Force Report,[1] India has been the one of worst affected countries from global cyber-attacks in the recent past. The 2017 WannaCry ransomware attack affected about 48,000 computers. Earlier, the Stuxnet malware attack in 2010 affected about 10,000 computers in India, some of which belonged to critical infrastructure facilities, including power grids and offshore oil rigs of the Oil and Natural Gas Commission. The Nuclear Power Corporation of India, by its own admission, blocks at least 10 targeted cyber-attacks a day. Cyber-attacks may include use of cyber capability for causing nuisance, espionage, denial of attacks, intrusion of electronic systems, causing damage to weapons or full spectrum cyber warfare.

Indian security forces regularly confront cyber radicalism from extremist groups who use the web to spread propaganda, incite violence and plan and carry out catastrophic attacks.[2] India has been targeted on a number of occasions, over the years. National Informatics Centre servers were reportedly beached in 2009. Defence Research and Development Organisation, Prime Minister's Office and Bharat Sanchar Nigam Limited websites were hacked in 2013–14. Indian Space Research Organisation webpage was defaced in 2015. Incidents of disinformation campaign by adversaries through social media sites have also been reported.

Information Technology and the Battle Space

Information technology has transformed the nature of the modern-day battle space and given way to electronic, cyber and space warfare. The information technology revolution is creating a new way of life, a different kind of economy and an enlightened society. The defence thinkers have been analysing the numerous ways in which the information technology has transformed modern-day warfare, changed the vulnerabilities and the arming methodologies of nation's war fighting machinery: many defence analysts feel that the next war will be fought not on physical but on digital borders. Information technology also offers much greater efficiency with fewer physical casualties through use of smart technologies and highly skilled armed forces. The vulnerabilities today include the ease of infecting computers with virus, denying connectivity to the adversary, disrupting daily life through delay/denial of financial transactions, defacing personal as well as business electronic data and spreading disinformation. Information technology may be used to disrupt, disable, delay and corrupt rather than physical destruction of the adversary's capabilities. Information technology had equally enabled even non-state actors, terrorists and criminals organisations to wage the information warfare. The need of the day is to prevent cyber-attacks on own data.

The main effort would be to gain electro-magnetic superiority with a view to neutralise the adversary's command, control, communication, computer, surveillance, intelligence and information acquisition systems. The focus of the information warfare activities would be to gain access to, tamper with, and exploit, information and information systems of the adversary to own advantage. Success of operations would largely depend upon achievement of superiority of electro-magnetic spectrum and speedy electronic isolation of adversary's armed forces. The aim will be to cause a psychological paralysis of an adversary rather than planning operations for capture of territory or destruction of material assets/forces. The armed forces would strive to achieve "information deterrence" against likely or visualised adversaries.

The greatest threat to Britain's security is posed by computer software and not military hardware, the head of the British Army warned recently. General Sir Mark Carleton-Smith said that the 'weaponisation' of data will mean that the Armies are soon judged on their ability to prevent cyber-attacks rather than on capabilities of their tanks and missiles.[3] "It might not be too far into the future before armies are no longer distinguished by the volume of their hardware—the number of tanks, infantry fighting vehicles—but much more accurately by the sophistication and integration of their software and associated artificial intelligence,"

'Information Warfare' involves use of battle space and management of information and communication technology to seek an advantage over the adversary. It is a conflict between two or more groups, with the aim of preserving the integrity of own information systems while manipulating information to make the adversary take decisions against his own interest. Information warfare may manifest as under:

- Electronic warfare is used to disrupt or neutralise electromagnetic transmissions. These include electronic counter measures and jamming to affect military communications and weapon guidance means. It also affects routine civilian functions like the aerial movements, navigation systems and rail traffic control systems—jamming and degrading of these would have severe repercussions.
- Cyber warfare includes actions by one side to penetrate opponent's networks to damage/disrupt their functioning while safeguarding own similar networks. The motives could be purely

commercial affecting civilian population or include military targets. Cyber warfare may cause major disruption of government, public and private sector resources and services and in turn impacting national security and citizens' lives. Cyber warfare adversely affects digital networks making every day routine business transactions impossible to operate, resulting in unbearable financial loss and may target industry control systems to render them dysfunctional or adversely affect their designed output. Cyber warfare against military targets will be directed against command and control communications, air defence systems, weapon control systems and guidance systems. Cyber warfare activities against state authorities would focus at causing uprising and chaos to make the government/authorities deploy additional security apparatus.

- Psychological operations aim at degrading the morale and well-being of soldiers and civilians alike. Psychological operations include all activities carried out in social, political and economic fields to influence the opinions, emotions and behaviour of the targeted population. These include spreading rumours/fake news/disturbing messages, building counter narratives and perception management primarily through social media platforms like Facebook, LinkedIn, Twitter, YouTube, Social Networking Sites, etc. Social media has become an essential tool for conducting psychological operations by the nation's military machinery as it is already being effectively used by terrorists and other non-state actors for their propaganda. Social media has exhibited its power to form/alter opinions through speedier sharing of information using internet, as was witnessed during 'Arab Spring' in 2010 and in various incidents of stone throwing in Kashmir over the last few years. In addition, intelligence collection from the social media platforms may lead to a host of effective counter actions by the state military/security machinery.

According to some thinkers, the various forms of information warfare are: Command and Control Warfare, Intelligence Warfare, Electronic Warfare, Network Warfare, Psychological Warfare, Economic Warfare and Cyber Warfare.

US Joint Doctrine for Information Operations, "JP 313" dated 13 February 2006,[4] and revised JP 313, describes in detail the various aspects of 'Information Operations'. As per the document 'Information Operations' are the integrated use of Electronic Warfare, Computer Network Operations, Psychological Operations, Military Deception, and Security Operations to influence, disrupt, corrupt or seize the adversary's human or automated decision making, while protecting own. 'Information Operations' consist of five basic capabilities, as under:

- Psychological Operations (PSYOPS)
- Deception Operations (MILDEC)
- Operations Security (OPSEC)
- Electronic Warfare (EW)
- Computer Network Operations (CNO)

  Note. The above five capabilities work closely with Public Affairs (PA) and Civil Military Operations (CMO).

British Army's Information Operations Doctrine is outlined in Joint Warfare Publication (JWP) 3-80, June 2002. The 'Information Operations' are defined as 'Coordinated actions undertaken to influence an adversary or potential adversary in support of political and military objectives, by undermining his will, cohesión and decisionmaking ability, by acting on his information, and his procedures and systems of information, while protecting one's own decision-makers and decision making processes.' Information Operations aim mainly at the will and capabilities of the adversary (undermining), of allies (protection), and of neutrals (persuasion and protection).

India's Approach to Information Warfare

India is presently facing numerous internal and external threats and it sees 'Information Operations' as the fifth integral dimension of warfare. Information Assurance are the 'Information Operations' that aim at protecting and defending information and its systems while guaranteeing their availability, integrity, authenticity, confidentiality, and acceptance. These operations include protection, detection and response. Informational Superiority is the status reached when à competitive advantage is gained from exploiting a favourable Informational position.

India has used information, as its recorded history and mythology suggest. In Mahabharata, Lord Krishna wrongly announces Ashwathama's death with drums, confuses his enemies, and the act assists in achieving victory. The objectives of information warfare are the creation and maintenance of databases; the protection of information; influence on the adversary's perceptions; influence on neutrals and noncombatants; the protection of decisionmaking system and destruction of enemy's systems. Information warfare may be conducted in the form of Command and Control Warfare, Electronic Warfare, Cybernetic Warfare, Network Centric Warfare, Intelligence Based Warfare, Psychological Warfare, and Economic Warfare.[5]

Although the approach to information warfare is fairly close to that of Western countries, the two major differences are the integration of economic warfare and the importance given to the content of psychological warfare. The psychological warfare aspect is strongly developed and is equally applicable to all levels of warfare, i.e. strategic, operational and tactical. The objectives of psychological warfare remain as creating doubt, causing dissidence and dissatisfaction among the adversary, strengthening the support of allies, and helping to resolve conflicts. It integrates civil military actions as well as public information. The integration of economic information warfare is a major aspect of the Indian approach.

The Indian Subcontinent

Figure 6.1: Preparing the Army for Future War

Source: IANS Infographics.

SWOT Analysis: The major aspects of an analysis of our capabilities for Information Warfare are discussed below:

Strengths

- A large battle hardened standing armed forces.
- Availability of highly qualified, technology savvy cyber experts with required infrastructure.
- Large population of inquisitive minds backed by technology.

Weaknesses

- Lack of formal education and training of staff to plan/execute information operations.
- Inadequate number of personnel dedicated for conducting cyber warfare.
- Lack of infrastructure to counter the emerging threats.

Opportunities

- Deployment of armed forces in active counter terrorist/insurgency operations.
- Joint operations and sharing of information between civil police and military establishments.
- On the job training of large number of armed forces personnel for gaining expertise.

Threats

- Speedy proliferation of hand-held, low-cost, high-technology electronic gadgets.
- Lack of in-depth understanding of nuances of information operations and cyber warfare.
- Limited number of assets.

Indian Subcontinent and Information Warfare

The Indian Subcontinent is a Southern region and peninsula of Asia. The subcontinent projects South, from the Himalayas into the Indian Ocean. The subcontinent includes Nepal, Bhutan, India, Pakistan, Bangladesh, Maldives and Sri Lanka. China, a strategic competitor in Asia, has significant influence on the political and security affairs of all constituents of the Indian Subcontinent. As India strives to emerge as a strong regional power, it faces formidable security challenges of terrorism—both external as well as internal. China continues to be and would remain a strategic competitor of India in foreseeable future. The security environment calls for a closer intelligence cooperation between US, India and all its neighbours.

Figure 6.2: Indian Subcontinent

Source: Global Plants Initiative, Kew.

Indian Subcontinent and Future Battle Space

A comprehensive report published by Vivekananda International Foundation (VIF) stresses that cyber-enabled armed forces and creation of cyber command are aimed at addressing a critical void in developing India's fifth generation warfare capability in a digitised battlefield.[6] In our context, the nature of warfare has changed the way we have to structure our armed forces. We are now capable of analysing a variety of inputs received through high technology communications means and are able to monitor an adversary's activities in real time enabling the commanders a timely and accurate placement of available military resources. The resultant enhanced battle field transparency and improved situational awareness enables the armed forces to act speedily and take decision without loss of time.

The weaponisation of space, reliance on unmanned military equipment and systems and extensive use of media are changing the character of warfare. Information operations targeting adversary's will to fight are the new tools of warfare during peace and war diminishing the existing boundaries between peace time and conflict stage. Further, the demarcation between civil and military resources is rapidly vanishing. This calls for a military structure that is capable of operating in multiple domains and handling multiple threats simultaneously. The open source systems increasingly being procured/used by the defence forces have further increased their vulnerability to cyber attacks. Commonality of equipment is desired for ease of maintenance; however, this also makes a higher quantum vulnerable to cyber attacks. Certain viruses may be either deliberately introduced during development stage and/or a vulnerability left in the operating software of the product.

Capabilities Employed For Information Warfare

Information Operations. The US Army document 'FM-100-6 Information Operations' defines "information operations" as "continuous military operations within the military environment that enable, enhance, and protect the friendly force's ability to collect, process, and act on information to achieve an advantage across the full range of military operations; information operations include interacting with the global information environment and exploiting or denying an adversary's information and decision capabilities.[7] The goal of these operations is "information dominance" or achieving a degree of information superiority that allows the possessor to use information systems and capabilities to achieve an operational advantage in a conflict or to control the situation in operations short of war, while denying those capabilities to the adversary.

Cyber Operations. Cyber warfare is a form of information warfare and includes means utilised to destroy, degrade, exploit or compromise the adversary's computer based systems while ensuring protection of own similar assets. It involves use of technology to gain intelligence, speedier processing and dissemination of intelligence, identification of friend and foe, jamming and overloading adversary's networks. Offensive cyber warfare aims at physical destruction of communication infrastructure/ assets as also to gain access into adversary's information systems or networks. Cyber warfare includes psychological operations whereby use of messages, pamphlets/leaflets and scam mails is resorted to. On the other hand, defensive actions aim at denying access to unauthorised persons or information and maintaining integrity of own data. Cyber operations through peace time espionage activities would assist, when required, targeting of military cyber assets, guidance systems, weapon control systems, civil communications and operations of air/rail traffic, leading to large scale breakdowns and disruptions. Cyberattacks on the websites of Estonia (2007) and Georgia (2008), possibly by non-state actors with no evidence of the involvement of state making attribution difficult, have been the trigger for many nations to consider setting up the infrastructure needed for conducting and/or countering cyber warfare.

Effects of Information Warfare Weapons

The role of information warfare has been gaining significance over the years. War fighting in the cyberspace involves planning and conduct of the offensive/defensive activities even during normal peace time. The exploitation of social media that caused uprising against the rulers and even lead to overthrowing of established regimes, during the Arab Spring exhibited another dimension of the potential of cyber warfare using space. Weapons available with the information warrior can have serious consequences, without any physical destruction and information warfare can seriously hamper functioning of both the civil as well as military information systems of an adversary. The ongoing activities of various nations, towards enhancing capabilities in this sphere, are discussed briefly to highlight the need to prepare ourselves adequately.

The United States declared cyberspace to be the fifth dimension of warfare in addition to land, sea, air and space, and established a Cyber Command in 2010. There are reports of British and France preparing cyber forces and South Korea creating a Cyber Warfare Command. Russia has been pursuing cyber warfare and had exhibited its superior information warfare capabilities in each of their military activities in Estonia, Georgia and Ukraine.

China

- China introduced its department for defensive cyber warfare and information security in 2010 and is engaged overtime to gain superiority through establishment of Strategic Support Force and acquisition of advanced telecommunications equipment with the aim of gaining information dominance in the years to come. The Strategic Support Force is a military theatre organisation tasked for space, cyber and electronic warfare missions as part of information warfare.

- The aim of information warfare, as per Chinese writings, is information dominance—the ability to defend one's own information while exploiting and assaulting an opponent's information infrastructure. It necessarily involves having the means to interfere with an adversary's capability to paralyze the opponent's strategic and operational military assets prior to actions directed at gaining superiority over land, sea and air.
- China has reportedly established at least twelve facilities for Integrated Network Electronic Warfare training at unit levels in computer network offensive/defensive operations, jamming, resorting to multiple forms of electronic and information warfare activities.[8] The facility is supposedly located at Zhurihe in the Beijing Military Region. The People's Liberation Army has been acquiring advanced communications equipment as information warfare seems to offer it options for asymmetric warfare, but their present capability may not promise information dominance.
- The Chinese accept that space will be an integral dimension of warfare in the 21st century. Operations in space may be through either use of weapons or support to operations. Weapons may include missiles travelling through space or space-based systems that can be used against missiles, satellites, or targets on the surface of the earth. Support to operations would include activities for communications, global positioning, intelligence collection, and weather systems.

Special Attributes of Cyber Warfare

Information warfare weapons can cause desired consequences without physical destruction of assets. Cyber warfare, a form of information warfare, can disrupt adversary's civil as well as military information systems. There being no agreed definition or scope, it is appreciated that cyberattacks may be directed against information systems for espionage activities as also for disruption/destruction of civil and military infrastructure. The vulnerabilities of systems and networks are increasing with the induction of newer technologies. Cyber warfare would have the following special attributes:

- **Non-Linearity**. Cyber operations can be simultaneously directed against a number of targets and can be launched at any time and from any location, achieving surprise and making adversary commit large quantum of resources and cyber assets in defence.
- **Asymmetric Nature and Low Cost Option**. Cyber attackers exploit the weaknesses in the software designs through use of malware, making it possible for a much weaker adversary, or a non-state actor to execute cyberattacks.
- **Launched in Real Time.** The multiplicity of actors makes the attribution of the act difficult. Cyber attackers are difficult to identify and would resort to denial, even when detected.
- **Deniability**. Cyberattacks may originate from anywhere. The servers in a friendly or some neutral country may be utilised even without their getting to know about the use/misuse.
- **Response to Cyberattacks.** The response of the attacked nation, its form and potency, would be largely dependent upon latter's capabilities and means available to counter the cyberattacks.
- **Intelligence.** Cyber activities/intrusions with the objective to gather military intelligence, effect industrial espionage or for stealing information of economic significance may not be easily determinable. The process of counter actions and identification/ selection of targets by the targeted nation may be inordinately delayed/inadequate, rendering it ineffective/even redundant at times.
- **Multiplicity of Targets**. Cyberattacks are equally effective against both civilian and military assets. The military targets may include some or all of the following systems/networks/assets:
  - Command, control, communications, computer, intelligence, surveillance, reconnaissance, and logistics networks.
  - Decision Support Systems.
  - Data storage systems, intelligence assessments and weapon control data.
  - Fire Control Systems.
  - Air Defence Control and Reporting Systems.
  - Navigation systems of aircrafts, ships and land-based platforms.

- Guidance systems of missiles and precision-guided munitions.
- Space based assets and their control infrastructure.
- Propaganda to undermine the morale of soldiers.

Indian Armed Forces and Information Warfare

India has been facing threat of cyber warfare from a host of agencies and actors. Indian Government, in 2010, had asked all concerned agencies to enhance their cyber warfare capabilities. The Government agencies were to develop cyber capability to break into adversary's communication and commercial networks, establish testing facilities and enhance countermeasures. National Technical Research Organisation, Defence Intelligence Agency and Defence Research and Development Organisation were to be the lead agencies. In the same year, India reported Chinese variant of Stuxnet worm in Indian installations and Pakistan Cyber Army hackers defacing India's Central Bureau of Investigation website.

Pakistan Military Establishment has been engaged in attempts to create havoc using internet and social media. Their cyber warfare agencies used morphed photographs of violence to mislead public by depicting these as acts of violence against Muslims in Myanmar and Assam. They also used short messages to circulate threat and create a false perception of insecurity amongst North-East people working in Bengaluru, Hyderabad, Pune and Delhi resulting in mass exodus from these cities for their home state(s). Such successful acts of cyber warfare are indicative of the catastrophe that can be caused by an adversary during war time when fighter aircrafts, missile guidance systems, weapon control systems and nation's nuclear and electricity power grids are likely to be targeted. The targeting of commercial and communication networks can cause disorder resulting in chaos.

India's National Security Advisor, Shri Ajit Doval, while speaking at Sardar Patel Memorial Lecture in New Delhi, on 25 October 2018, stressed on the need to prepare for fourth generation warfare with an invisible enemy.[9]

Economic Times dated 10 December 2018[10] reported that as per panel discussion at Military Literature Festival 2018 held in Chandigarh on Saturday 08 December 2018, defence experts called for development of more indigenous equipment for 'Information Warfare' in the country to build an edge against adversaries in the battlefield. During the discussion on 'Information Warfare—the new face of war', Lieutenant General Vijay

Oberoi, former Vice Chief of Army Staff said that despite major advancements in the field, India was still banking on Information Warfare Techniques imported from other countries and Lieutenant General R S Panwar (Retired) said while countries like the US, China and Russia had already taken concrete steps to strengthen their 'Information Warfare' techniques, India was still to take an appropriate call on it (Information Warfare Techniques).

The Joint Information Warfare Doctrine for Indian Armed Forces was published in 2005 and further revised in 2010. The Joint Doctrine of Indian Armed Forces released in April 2017 highlighted the need for India to prepare for the triad of space, cyberspace and special operations. Creation of Defence Cyber Agency, Defence Space Agency and Special Operations Division are steps in the right direction. Defence Cyber Agency is likely to perform the following functions:

- Safeguarding own computer networks, platforms and weapon systems from cyberattacks.
- Defence against unfriendly cyberattacks, especially when loss of life, property, or significant foreign policy and economic consequences are expected.
- Carry out a comprehensive threat analysis by synergising actions/ inputs of all agencies concerned with information warfare to include Cyber Intelligence, Signals Intelligence, Electronic Intelligence, Human Intelligence and Operational Security.
- Formulate offensive cyber options including covert operations, for execution on approval of designated authority.
- Plan and execute cyber deception, when required for facilitating conduct of operations by armed forces.
- Human resource development to include recruitment of personnel and their training.
- Equipping of establishments/agencies for efficient conduct of information warfare, ensuring interoperability of systems.
- Liaison with civil establishments/agencies, for formulation of cyber-related policies.
- Exchange of information with friendly foreign countries.

India, located in a region where neighbours have acquired/created the cyber capability has been most vulnerable. India has reportedly stepped up its efforts in offensive cyber capability and create capability to defend own networks.

Organisational Structures for Effective Information Warfare

At National Level. We need an apex body at the national level to formulate, coordinate, synergise resources and efficiently execute Information Warfare plans. It is suggested that the apex body under the National Security Advisor have separate national board for Information Warfare. The board should have agencies for information warfare and its infrastructure development functioning under it. Defence Planning Committee constituted under the Chairmanship of National Security Advisor in April 2018, is a right step to deal with emerging security threats, evolve military strategy and plan military acquisitions. The Committee has members from the civil and military services including the three service chiefs, the Defence Secretary, Foreign Secretary, and Secretary (Expenditure) of the Ministry of Finance, with the Chief of Headquarters Integrated Defence Staff performing the task of member secretary. As per Laxman K Behera, Research Fellow, Institute of Defence Studies and Analyses, April 2018, the new mechanism provides for four sub-committees, one each on Policy and Strategy, Plans and Capability Development, Defence Diplomacy and Defence Manufacturing Eco-System.[11] Defence Planning Committee is tasked to analyse all inputs relating to defence planning including dealing with the strategic and security-related doctrines, defence acquisition and the 15-year Long-Term Integrated Perspective Plan. The committee is also to prepare draft documents on national security strategy, strategic defence review and doctrines, defence manufacturing eco-system and prioritised capability development plans for the armed forces. With the constitution of Defence Planning Committee at the apex level, it is assessed that the requisite impetus would be imparted to equip and arm the defence forces to meet the challenges of fighting the fourth generation warfare. A centralised control of all information warfare agencies under the National Security Council and an integrated approach by all agencies is desired for optimising their efforts towards proactive cyber defence. National Security Council Secretariat also synchronises efforts by all agencies dealing with cyber activities through National Cyber Coordination Centre under the Ministry of Communications and Information Technology. A separate wing, for cyber operations, in the National Security Council may be considered to meet the challenges.

At Joint Services Headquarters Level. The Chief of Staff Committee/ Headquarters of Integrated Defence Staff should have a board for

Information Warfare as also a Joint Information Warfare Committee to coordinate sharing of assets held with individual services and synergising the operations of various sub components. Defence Information Assurance and Research Agency and the Defence Intelligence Agency are already functioning under the aegis of Integrated Defence Staff. Defence Information Assurance and Research Agency is the nodal agency concerned with all cyber related needs of the tri-services and Ministry of Defence[12] and is being upgraded to the Defence Cyber Agency. Defence Intelligence Agency coordinates intelligence acquisition by three services, civil intelligence agencies and also controls tri-services agencies, namely Defence Imagery and Photo Analysis Centre (established to process the satellite imagery requirements and maintain a data bank for meeting imagery requirements of the armed forces) and Directorate of Signals Intelligence.

At Army Headquarters Level

- Presently, Additional Director General Military Operations (Information Warfare) at Directorate General of Military Operations in concert with Directorate General of Military Intelligence coordinates all aspects of Information Warfare to include Cyber Operations, Electronic Warfare and Psychological Operations. The staff at Directorate General of Military Operations would coordinate development of information warfare software, information assurance technology and cyberattack capability. Army Cyber Group is designated to carry out cyber operations for the Army. Directorate General of Military Intelligence should provide the necessary expertise for conducting the psychological operations.
- As reported in the media, Army has also set up a cyber-monitoring cell recently to monitor the use of social media by its personnel, especially on non-encrypted sites.[13] The cell reportedly keeps tabs on malicious software, imposters on social media and hackers, primarily to safeguard personnel from fraud, imposters and honey-traps by carrying out random checks of the social media accounts of personnel to monitor them.
- As reported in the media,[14] the Defence Ministry has approved a new branch in the army for 'Information Warfare' to combat misinformation and false propaganda being spread through social media for adverse psychological impact. The report further adds, 'In

keeping with the needs of the future battlefield, hybrid warfare and social media reality, the new Director General Information Warfare will have under him the erstwhile Additional Director Generals of Public Information and Information Warfare'. A cyber unit will also be placed under the aegis of the Director General Information Warfare.

At Headquarters Command and Corps. Information operations are being handled by the available staff and specific information warfare related set-ups exist at Army Command and Corps Headquarters. Electronic Warfare Groups and Sub-Groups function under Command Headquarters. Brigadier General Staff (Information Warfare) with adequate trained staff should be capable of coordinating and conducting electronic warfare, psychological operations, military deception and also ensure operational security.

At Division Headquarters. There is a need to incorporate a Grade-1 level staff officer, under the Colonel General Staff, to deal with various aspects of information warfare.

The Way Forward

Training. Information Warfare courses are presently being conducted for the three services at Mhow. The aspect needs greater attention to achieve required level of understanding of threats and vulnerabilities, and generating requisite expertise at all levels in the three services. We must create a core group with adequate insight into the nuances of information operations. Suitably trained personnel in languages of our adversaries would have to be employed for efficient monitoring and timely offensive cyber actions. A partnership program with the private sector would assist in developing required number of cyber trained personnel. A training capsule at all levels and for personnel (civil and military) of all streams would enhance awareness and, in turn, act as deterrence.

Doctrine and Organisational Infrastructures. Joint Electronic Warfare Doctrine as also individual Services Doctrines should lay out all possible nuances of electronic warfare and recommend modalities for synergising the available resources with the three services for an effective utilisation of cyber assets. Suitable initiatives for developing the 'Information Psychological Operations' in accordance with the prevailing strategic environment and to create a tri-services training institute, are required. Effective organisational structures required at national, strategic and operational levels be discussed in detail, established with requisite technology/equipment, and geared up to ensure an enhanced information warfare and deterrence capability.

Public Information. The Defence Public Relation Office should be remodelled to meet the challenges of the Information Warfare, and to cater to operational needs of the Armed Forces. The Defence Ministry has approved a new Information Warfare branch for Indian Army.[15] In a clear reference to Pakistan, a press statement issued said, "In the last three weeks, disinformation campaign by the adversary on digital media has increased. All ranks have been well sensitised of these disinformation campaigns by the adversary on digital media has increased. All ranks have been well sensitised of these disinformation campaigns and all ranks can see through the lie, deceit and deception of the terror sponsors." The Defence Public Relation Office may actively engage with the services elements to understand the latter's operational requirements.

Indigenisation. Indigenisation of cyber technology to include electronics and software in service with the armed forces needs to be given impetus for making the defence sector secure and reliable under all situations. Our efforts must be focused on reducing our dependence on other nations for high technology systems, to negate the threat of sabotage and intrusion into defence-related electronic systems. The growth of information technology and related services and the intellectual potential in India, makes it possible for us to achieve much higher levels of indigenisation that are needed for a self-reliant defence sector as also to meet our requirements of systems for nonmilitary purposes. Environmental aspects that must be addressed to encourage indigenisation include creation of requisite infrastructure, incentives to private sector for research and development, investment friendly policies and labour laws. Priority for domestic production of strategic defence electronics and additional incentives offered by all states would be steps towards India's national security. A healthy competition between public and private sectors, through ensuring equal opportunities and a level playing field, would enhance the quality of the end product and an increased production.

The need for indigenisation of information technology was amply stressed by various defence experts in the Military Literature Festival 2018 held in Chandigarh on 08 December 2018, as highlighted in *Economics Times* of 10 December 2018.[16]

Social Media. The armed forces may exploit social media platforms for gathering day-to-day intelligence during peace time and on outbreak of hostilities. The intelligence so collected must be utilised in profiling of terrorists/anti-national éléments/organisations, and to initiate necessary measures towards countering their malicious narratives. Real time intelligence gained from the social media platforms helps in launching timely counter terrorist operations with precision. During active hostilities, psychological operations using social media platforms would focus at demoralisation of the adversary's civilian public support systems and the leadership. Social media enables accurate and faster (real time) communication to larger audience the world over—the need, therefore, is to incorporate it as a tool for strategic communication to achieve the nation's goals while minimising own vulnerabilities. Equally important is the need to educate the armed forces personnel about the ways an adversary can exploit the social media to track our strategic movements, engage certain unsuspecting lobbies for perception management and to maintain surveillance over activities of groups using social media platforms for routine communications affecting opinions of masses. As reported in the media,[17] the Indian Army has issued specific guidelines to its personnel on the use of social media, banning using photographs in uniform as profile pictures, exposing official identities or ranks, disclosing unit names and locations.

Cyber Defence. The requirement is to safeguard own networks and assets, in order to protect information and to effectively counter the potential threats of cyberattacks. Effort at the policy level needs to be put in to ensure safety of our equipment and its operating software so that an adversary cyberattack does not paralyse the security set up. A design that permits operation of the system during the conflict stage withstanding adversary cyberattacks is desired. The movement of our society and the world from the industrial age to the information age has been hastened by the liberalised availability of frequency spectrum. India has plans to roll out 5G services for consumers by 2020. This has an impact on the Armed Forces too as it provides equal opportunities and challenges to the two opposing sides.

Technologies. Information Technology and Information Warfare Technologies are assisting in focusing on key result areas during a conflict and signify a synthesis of technology and human intelligence with force capability. These technologies have major force multiplication effect on the conduct of warfare and exploit the vast potential of technology to gain major advantages over an adversary. Information warfare can be continuously exploited even during peace-time. The information technology and information warfare environment significantly assists in gaining timely and accurate intelligence, achieving surprise during operations, and to effect a psychological degradation of the adversary.

Perception Management. The Industrial Age had given the concept of mechanised warfare and destruction of the enemy's war waging capability and today the information era demands suppression of enemy's information systems in order to achieve national and military objectives. The public perception and the contribution of operations towards influencing public opinion need to be factored into the operational plans. The military campaign has to plan comprehensively to influence the adversary, own citizens, and the international opinion. Armed forces would have to be prepared to conduct information warfare. A conventional war in the Indian Subcontinent, is likely to be a hybrid of the industrial age and knowledge based warfare.

Conclusion

Indian Armed Forces are rapidly adapting to the information age and are in the process of acquiring offensive and defensive capabilities for information warfare. Establishment of Indian National Defence University and Defence Cyber Agency would give it the requisite reservoir of human resources and technology prowess.

Indian National Defence University is being established to inculcate and promote coordination and interaction among the three Services and also with other agencies of the government. It would encourage higher education in defence studies, defence management, defence technology, defence acquisition/procurements and promote policy-oriented research on aspects related to National Security.

Incorporation of private sector in defence research and development and strategic partnership agreements with global powers with expertise in cyber warfare are seen as positive steps to gear up for the 21st century battlefield. National and military doctrines laying down the objectives, an efficient cyber agency and induction of advanced technology at a faster pace are the needs of the moment.

War fighting, in future, will need a much advanced and integrated planning, detailed coordination and perfect execution at the national level with military being involved throughout. All sub-components of national defence must necessarily prepare, equip, acquire the requisite knowhow and train to fight a coordinated battle in the information environment. India must step up its efforts to prepare for a future war in cyber domain. India needs to initiate steps towards enhancing cyber security and information warfare capability.

NOTES

1 Credible Cyber Deterrence in Armed Forces of India, Part II, Section Two, Policy and Strategy For Developing Cyber Capability of The Indian Armed Forces, published 28 Mar 2019, pp. 53–58.
2 Ibid.
3 Mail On Line, dated 05 June 2019
4 http://www.dtic.mil/doctrine/jel/new_pubs/jp3_13.pdf
5 Sapan Kumar Chatterji. "An Overview of Information Operations in the Indian Army", IO Sphere (Special Edition 2008).
6 VIF Task Force Report on Policy and Strategy for Developing Cyber Capability of The Indian Armed Forces, June 2019, pp. 54–55.
7 Field Manual 100-6 Information Operations, August 1996.
8 Desmond Ball, China's Cyber Warfare Capabilities, Security Challenges, Volume 7, Number 2, Winter 2011, pp. 84. https://indianstrategicknowledgeonline.com/web/chinacyber.pdf
9 https://timesofindia.indiatimes.com/videos/news/sardar-patel-memorial-lecture-nsa-ajit...
10 https://economictimes.indiatimes.com/news/defence/defence-experts-call-for-development, December 10, 2018. Accessed on October 31, 2019.
11 Behera, Laxman K, Creation of Defence Planning Committee: a Step towards Credible Defence Preparedness, Institute of Defence Studies and Analyses, 19 April 2018, https://idsa.in/idsacomments/creation-of-defence-planning-committee-lkbehera-190418
12 Joint Doctrine Indian Armed Forces, April 2017, p. 49.
13 Sputnik News dated 10 Jul 2019, available at https://sputniknews.com/asia/201907101076204660-indian-army-sets-up-cyber-monitoring-cell-to-check-social-media-use-by-its-personnel
14 Shaurya Karanbir Gurung, ET Bureau. *Economic Times*, dated 09 March 2019, available at//economictimes.indiatimes.com/articles how/68329797.cms? from =mdr&utm_source=content ofinterest&utm_medium=text&utm_campaign=cppst
15 Ibid.
16 https://economictimes.indiatimes.com/news/defence/defence-experts-call-for-development...
17 Sputnik News, 10 July 2019, available at https://sputniknews.com/asia/201907101076204660-indian-army-sets-up-cyber-monitoring-cell-to-check-social-media-use-by-its-personnel

7

Manoeuvre Warfare and Firepower

Major General (Dr.) PK Chakravorty

ABSTRACT

It is an indisputable fact that Firepower and Manoeuvre have been two components on which battles were won. The classical use was seen during the two Gulf Wars in 1990s. However, that was in open terrain which permitted freedom of movement. When we narrow it down to our mountainous borders with Pakistan and China the issues become entirely different. Mountainous terrain on the Indian borders provides limited space for manoeuvre. Accordingly Firepower assumes greater importance. Therefore Asymmetry of Firepower will decide victory in the Indian subcontinent. Accordingly making it extremely important to have a good assortment of Guns, Rockets and Missiles who could complement the manoeuvering forces.

The chapter would be dealt under the following headings:

- *Complementing Firepower and Manoeuvre Warfare*
- *Elements*
- *Technological developments visualised in Firepower*
- *Futuristic Developments*
- *What is Manoeuvre Warfare?*
- *Issues which merit importance*
- *Analysis*
- *Manoeuvre Warfare in the present context*
- *Force Structuring and Training*
- *Conclusion*

The Chapter would focus on the scope of undertaking these operations visualised in the next 15 years. Despite the nuclear backdrop scope exists to undertake these aspects in the existing battle space.

Complementing Firepower and Manoeuvre

Warfare quintessentially comprises two ingredients Firepower and Manoeuvre. Both complement each other and synergise to defeat the enemy. Manoeuvre entails moving to positions of advantage with dexterity thereby outwitting the enemy.

Firepower essentially comprises Weapons and Missiles. These constitute the combination of Small Arms, Artillery, Air Defence, Tanks, Aircraft, Unmanned Combat Air Vehicles (UCAVs), Ships, Submarines and Unmanned water vehicles. The payload from these weapons could be Conventional, Chemical, Biological, Radiological and Nuclear (CBRN). The use of nuclear bombs delivered by an aircraft at Hiroshima and Nagasaki saw the capitulation of Japan during the Second World War. Thereafter these elements have been used efficiently in numerous conflicts. In India's case the Kargil Conflict of 1999 terminated in favour of India due to preponderance of Firepower delivered by these weapons by the Indian Army and the Indian Air Force. The use of 155 mm Bofors Gun in effectively engaging Tiger Hill and Tololing as also the Indian Air Force using Mirage 2000 aircraft to release Laser Guided Bombs on Tiger Hill in the third week of June 1999 paved the way for assaulting troops to reach their objectives. Similarly the effective use of weapons by the Indian Army compelled Pakistan to declare cease fire on the Line of Control in 2003.

It is an indisputable fact that Firepower and Manoeuvre have been two components on which battles were won. The classical use was seen during the two Gulf Wars in 1990s. However that was in open terrain which permitted freedom of movement. However, when we narrow it down to our mountainous borders with Pakistan and China the issues become entirely different. Mountainous terrain on the Indian borders provides limited space for manoeuvre. Accordingly Firepower assumes greater importance. Therefore Asymmetry of Firepower will decide victory in the Indian subcontinent. Accordingly making it extremely important to have a good assortment of Guns, Rockets and Missiles who could complement the manoeuvering forces.

Globally modernisation is being undertaken by all Armed Forces to enable them to fight in a Network Centric Warfare environment. Armed Forces networking essentially link the elements comprising the sensor, command elements and the shooter to engage targets instantaneously. Therefore the current focus is on precision standoff and strikes in real time. Firepower presently is undertaken from all four dimensions which include land, sea, air and submerged surfaces of the sea. Outer space is being used currently for surveillance. However, despite the various space treaties, it is gradually becoming an area for deployment of weapons. Technologically, it would be practicable to consider deployment of Anti Satellite and Direct Energy weapons in this region with developments taking place in this field. Extrapolating to the year 2035, Firepower should be capable of breaking the enemy's will to fight. This would entail causing physical damage as also psychologically attenuate his mental capabilities so as to set in a fear psychosis.

Firepower from weapons and missiles essentially comes down to bringing effective fire on selected targets. The entire process entails getting details of the area to be engaged commonly referred as Surveillance, followed by selection of targets, thereafter engaging the target. It is natural that the target may not have been effectively decimated. Accordingly there is a need to undertake a Post-Strike Damage Assessment (PSDA). These could lead to a Correction or a Reengagement to ensure destruction. Destruction of critical targets would break the enemy's will to fight, thereby paving the way to success. Asymmetry of Firepower in future wars will lead to victory.

Eléments

Results will be achieved at the target end based on the diversity of application of weapons and missiles. The principal elements are weapon and missile platforms with ammunition, which can deliver from five dimensions; Land, Air, Surface of the sea, below the surface of the sea (hereafter referred as sub-surface) and possibly in times to come Outer Space. These are Small Arms, Guns, Mortars, Rockets of Artillery, Tanks, Aircrafts, Missiles, Unmanned Combat Aerial Vehicles (UCAVs), Armed Helicopters, Submarines and in future possibly stations in Outer Space. The ammunition which is the payload is the most important element of these systems. The various types of ammunition would constitute the conventional series which would comprise of High Explosive, Smoke, Illuminating, Armour Piercing, High Explosive Squash Head, Fuel Air Explosive, Cluster, Precision, Sensor Fuzed, Incendiary and Propaganda. Apart from this there is a strategic variety of ammunition which comprises of Nuclear, Biological and Chemical. Further entering the field of Direct Energy this consists of Laser, Electro Magnetic Pulse and other scientific applications. These ammunition with their associated platforms are able to cause destruction which would severely impact the capability of the adversary to fight.

The new domain of warfare is Cyber. As per 17 intelligence agencies of the United States, Russia had penetrated into the Democratic National Convention using cyber techniques thereby influencing the Presidential elections of the United States in 2016. Cyber warfare is the new entrant and is currently known as the fifth domain of warfare. Cyber weapons perform a series of tasks which can physically or technically destroy a target. The purpose of Cyber Warfare is to sabotage or damage the information system of a sensitive target. Cyber weapons are primarily used against network to disrupt, deny, degrade and destroy critical components of a network. The effects would be termed as physical, syntax and semantic.[1] Cyber weapons impact all platforms and can subvert communication signals as also data thereby becoming an important tool for undertaking operations.

The elements are distributed in all the three services. These systems used in the Army are distributed to the role of the corresponding arm in battle. Small arms are primarily with the Infantry, Tanks with the Armoured Corps, Armoured Personnel Carriers with the Mechanised Infantry, Guns, Rockets, Missiles, UCAVs (Unmanned Combat Aerial Vehicles – possibly moving to Aviation), Surveillance Equipment with the Artillery, Air Defence Equipment with Army Air Defence and Helicopters with Army Aviation. It is currently reported that Unmanned Aerial Vehicles (UAVs) are moving under the Army Aviation. Engineers play a critical role in mobility of Firepower platforms and ammunition, The Corps of Signals provides a substantial proportion of C4I2SR requirements. Further cyber warfare equipment will form a part of possibly Signals, Artillery and Air Defence. Firepower elements in the Navy comprises of frigates, destroyers, cruisers, corvettes, aircraft carriers, air defence ships, submarines, fighter aircrafts, maritime surveillance aircraft, helicopters, UCAVs, coastal guns and missiles. Air Force systems would include aircrafts which are fighters and bombers as also armed helicopters, UCAVs, missiles for engaging wide range of targets. The Air Force would also include surveillance equipment like Aerostats, UAVs, Radars and C4I2SR aircrafts like AWACs. These elements would need to be modernised to undertake a net-centric warfare in a full spectrum conflict. This would entail synergy of these constituents to ensure precise standoff strikes from long ranges with increased lethality. Further Battle Field

Transparency (BFT) needs to be enhanced to ensure everything tactically important is seen and what is seen can be hit in real time.

These elements would be used in operations which could be counter insurgency, sub conventional, limited, conventional, nuclear, chemical and biological. The operations would have to be Effect Based with possibly no collateral damage. Other aspects which characterise future operations are non-linearity, enhanced battle space and low threshold against the use of nuclear weapons. It is pertinent to note that more and more countries are developing nuclear weapons covertly to ensure security. However, conventional conflicts can still take place between countries holding nuclear weapons as has been observed during the clash on the Ussuri River between Russia and China as also the Kargil conflict in 1999. Further our surgical strikes post Uri and Pulwama bear testimony to this fact.

Technological Developments Visualised in Firepower

There are numerous technological developments in Firepower. A new class of weapon system which is currently under development is the Direct Energy Weapon System. These weapons emit energy in an aimed direction without the means of a projectile. It transfers energy to a target for desired effect. The energy can come in the form of Electromagnetic radiation in lasers or masers, particle beam weapons, flame throwers and sound in sonic weapons. Laser weapons usually generate brief high energy pulses. Most existing weaponised lasers are gas dynamic lasers. They use a low-powered oscillator to generate a coherent wave which can destroy a target. The pulsed energy projectile emits an infra-red laser pulse which creates rapidly expanding plasma at the target. The resulting sound, shock and electromagnetic waves stun the target and cause temporary pain and paralysis. Further there are particle beam weapons which can use charged or neutral particles to decimate targets. The last weapon in this category is a sonic weapon. These weapons utilise sound to injure, incapacitate or kill an opponent. Currently, they are in the development phase. These are in the form of sonic bullets, sonic grenades, sonic mines or sonic cannons. They either make a focused beam of sound and some make sound over an extensive area. Sound waves of high power emitted by these weapons can disrupt ear drums and cause severe pain or disorientation. On the contrary less powerful sound waves can cause nausea and discomfort. These weapons would be optimised once the development phase is completed.[2]

The next aspect which needs focus pertains to Command, Control, Communications, Computers, Information Intelligence Surveillance and Reconnaissance (C4I2SR). Evolution of technology has changed dimensions of war from human centric to platform centric and currently the move is towards Network Centric Warfare. This warfare integrates Sensors, Decision makers and Firepower. The entire process in the current battle space has integrated these elements resulting in synergy during operations.

Broadly there is a wide array of surveillance equipment. Sensors are located on land, sea, under water, air and outer space. Ground-based surveillance equipment comprises the Thermal Imaging Integrated Observation Equipment (TIIOE), Long Range Observation and Reconnaissance Equipment (LORROS), Short Range Battlefield Surveillance Radars, Medium Range Battle field Surveillance Radars, Weapon Locating Radars and Sound Ranging systems. Naval surveillance equipment comprises Radars, Sea bed arrays and Sonar. Surveillance. The Air component comprise Aerostats, Airborne Warning and Control System (AWACs), Tactical Reconnaissance, UAVs and UCAVs. Space based systems comprise Geo synchronous satellites, Remote Sensing satellites, Low Earth Orbiting satellites and space stations. Information provided by these sensors is interpreted by the command and control elements leading to decisions regarding target engagements. A tactical C^4 I^2 system would be primarily based on Command Information Decision Support System (CIDSS) with affiliated systems comprising of Artillery Combat Command & Control System (ACCCS), Electronic Warfare System (EWS), Battlefield Surveillance System (BSS), Air Defence Control & Reporting System (ADC&RS), Operational Air Support (OAS), Air Space Control System (ASCS) and Communications & Data Network System (CDNS). These systems enable the data to be processed leading to selection and engagement of targets resulting in effective Firepower at the objectives to accomplish the operational aim.

Futuristic Developments

The present battlefield environment provides for good surveillance, creditable reconnaissance leading to systematic target acquisition followed by engagements with an aim to degrade or destroy, thereby breaking the enemy's will to fight and paving the way to victory. The developments described above are likely to fructify by 2030. Technology keeps on improving and the areas which would be impacted are as stated below:

- In the next two decades, warfare will possibly include five domains, Land, Sea, Air, Cyber and Outer space. Firepower of Guns and missiles will be a part of all five domains including Cyber which would possibly entail Hard Kill of Cyber assets.
- Technology will enable surveillance of land and sea assets as also movements under water and in Outer Space. Recent operations between Israel and the Hamas in Gaza strip have indicated the use of tunnels by Hamas to link various locations in Israel and Egypt. Surveillance of underground would be a major area for scientific research. Further technology will ensure real time imaging in terms of targets to enable accurate observation while undertaking engagement.
- The entire operations will be Net Centric. Communications will be with every soldier and he would be in a position to call, observe and correct fire. He would also have a Hand held computer which would provide necessary information.
- Warfare will essentially be Non-Contact and would entail the issues of Engagement, Adjustment and Post Strike Damage Assessment to be done with minimum human interference.
- The human being would be gradually replaced by robots that would constitute about 30 per cent of the forces. It is visualised that aircraft, ships, submarines and ground vehicles would be unmanned. Robots would also be used in offensive operations duly guided by commanders from remote locations.
- Conventional ammunition will become more lethal and accurate. Use of thermobaric and other developed explosives will cause higher casualties. A large percentage approximately 60 per cent of all ammunition will be Precision Guided Munitions (PGMs).
- Ranges of Guns firing shells at ranges of 190 to 200 km would be developed to engage targets. Currently two developments are on in the USA. The Long Range Land Attack Projectile (LRLAP) is a developmental programme to produce a precision guidance 155 mm naval artillery shell for the US Navy. The system is under development by Lockheed Martin Missiles and Fire Control, the prime contractor being BAE Systems. In cooperation with BAE a version of LRLAP has been designed to be used with 5 inch/54 naval cannon. The 155 mm/62 AGS shell weighs 102 kg and has a bursting charge of 11 kg. The guidance of the projectile is GPS and INS. The Circular Error of probability is less than 50 metres.

The warhead is Unitary High Explosive and the range is 190 km.[3] By June 2013 four full cycle live tests have been conducted. In September 2013 Lockheed received $18 million contract to transition the LRLAP to production. The fielding is planned in a few years based on Service requirement. By 2025 the equipment would not only have been operationalised but stabilised.

- In addition to that the United States have dropped a 21000 lb. bomb at Achin district of the eastern province of Nangarhar in Afghanistan. This is close to the Pakistan Border and the ISIS was based in a tunnel complex in that area. The bomb exploded at 7:32 pm local time on 13 April 2017. The bomb, a GBU-43B, is a Massive Ordnance Air Blast Bomb. It weighs more than 10,000 kg and contains 8100 kg of explosive. Its explosion is equivalent to 11 tonnes of TNT and the radius of the blast is 1.6 km. The bomb exploded and shrapnels killed people, and also caused shock and awe which psychologically paralyses an individual. As per reports received about 94 ISIS militants were killed in the attack.[4]
- Unmanned platforms in the form of aerial vehicles, land systems, ships, patrol vessels and submarines would gradually replace human beings. Currently all gas stations in the US are gradually becoming unmanned. There are numerous unmanned trains being run in the US airports. Recently, even Delhi Metro started unmanned metro trains in the newly constructed lines. Taxis are soon going to be run by robots and possibly there would be no manmade taxis in the US by 2030. A conscious decision has been taken by the US Air Force that 30 per cent of their aircraft of all categories would be unmanned. As stated, in the next 20 to 30 years, these are going to explode and create innovations in use of Air Power and Firepower.[5] Further the entire logistics system would possibly be unmanned. The weapon of the Artillery is ammunition and the entire logistic chain could be unmanned. Further, PGMs would reduce the logistics load that would be required to be maintained. The use of loitering missile system would gain prominence.
- Cyber warfare will be the most important component directly affecting operations at Land, Sea, Air and Outer Space. Firepower of Guns, Rockets and Missiles are entirely dependent on electronics and interference in these would cause serious impact

on surveillance, engagement and adjustment of fire. Cyber could also be used in peace to disrupt power distribution, tamper with firepower logistics networks and thereby cause confusion.

- Nano technology is likely to be used extensively. Military equipment including weapon platforms is going to be lighter enabling them to be easily operationalised in mountainous terrain.
- Biotechnology weapons causing awkward sounds by shells resulting in loss of hearing or use of chemicals to induce sleep could be covertly used by 2050.
- The field of Avionics is likely to witness fighter aircrafts flying at Hypersonic Speed which entails flying at a speed greater than 5 Mach.
- ABM Systems would be more effective and possibly Outer Space would be used for detection and engagement. Cruise missiles would be ideally tackled from Outer Space.
- Directed Energy Weapons would be inducted and optimised by 2050. Laser and particle beam weapons would be capable of decimating targets. As explained earlier these weapons emit highly focused energy, transferring that energy to a target would damage it. These weapons would be line of sight and could be deployed sensibly.
- Developments in the nuclear field particularly of Electro Magnetic Pulse need to be researched and carefully applied to Firepower.
- Navigational systems would be numerous and it would be incumbent for any country using firepower to have its own navigational satellites. Currently the US has the Global Positioning System (GPS), Russia has GLONASS, European Union has the Eurosat and Chinese have the Beidou system. India is also planning to have her own navigation system.
- By 2035 there would be a Counter for every weapon in terms of Soft and Hard Kill. This must be borne in mind as in applying Firepower deception will become extremely important.
- Critical technologies for future requirements would be Nano technology, Robotics, Artificial Intelligence, Bio technology, Micro Optronics / Electronics, Cyber, Radar, Microwave, Directed Energy systems, Avionics, Nuclear, Missile, Rockets and Material Science.

What is Manoeuvre Warfare?

The dictionary meaning of Manoeuvre is a planned and control move or operation by the armed forces for purposes of training and war.[6] It is a movement or a series of movement that requires skill and care. This relates to undertaking movement to avoid direct observation. This would result in avoiding aimed fire from the enemy's direct firing weapons. It is an approach to War which emphasises disrupting the cohesion of the enemy's tactical units, and the mental process of the enemy commander, thereby interrupting his ability to make correct and timely decisions rather than get involved in Attrition which involves inflicting casualties without achieving the Aim of the operation.[7]

The concept of Victory through Manoeuvre has been paramount at various periods of military history. Sun Tzu was perhaps the first to state an important aspect of the Manoeuvre theory. He stated, "To subdue the enemy without fighting is the acme of skill." In his book, the *Art of War*, Sun Tzu enunciates manoeuvre as the art of victory throughout. Destruction of the Army was not the key to victory. Disruption caused by speed, surprise and deception were the keys to preserving own forces and attaining the surrender or withdrawal of the enemy.[8] Manoeuvre Warfare was a discussed subject after the First World War by Liddell Hart and Fuller. Applications of the same were undertaken during the Second World War. The defeat in the Vietnam War caused a fresh thinking on the subject. There was a need to analyse the faults and find the remedies. The analysts felt that they must find an alternative to Attrition. Here in Manoeuvre Warfare was thought of in which the commander uses Manoeuvre to create a succession of unexpected and dangerous situations which occur too quickly for the enemy to react to them. However, by no means does Manoeuvre Warfare negate the use of firepower to destroy enemy forces or the use of manoeuvre to engage the enemy in close combat. This is a mental and physical type of warfare. You are mentally trying to engage the enemy commander. It is methods of fighting outnumbered and still win.

Issues which Merit Importance

John Boyd is the initiator of the Manoeuvre Warfare theory.[9] He derived a theory of conflict based on observation of air-to-air combat between MiG-15 and the F-86 fighter aircraft during the Korean War. During fighter combat, the F 86 often beat the MiG-15. The cause of this disparity was due to several factors which are stated below:

- F 86 was a more powerful aircraft.
- Easier to control in flight.
- F 86 pilots were better trained with better skills.

Accordingly the MiG-15 pilots passively gave up before being shot down.[10] Boyd through analytical research found that the F-86 pilot was trained to go through the process of Observation, Orientation, Decision, and Action (OODA) loop faster than the MiG-15 pilot. The MiG-15 pilot was outwitted by the tempo of the F-86 in combat and was beaten psychologically before being shot down.[11]

This is a mental and physical type of warfare. The intention is mentally trying to engage the enemy commander. It is a method of fighting outnumbered and winning. It requires sound tactical judgment and a great deal of subordinate initiative. The fundamentals are as enumerated below:

- Focus on the enemy: not on terrain objectives. The enemy can be the objective vis-à-vis terrain. If terrain is to be the objective that should be because it is useful to you or dear to your enemy, (Disruptive to him if captured). Terrain can be used as an aiming point or reference point such as "destroy mortar position in vicinity of hill 1800" instead of "capture hill 1800". We don't always have to seize terrain to accomplish our mission. It is not always necessary to assign an objective as long as we have a mission.
- Act more quickly than the enemy can react. Manoeuvre Warfare is as much a mental approach to warfare as it is a physical one The essence of Manoeuvre Warfare is to make and implement operational and tactical Decisions quicker than the enemy. However this does not mean making rash decisions and executing incomplete plans. The commander who generates a faster operational tempo gains a significant advantage. He seizes the initiative and dictates the course of battle until the enemy is overcome by events and his cohesion and ability to influence the situation are destroyed.
- This can be understood by the Boyd Cycle or OODA Loop. This is viewed as a time-competitive decision cycle where the goal is to go through your decision cycle faster than the enemy:

(i) Observation—observes one's self, physical surroundings and enemy.
(ii) Orient—take a mental image or a snapshot.
(iii) Decision—analyse, make a decision and communicate orders.
(iv) Action—speedy action to enhance the tempo.

- The key to out cycling the enemy is to maintain a faster tempo. Tempo is a function of several issues enumerated below:

(i) Focus on the enemy—find his weaknesses exploit them, and pit your strength against his weaknesses.
(ii) Seize the initiative.
(iii) Retain the initiative (keeps enemy off balance).
(iv) Act quickly and aggressively.
(v) Use mission orders. This generates timely action, decentralised decision making and initiative.
(vi) Support manoeuvre by fire. Firepower supports manoeuvre by creating gaps, suppressing and disrupting enemy forces, or physically destroying the remnants of enemy unit whose cohesion has been destroyed. Tempo must not be sacrificed for the need for immediate fire support. A few rounds that are immediately available may be worth more than a massive artillery pounding later.

John Boyd also described three categories of conflict as: Attrition Warfare, Manoeuvre Warfare and Moral Warfare. In Attrition Warfare the enemy is compelled to surrender and sue for peace. The essence of this type of Warfare is Destruction to break the enemy's will to resist. In Manoeuvre Warfare the aim is to generate many non-cooperative centres of gravity as well as disorient, disrupt or over load those that adversary depends upon. This would magnify friction, shatter cohesion, and produce paralysis leading to the enemy's collapse. In Moral Warfare the Aim is to destroy the moral bonds that permit an organic whole to exist. The essence would be to create, exploit and magnify fear, anxiety and alienation in order to generate many non-cooperative centres of gravity as well as subvert those that adversary depends upon, thereby magnify internal friction.[12] Boyd drew examples from history and summarised issues as under:

- Consistent victory by smaller forces. It implies that numbers are less important since the aim is to disrupt the enemy's mind.

- Tactical Victory is caused by psychological disruption. This is caused by speed of movement, surprise and deception.
- Further destruction is incidental to Victory.[13]

With Boyd's theory as basis William Lind described the tactical applications of this theory in his book *The Manoeuvre Warfare Handbook*. He provided a list of principles, mental reference points and tools through which the tactical unit commander could seek disruption of the enemy's cohesion as a fighting force. His principles of the tactical manoeuvre doctrine are Decentralisation of Command, Accept Confusion and disorder as the natural state of affairs and all patterns, recipes and formulas are to be avoided. The mental reference points are Mission Type Orders. Main force applied through gaps and avoids the surface of front line. The tools would be to use Firepower only as suppression to help a unit manoeuvre. Counter-attack must be used to obtain decisive results. Further a strong reserve must be maintained and lastly Monitoring must be the basis of Command and Control.[14]

Lind therefore, like Boyd, felt that Victory in future battle is to be sought not in physical destruction of the enemy but in his cohesion to act. The essence down to the lowest level is to avoid battle, seek disruption of enemy forces rather than their physical destruction. It is victory through psychological disruption than physical destruction.

Analysis

Manoeuvre Warfare emerged after the Vietnam War and it was conceptually different as you attacked the enemy's weakness instead of strength. The martial art of judo is often used to illustrate the theory of manoeuvre. In a judo match, the skilful competitor exploits opportunities presented by the opponent's shift in balance or commitment.[15] Manoeuvre Warfare intelligently synergises, Sun Tzu's Art of War to Basil Liddell Hart's Indirect Approach. Brigadier Richard Simpkin's book, *Race to the Swift*, provides a good theoretical analysis of Manoeuvre Warfare. He analyses the Soviet Deep battle which includes Airborne and Mechanised Forces.[16] Manoeuvre Warfare definitely lays down a technique but has to be applied in conjunction with Attrition Warfare. Often in areas where there are limited gaps and constraints for space, penetration by forces to create gaps is necessary prior to break out by forces using Manoeuvre Warfare. Accordingly Manoeuvre Warfare takes into consideration the strengths and weaknesses of the enemy. The United States intelligently applied Manoeuvre Warfare in the Gulf War with Colonel Warden's theory of targeting by concentric circles which ensured that the enemy was defeated psychologically. It would be best to pragmatically apply Manoeuvre Warfare. It would be pragmatic to link Manoeuvre Warfare in the Indian context.

Manoeuvre Warfare in the Present Context

In the current milieu, our Western adversary is doing its best to nullify India's conventional superiority by lowering its threshold on the usage of nuclear weapons. The Tactical Nuclear Weapons (TNWs) which Pakistan boasts of is cold tested and its usage against mechanised columns would cause limited casualties. Indian Armed Forces must realistically view the situation and respond to the proxy war in a calibrated manner and undertake operations where our superiority in conventional strength must expose its nuclear bluff. It is indeed creditable of our Prime Minister to point out his fault lines in Baluchistan, Gilgit Baltistan and Pakistan Occupied Kashmir (PoK) to caution him from interfering in India's domestic policies. This has been vindicated when India undertook surgical strikes in September 2016 and Pakistan did not threaten to use TNWs. Neither did they threaten to use TNWs even when Balakot was targeted by our Air Force.

Pakistan has been fighting a proxy war with India since 1990. It has realised post the Kargil Conflict of 1999, that it is the best manner in tackling India which enjoys a Conventional superiority. There have been a series of events with the crescendo being reached in Mumbai on 26 November 2008 and the openly supported agitations in the Kashmir valley since 08 July 2016, consequent to the killing of Burhan Wani, a terrorist who was the Commander of the Hizbul Mujahideen. In all these events it is interesting to note that events are launched by non-state actors from Pakistan. They undertake these operations as Fourth Generation warriors and cause chaos, consternation and casualties in India's hinterland. Pakistan perpetually denies any hand in these activities. Diplomatically, India has left no stone unturned in giving details to Pakistan about its covert support to the militants. The Pakistanis are good listeners and understand that issues get diluted with the passage of time. They continue protracted negotiations taking one step forward followed by two steps backwards. The media and the Indian establishment speaks optimistically that issues would improve and soon a militant attack takes place and we are caught unaware as to how it happened. In the debates and statements Pakistan denies and at the same time cautions India, that they are a country possessing nuclear weapons and India should not cross the rubicon and settle outstanding disputes.

In such a situation where diplomacy does not work we are left with the option to curtail water flowing into Pakistan or use Hard Power. These are often discussed at all forums but when push comes to shove, we as a country buckle down. Now that the United States is going to treat us with the same respect as allies of the North Atlantic Organisation, it is time we change our stance and stop our sweet behaviour when fourth or possibly fifth generation warriors are attacking our police stations, Army and Air Force Bases. It is assessed that these attacks are the handiwork of the ISI which functions directly under the Chief of Army Staff of Pakistan. Since the Army and the Pakistan Civil administration are not on the same page, these attacks will continue to keep the Indian Armed Forces bleeding. It is pertinent to note that for the first time in its history the Pakistan Army is fighting militancy in all its four provinces. This would continue as it continues to irrationally differentiate between a good and bad terrorist, little realising that both are one and the same.

It is gradually clear to our entire country that present methods are only skirting the problem to deal with Pakistan using Covert Hard power and our response has been a defensive reaction with limited results. It is time we changed our approach and start giving an effective response to these attacks. On the civilian side due to the current dry season we can calibrate the flow of water in a manner that Pakistan feels the pinch of receiving lesser quantity of water. The next step is to activate the line of control. This should be done carefully after removing the civilians to safer places and use Artillery to hit their field works, Command and Control Centres as the Gun Areas. Pakistan's capability in terms of Guns and Ammunition is lesser than ours. Pakistan always prevents us from using our Artillery as they know that the Indian Artillery is stronger and has the capability to undertake sustained fire which would play havoc with their Command and Control system, Line of Communications and day-to-day routine in their defences on the Line of Control. With our detailed knowledge of their Gun Positions, we have the capability to silence their Guns and decimate other targets. To take our minds back to November 2003, when Pakistan unilaterally declared ceasefire which we later accepted gracefully. It is essential to note that our domination of Artillery fire was complete and Pakistan was running out of its capability to undertake sustained Artillery duels.

The next aspect pertains to our superior conventional forces. It is here that India must use Manoeuvre Warfare. If the Pakistan Army does not alter its path by our domination of the Line of Control we must undertake Conventional operations which would entail use of Intermediate Battle Groups in the Mountains and Riverine terrain in conjunction with Deep Strikes in deserts. While the Battle Groups would be used in Shallow thrusts, the Strike formations would undertake Deep Strikes. Pakistan has lowered its nuclear threshold and threatens to use Tactical Nuclear Weapons against these offensives.

The TNW is a Cold-tested weapon and its range being limited would have to be deployed in the field at about 40 km from the border making it vulnerable to own air and missile attacks. Nuclear weapons of Pakistan are for Deterrence and providing parity with India in a politico-strategic realm. The actual possibility of use of tactical and strategic nuclear weapons is zero. Senior Pakistani officers have categorically stated that the Indian response to Pakistan's first use would be total Holocaust. In late 2010, with 90 TNWs it was found difficult to stop an Indian Armoured Division moving dispersed on a 30 km frontage. There would be a minimum inescapable requirement of 436 TNWs to stop an Armoured Division. With the reported accelerated production of plutonium from three military dedicated reactors in Khushab and a fourth under construction it would result in an inventory of 200 warheads by 2020. To further compound to the existing problem, the issue of miniaturising the warhead to fit into the Nasr missile with a 30 cm diameter is a complex engineering problem. Further data shows that a TNW use against a Combat Group moving dispersed over an 8 km front would at best produce 25 casualties and damage to about four tanks. Accordingly not much should be read against the TNW and the Indian Army must retain the option of Deep Strikes particularly in the Southern theatre. The Artillery must work towards locating the Nasr and develop possibly with external assistance a Make in India project to destroy the Nasr in flight.

The entire response must be synergised and it is high time we took the fight back to Pakistani soil. The entire strategy calls for a changed Offensive Mindset which must work out the details and synergise the leaders, bureaucracy and the Armed Forces to meet the Pakistani threat.

In our area of operations, the ideal terrain for executing manoeuvre would be the desert region. Our mountains lack space and the plains are full of water obstacles which would result in time consuming break in operations which would be deliberate and enable us to undertake shallow thrusts. The deserts would have a set of minefields which could be negotiated with greater speed and intervening strong points as also nodes based upon the operational plan of the formation could be bypassed, isolated, invested or finally captured. Normally a mechanised formation with an Armoured Division, about two Reorganised Army Plains Infantry Divisions (RAPID), an Independent Armoured Brigade, an Engineer Brigade, Air Defence elements and an Artillery Division with adequate Air Support from the Indian Air Force.

The aim of the operation would be to capture an important Communications Centre as also destroy its mechanised reserves. Prior to the operations Surveillance would be undertaken in the Areas of interest using all surveillance equipment with heavy reliance on Remote Sensing satellites and Unmanned Aerial Vehicles (UAVs). The operations would involve possibly the following phases:

- Degradation of key objectives by Air, Artillery including rockets and missiles. The Artillery Division to suitably decimate forces and ensure effective engagements wit Post Strike Damage Assessment by UAVs.
- Capture of selected enemy Border out Posts. They must be pulverised by Artillery Fire to facilitate quick capture.
- Advance across three thrust lines using the mechanised spearheads.
- Speedily cross its Forward Defensive Minefield, Intermediate Defensive Minefield and Depth Defensive Minefields. Undertake encounter and opportunity crossings wherever possible. Reach the projection area to undertake a tank versus tank battle against strategic reserves of the enemy.
- Based on the operational plan mechanised forces would bypass, contain and isolate strong points on the axis of advance. To open an axis of maintenance a selected node or a strong point to be captured using the formation and thereafter suitable track be developed for move of ammunition and supplies.
- Launch a sizeable Heli-borne Force to capture a lightly held objective in depth. One of the mechanised spearheads to link up as early as possible with this force. Medium Artillery and Close

Air Support must be provided to the force.

- Entire operations should be completed as early as possible. Likely time would be about 96 hours.

It is envisaged that the enemy would try and impede the momentum of advance by employing his reserves at the divisional level, Operational level and Strategic level. The manoeuvres would be in consonance with other thrusts in the mountains, which would be against terrorist training centres, in the plains on enclaves and the deep strike in terrain stated above. The entire operations would be short, swift and lethal. It is essential that the Indian Army acquires two major weapon systems for the manoeuvres. These are the Unmanned Combat Aerial Vehicles (UCAVs) and the Loitering Missile. Both these weapon systems would enable us to undertake precise destruction of targets which causes an effect of morale on our troops.

During the manoeuvre Cyber operations must be undertaken to ensure degradation of enemy Communications and Data links, Synergy of these will pay rich dividends. Our Western adversary needs to be dealt in an offensive manner to ensure that they stop interfering with our internal affairs. Further, we must exploit our conventional superiority to exploit issues to our advantage without buckling to its ineffective nuclear threat. Our mechanised spearheads are trained and they must be used if push comes to shove.[17]

Firepower and Manoeuvre Warfare in the Changing Character of Conflict

The changing character of warfare has brought in two terms to classify conflict, Low-intensity Conflict and Hybrid Conflict. Low-intensity Conflict may be non-violent or violent. Non-violent forms would be subversion, show of force and peace keeping under Chapter VI of the United Nations Charter. The violent form would be revolutionary or guerrilla warfare, counter-insurgency, terrorism, prolonged confrontation along a Line of Control and peace keeping under Chapter VII of UN Charter. To be clear it is important to see the definitions of Low-intensity Conflict. These are as elucidated below:

- The United States definition is, "Limited politico military struggle to achieve political, social, economic or psychological objectives. It is often protracted and ranges from diplomatic, economic and psychological pressure through terrorism and insurgency. Low Intensity Conflict is generally confined to a geographical area and is often characterised by constraints on weaponry, tactics and the level of violence."[18] The Indian definition encompasses a few more issues. "Low Intensity Conflict is a generic term encompassing all kinds of armed conflicts that are above the level of peaceful co-existence among states and below the threshold of war. These include proxy war, terrorism, and insurgencies. Border skirmishes also fall in this category. It involves protracted struggle of competing principles and ideologies."[19] A Low-intensity Conflict is characterised by one of the following conditions:

- Asymmetry of force levels between the regular forces and irregular opposition forces.
- The force applied and the violence generated depends on the modalities adopted by the weaker side.
- Action of security forces are constrained by the laws of the land.

The next aspect which is of essence in the current environment is Hybrid Warfare. While there is no universal definition, Hybrid Conflicts are full spectrum wars with both physical and conceptual dimensions. The physical part a struggle against an armed enemy and the latter, a wider struggle for, control and support of the combat zone's indigenous population, the support of the home fronts of the intervening nations and the support of the international community. To secure and stabilise the indigenous population, the intervening forces must immediately rebuilt to restore security, essential services, local government, self-defence forces and essential elements of the economy.[20] Further a hybrid threat would entail simultaneous employment of a mix of conventional, irregular, terrorism, and criminal means in the operational battle space.

How do Firepower and Manoeuvre Warfare get applied in Low-intensity Conflict and Hybrid Warfare? As far as firepower is concerned it would be ideally used in Low-intensity Conflict and in Hybrid Warfare on Targets across the Line of Control. Further Small Arms and where necessary Rocket Launchers could be used for engaging terrorists in these types of conflict.

Utilisation of Manoeuvre Warfare would be at Strategic and Operational level. While the enemy would use Low-intensity Conflict in a particular region it would be appropriate to use our strike elements duly synergised with Firepower to be used in other regions which would compel the enemy to reconsider undertaking operations on the Low Intensity Conflict and Hybrid Warfare to be scaled down or halted as a result of Manoeuvre Operations. This would result in optimisation of our assets.

Necessary Force Structure and Training

While the Indian Army must undertake Manoeuvre Warfare as explained above there is a need to examine our Force Structures, Selection and Training to undertake manoeuvres successfully. All our formations be it pivot or strike irrespective of Terrain must be capable of Manoeuvre Operations. Special Forces have a particular place in Manoeuvre Warfare. There is a need to raise another Special Forces Brigade Headquarters for the mountains and be located as a part of the Mountain Strike Corps. Further the equipment of all Manoeuvre Arms must be designed for undertaking Manoeuvre Warfare. This includes light equipment for the infantry, Guns like the Ultra-light Howitzer, Precision Guided Munitions, light tank for Mountains and High Altitude, Attack Helicopters, Utility Helicopters, Unmanned Aerial Vehicles (UAVs), Unmanned Combat Aerial Vehicles (UCAVs), Unmanned Underwater Sea Vehicles, Satellites and Hypersonic Glide Vehicles.

There is a need for training Officers, Junior Commissioned Officers and Other Ranks in this type of Warfare. They need to be selected with a Psychological Test which enables them to undertake Manoeuvre Operations. Further Manoeuvre Warfare must form a part of the Syllabus of important Courses of Instruction. This would enable us to encourage thinking at all levels in the Indian Armed Forces. Further Strategic and War Games at all levels must include this aspect to ensure its pragmatic application at all levels. We have to understand that Attrition and Manoeuvre Warfare are both required and would have to be applied based on the Situation. All this would help us to synergise Manoeuvre in our Armed Forces.

Conclusion

Necessity is the mother of invention. The loss in Vietnam caused John Boyd and William Lind to formulate the concept of Manoeuvre Warfare. It is a warfare which addresses the weaknesses of the enemy and the objective is to win by disruption. Disruption can be created by high tempo where we outwit the decision of the enemy. Manoeuvre Warfare has to be used pragmatically and may require a combination of Manoeuvre and Attrition.

In the Indian context Manoeuvre Warfare will be important against both our adversaries and has to be applied in varying degrees depending on terrain and the prevailing situation. The application requires synergy with other Services and use of Special Forces, Cyber Warfare and a high degree of Surveillance, Reconnaissance and Target Acquisition. This would call for Satellites, UAVs, UCAVs and other Surveillance Equipment. Our weapon systems would also need upgradation and it is high time we have reliable PGMs in our inventory. All this would result in transforming our doctrines to ensure victory against our adversaries.

NOTES

1 Colonel Sanjeev Relia, "Understanding Cyber weapons," United Service Institution of India Journal, October-December 2013, pp. 584–87.
2 Ray Guns, "Laser Warfare," www.spacewar.com, 29 March 2017.
3 Long Range Land Attack Projectile, United States of America, www.naval-technology.com,down loaded on 14 April 2017.
4 Massive bomb dropped by US in Afghanistan", cbc news /world, www. cbc.ca/news/world/Afghanistan-mother, updated on 15 April 2017.
5 Colonel Bradley T Hoagland, "Manning the Next Unmanned Air Force", Centre for 21st Century Security and Intelligence, Policy Paper August 2013.
6 Meaning in the Cambridge English Dictionary, http://dictionary.cambridge.org.manoeuvre
7 Marines Corps Gazette, 21st century Manoeuvre Warfare absorbing the lessons, Author: Ellis Group, mca-marines.org
8 Major G S Lauer, "Manoeuvre Warfare Theory: Creating a Tactically Unbalanced Marine Force?" School of Advanced Military Studies, US Army Command and General Staff College, Fort Leavenworth, Kansas. Mil, pp. 6-7.
9 William S. Lind, "Manoeuvre Warfare Handbook," Boulder, Colorado: West View Press, 1985, p. 5.
10 John R Boyd, "Patterns of Conflict-Proceedings of Seminar on Air Anti-Tank Warfare", Columbus, DH, Battle Laboratories, May 1979, p.8.
11 John R Boyd, "A Discourse of Winning and Losing, "Unpublished Manuscript", presented to U.S. Marine Corps Command and Staff College Quantico, VA, p. 115.
12 Ibid., p. 125.
13 Ibid., p. 136.
14 William. S. Lind, *Manoeuvre Warfare Handbook*, p. 7.
15 Colonel Pat Stogran, "Manoeuvre Warfare: Using Clever and Unexpected Tactics to Defeat an Enemy by attacking their Weakness," The Arm Chair Colonel, espiritcorps.ca, 09 February 2017.
16 Richard Simpkin, "Race to the Swift", Brassey's Defence, London, 1985, ISBN 0-08-028341-1.

17 P K Chakravorty, "Manoeuvre in Indian environment, "Salute magazine, edited by Major General Dhruv Katoch, September-October 2016.
18 Gurmeet Kanwal, "The Changing Character and the Taxonomy of Conflict", Hybrid Warfare, Institute for Defence Studies and Analyses, Pentagon Press, New Delhi, p. 14.
19 "Types of Wars", in Indian Army Doctrine, Shimla: HQ Army Training Command, October 2004, p. 16, Chapter 2, Section 5, as stated ibid., on p.14
20 Gurmeet Kanwal, "The Changing Character and the Taxonomy of Conflict", Hybrid Warfare, Institute for Defence Studies and Analyses, Pentagon Press. New Delhi, p.16

8

Special Forces (SF) in the Indian Context

Major General Bhupesh Kumar Jain

"First punch is as good as two"

– Maharaja Ranjit Singh

ABSTRACT

Proxy war employing asymmetric means and hybrid tools is emerging as a global strategic trend in warfare. India has been facing proxy war for the last four decades. Our northern neighbour, besides aspiring to be a world-class military power, has shown adeptness in employing asymmetric means. India has been a reactive power. Diplomacy, conventional capabilities, and limited cross border actions have not proven to be adequate deterrence to non-state actors backed by the state. Indians recently seem to have had enough and are seeking punitive actions against entities waging proxy war. Special Forces (SF) have emerged as a viable tool to counter asymmetric means and hybrid tools waging proxy war. Currently, Indian SF are organised and structured to support conventional warfare in the Tactical Battle Area (TBA), are reactive in waging counter-terror operations and are Army/ Navy/NSG/Cabinet Secretariat specific. They need to be reorganised and restructured. Indian SF need to acquire capabilities to support Intelligence Support Operations, covert operation and soft-skill capabilities (Info Operations, Civil Affairs) so that they are able to operate successfully in the emerging fields and domains of warfare. The SF organisation needs to incorporate political decision-making, integrate intelligence and synchronise with other ingredients of national decision-making, such as diplomacy.

Introduction

Robert Gates, the United States (US) Secretary of Defence, speaking at West Point in February 2011 said, "I must tell you, when it comes to predicting the nature...of our next military engagements, since Vietnam, our record has been perfect. We have never once gotten it right."[1] He also added, "...there has been an overwhelming tendency of defence bureaucracy to focus on preparing for future high-end conflicts—priorities, often based ironically on what transpired in the last century—as opposed to the messy fights in Iraq and Afghanistan."

India has been facing a proxy war, being waged against her for the last over four decades. The proxy war has been targeting the people's mind, material, image and most importantly, their security. It is not to be mistaken as insurgency or terrorism; for all forms of coercive power are engaged in to achieve political objectives. What India is facing is war. In another two years, India would be celebrating 50 years of the 1971 Indo-Pak War and the creation of Bangladesh. The Indian Army, during this period, has been facing Pakistan-sponsored as well as abetted cross-border proxy war in Punjab (now defeated) & Jammu and Kashmir (on-going). In the same period, the Indian Army undertook peacekeeping operations in Northern Sri Lanka & Africa (under the UN flag). The Army continues to confront threats to national integrity from insurgent groups in the North East, with some of these groups possibly operating from across the international border. Our Northern neighbour has started asserting its growing military capabilities. The creeping construction of roads and patrolling have often led to face-offs.

Post-26/11, the Indian cabinet was briefed in the Operations Room to discuss the options to respond. The briefing covered what could be the military options to punish Pakistan. During the said briefing, a visibly irritated Defence Minister said, "Are you mad!"[2] The honourable minister appeared to be aghast that the Armed Forces were considering the option of a full-scale conventional war to punish Pakistan. The organisation and structure of the Indian Armed Forces has been designed for warfare in the conventional domain from the lessons learnt from the past conflicts, rather than how the future conflicts shall unfold. Regular and conventional force-structures, historically, have often found themselves unable to address the emerging technologies and spectrums of the conflict. Unconventional forces have often evolved to support the war-effort and have acted as a force-multiplier.

The Indian Army has a history of coming up with new organisations and structures based on the emerging requirements, e.g. Rashtriya Rifles units. The Army has added to the number of SF units in its orbat by reorganising the airborne units. Recently, the Ministry of Defence has acted on a long pending proposal and announced the formation of Special Forces Division, along with organisational changes to address the emerging challenges in cyber and space. However, for some reasons, the three services have been slow to undertake reforms to provide the Special Forces the requisite capabilities to address the emerging threats.

SF are trained for counterterrorism, insurgency and guerrilla warfare, using superior tactics, equipment, and mobility to defeat terrorists, guerrillas, and insurgents who adopt unconventional tactics out of necessity.[3] To prepare for and align to the emerging changes and challenges to land warfare, there is a need for the Indian SF to transcend the existing thinking and prepare them to defeat the proxy war being waged against India. The SF ought to also prepare for the future threats, which are likely to emerge in India's area of interest.

Historical Account

In 1846, the British Indian Army employed the Corps of Guides in the erstwhile North-West Frontier Province. In 1897, they employed the Gurkha Scouts in the Tirah Campaign. During the Boer War, the Boers successfully employed Boer Kommandos—an all-volunteer force which operated in the enemy's rear, armed and controlled always by the state. During the Second World War, both Britain and Germany experimented with unconventional forces. David Sterling of Special Air Service (SAS), Otto Skorzeny of German Waffen-SS, and Maj General Wingate's Chindits in Burma have all left behind a legacy and are part of folklore among the SF fraternity.

Post-World War II, many countries retained the core of these unconventional units. The erstwhile USSR, USA and the UK were among them. Among the newly independent countries, Unit 101, followed by Unit 269—Sayeret Matkal—of Israel crafted fearsome reputation of professional excellence, particularly among its adversaries. The raising of Pakistani Special Forces was facilitated by USA after their treaty agreement in 1956. A number of writers world over have vividly documented the role played by Inter-Services Intelligence-Special Service Group (ISI–SSG) combination across both the Eastern and Western borders of Pakistan over the past four decades in waging proxy wars and employing non-state actors. India inherited Gurkha units, which were part of Wingate's Chindits. These units were reverted to their conventional infantry roles post-independence.

During the 1965 Indo-Pak War, a few volunteers were cobbled together to operate behind enemy lines under Lt Colonel Megh Singh. This led to the raising of India's first Commando unit in July 1966. In 1967, the unit was split to have separate units for operations in mountains and in deserts. Both these units participated in the 1971 War and performed to the satisfaction of the Army. In the eighties, the Indian Army designated the Commando Units into SF units after carrying out suitable reorganisation of structures and tasking. Currently, all the three Services, the National Security Guard (NSG), and the Special Frontier Forces (SFF) have units with *special capabilities*.

SF Pedagogy

What is special?

It is imperative to understand what qualifies to be called "special". For any force to be known as "special", it ought to act as a force multiplier, expand the space for operation of the (own) force and quicken its Observe-Orient-Decide-Act (OODA) loop. By implication, the Special Force of a nation ought to slow down the OODA loop of the adversary, circumscribe the space for application of his Force, and limit the options for application of Force. It is essential to avoid confusing Special Operations with "Commando" operations; the latter are tactical in nature and refer to specially equipped units/sub-units undertaking raids or other such operations in the enemy held area. The impact of the Commando operations is meant to be immediate and directly on the Tactical Battle Area (TBA). The Special Operations, on the other hand, are meant to make an impact at the operational level and above. Special Forces are not necessarily in the kinetic domain only.

Principles of Special Forces

The following are the principles of Special Forces:

- SF is a precious asset that takes time, effort and investment to develop.
- The SF are not always capable of large-scale tasks. Enhancing their numbers and capabilities in a hurry is not feasible.

- SF are part of nation's strength and are not meant to replace any part of its military capabilities.
- SF operations, to be successful, need the support of other non-SF assets.

Categories of SF Operations

SF can undertake four categories of operations: Direct, Indirect, Information and Civil Affairs.

- Direct approach: Conducted by a small unit, lethal, based on focused intelligence, surprise, achieve shock action, high risk, precise execution, high payoff, deniability or could be made visible to public, immediate impact. Tend to be more kinetic.
- Indirect approach:—Empower friendly nations/agencies, engaging key population to support Indian programmes, support allies, provide thorough humanitarian assistance, address their local needs to advance own ideas and discredit and defeat ideas of adversary. Tends to be long term, low on investment of assets.
- Info Operations: To influence actions, behaviour, values, beliefs and attitudes of citizens & communities in support of SF teams, assist diplomats, allies and partners. A typical Team could comprise 3 to 12 persons, depending on the role or task, each a specialist in his own domain. Frequent use is made of specialists employed as reserve. Territorial Army (TA) model is also employed.
- Civil affairs: Well-versed in the culture of the target, work with local communities, weaken hostile opposition to Indian interests, join disaster relief efforts of India, e.g. immunisation, provide running water during natural calamities, etc. Team could comprise of an officer, two NCOs, one medic with enhanced skills.

Levels of SF Operations

The following could be one such example of multiple tiers of Special Operations. Depending upon the threats and the nation's aptitude, these could be reviewed.

- Tier 1 – intelligence support apparatus.
- Tier 2 – covert capabilities, unconventional tasks in hostile territory.
- Tier 3 – direct action capabilities, unconventional task for friendly regimes.

- Tier 4 – support for conventional operations, capture of lightly held objectives, holding territory for limited time, ambush, raid, etc.
- Miscellaneous – soft power component such as civil affairs and information operations. This support may be provided across all tiers and even to other organs of the state such as diplomacy.

Limitations of SF Operations

SF operations have the following limitations:

- They cannot achieve decisive strategic success on their own.
- The risk is high. It can be managed but not eliminated.
- They are a limited liability option.
- Indirect approach missions are sub-optimally effective.

Imperatives to Reorganise SF-Emerging Global Strategic Trends[4]

In its publication—Global Strategic Trends 2045—the Development, Concept and Doctrine Centre (DCDC) of UK brought out the following trends which will impact the South Asian region:

- Kashmir and India-China border shall continue to remain areas of tension.
- China's military shall be close to matching that of the US.
- The US will continue to be the pre-eminent military power.
- Behind US and China, India could have the "second tier" of global defence expenditure equal to that of the EU (Russia, UK, and France could form the Third Tier).
- State on state conflict not ruled out.
- Islamic fundamentalism will continue to fuel terrorist network.
- Terrorism will continue to pose a threat in South Asia.
- Quantum computing could make all codes crackable. Need to keep classified computer network of defence separate with reasonable air gap.
- Possibility of fissile material being obtained by non-state actors.
- More frequent need for humanitarian assistance and disaster relief.
- Increased level of surveillance due to increased urbanisation.
- Increasing role of unmanned system in combat.
- Non-state actors, e.g. Multi-National Companies (MNCs) may develop highly capable security forces.

The Conflict-Spectrum

The conflict spectrum, meanwhile, is continuously evolving too, driven by new technologies/opportunities. The erstwhile linear spectrum is adding additional domains, such as narco, information, unrestricted/ asymmetric, cyber, space, hybrid, legal, economic, etc. Thus, the trends shaping the conflict-spectrum indicate that it shall extend to all possible domains.

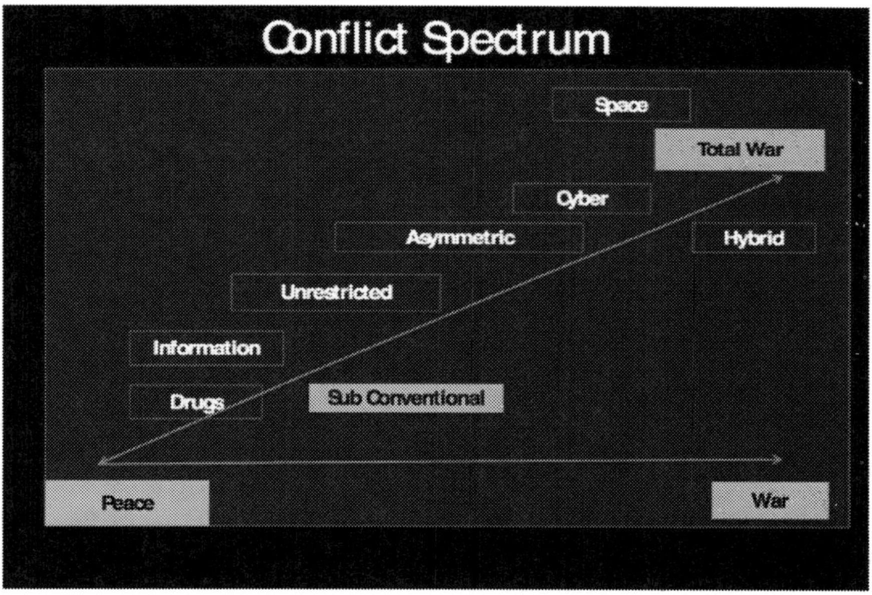

Figure 8.1: Conflict Spectrum

Operational Imperatives

Impact of battlefield-transparency and precision-strikes may lead to militaries undertaking operations, which instead of seeking destruction in the material domain may endeavour to impact the cognitive domain. Recently, the Chief of the Indian Army Staff spoke of Indian Army being called upon to undertake operations without military engagements. Possible operational imperatives in such an environment would be:

- **Battlefield**
  Manipulation of the population of the adversary.
- **Entities**
  Trans-national and trans-regional actors, irregulars, terrorists and criminals besides the armed forces of the adversary.

- **New tools**
  Cyber, social media, etc.
- **Military Backing**
  Backing of conventional armed forces and Weapons of Mass Destruction (WMDs).
- **Methodology**
  Dynamic and diverse, multidirectional mix of threats, methods and activities with unclear links which are difficult to verify.
- **Incremental Aggression**
  Individually, the actions may fall short of warfare, but if not responded to, their sequencing may lead to attaining of desired goals by the adversary.
- **Threats**
  If not detected, analysed, and defeated in time, the threats could cross the critical threshold.
- **Victory**
  Forcing change of political course of adversary by a nation can be termed as attainment of goals or success.

The proxy war being waged by *Jihadists* against perceived adversaries shall persist. Actions by white supremacy ideologues and right wing activists, such as the one recently in New Zealand, provide motivation and recruits to the *Jihadist*. Possibilities of acquisition of WMDs by hostile non-state actors are real. Threats from highly capable non-state actors need to be deterred without the need for application of conventional forces. Application of conventional force ought to be the last option. Israel realised that after a bitter experience of waging a conventional conflict against *Hezbollah*.

Terror acts such as the recent suicide bombing on the Central Armed Police Forces (CRPF) convoy in February 2019 is an example of the challenges India shall face in responding to such grave provocations. It is imperative that India responds with firm control over the escalatory ladder. Indian political leadership has been historically reluctant to join military groupings, but has been open to engage with friendly nations to fight terror. SF, closely working with the intelligence agencies in close collaboration with National Security Structure, would provide such options. The options exercised so far have been Trans-LC, Covert and Intelligence Support Operation. Additional option and lesson for India is to up-skill its SF. India should not only to be prepared for a conventional conflict, but also create capabilities (SF) to deter aggression as well as seek and create axes of allies to defeat proxy war.

A thorough analysis of the emerging global strategic trends and the operational imperatives on the doctrine for war fighting and the likely conflict for war fighting shall help us arrive at a doctrine and the role for employment, organisational structures, policies for manning and equipping the SF. They will also facilitate in identifying battle drills and battle procedures for their application.

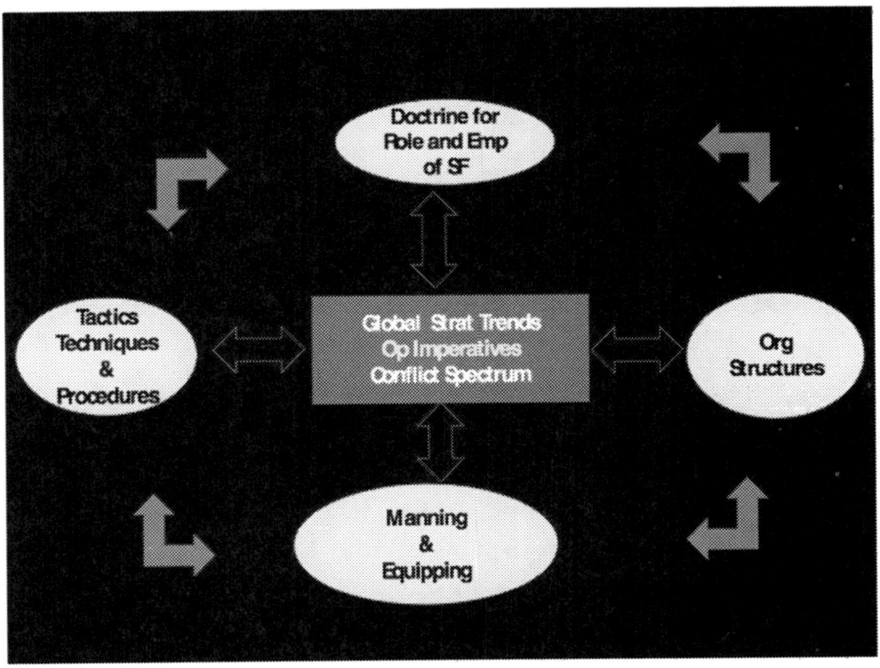

Figure 8.2: Global Strategic Trends

Existing Models of Application of SF Capabilities

US

It has one of the largest components of the Special Forces due to its global aspirations. A four star officer commands the US Special Operations Command (SOCOM). Its Army component is 28,500 strong comprising 5 SF Groups. Each Group comprising 3 to 4 Battalions is affiliated for operations in an area (continents). The Army component also has a Ranger Regiment, Special Aviation Brigade, two Military Information Support Group and a Sustainment Brigade. Naval SOC has strength of 9,000 SEALs.

The Air SOC component has seven Air Wings, which includes Combat Controllers and Aviation Advisers. The Joint SOC has SEAL Team 6, SF detachment Delta, Intelligence and Communication units and a Test and Evaluation Unit. The counter-terrorism and special mission tasks are undertaken by Joint SOC. US SOC is responsible for equipping and training, testing and evaluation of the SF units. Manning is a Service-specific responsibility. The equipping of SF is undertaken by SOCOM. The US Congress provides separate funding for the same in the Defence Budget. US Special Forces' application takes place across all the levels. One of the recent examples of it recently is elimination of Osama bin Laden. It is imperative to understand that even with such impressive budgets and capabilities, the time US SF took to identify his hideout and then eliminate him in spite this being a national obsession, was in years. Furthermore, US agencies did not know for years that Mullah Omar was living inside Afghanistan. On October 26, 2019 the US Team Delta of Central Command in a heliborne operation killed Abu Bakr-al Baghdadi in Idlib Syria. The operation proves the professionalism of the US Special Forces.

UK

The UK has a different model of SF. Its SF, The Special Air Service (SAS), has three regiments with a total of 10 squadrons. The squadrons have a mix of air, boat, mobility and mountain troops. A special team is responsible for counter-terrorism tasks. After continuity training lasting a year, a squadron is on alert for six months. To join SAS, a soldier in the UK Army has to volunteer. Equipment is funded from the defence budget. Unlike the US, the UK has kept its intelligence agencies a bit distant from the SF. SAS has superior unconventional and covert capabilities rather than Intelligence Support Operations. Intelligence agencies often employ ex-SAS manpower.

Russia

It inherited the Spetsnaz from the erstwhile Soviet Union. It has recently formed Special Operations Command (KSO). They undertake reconnaissance and special security missions. Spetsnaz led the security of air and naval bases in Syria, as Russia began its deployment. Their role in Eastern Ukraine and Crimea need to be analysed and understood. They worked with Russian-affiliated Ukrainian groups to orchestrate the insurgency and later led the operations to secure Crimea. Spetsnaz operates across a very wide spectrum in multiple domains.[5] Alpha Group is the equivalent of Team 6 or Delta Force of US' SF, and SAS of the UK. The tactics of Alpha Group are distinctly unique.[6] Alpha Group operates in all domains as is expected in a centralised system of governance. Recently, there were reports in the media of Russian SF undertaking covert cyber operations in Scandinavian countries and operations in the UK. A number of hostile ex-Russian citizens have been eliminated in the UK. The Russian cyber-cum-info operations have spooked the US polity and there is a perception in a section of US populace that Russia successfully influenced the 2016 US Presidential elections.

China

The Chinese are in the process of developing their SF capabilities.[7] Very little is available of their SF capabilities in the open domain. It would be safe to assume that the Chinese have observed the SF capabilities of their potential adversaries and would be developing matching capabilities to counter the threats in the cyber, information and direct actions fields.[8] The Chinese seem to be following a path dissimilar to other nations. They have come up with Strategic Support Forces by amalgamating their Space, Cyber, Electronic, and Perception Management assets. The SF Regiments are part of the respective.[9] Theatre Commands so as to attain theatre-specialisation. It would be reasonable to assume that the Chinese Communist Party would retain some sort of central control, although the structures for the same are not in the open domain. The Central Military Commission, has political control and hence, most likely to control the Chinese SF.[10] The Chinese are determined to keep strengthening the military, comprehensively promote national defence and military modernisation, including "a modern army, navy, air force, rocket army, strategic support force, and a strong and efficient command agency for joint operations". Additionally, Xi also set the goal that by 2020, the Chinese military "should have basically realised mechanisation, made significant progress in information technology, and made a big leap in strategic ability; by 2035, modernisation of national defence and military should be basically achieved; and by 2050, the Chinese military should be a world-class power". Some of the US military Sinologists believe that the Chinese have done things differently in the SF domain. One of the key Chinese SF mission was to support acquisition of high-end dual technology. In order to do that, the Chinese led their operation by developing cyber capabilities besides all-of-government approach. Legal warfare, control of fishing fleet in the South China Sea, etc., are some such additional missions attributed to the Chinese SF. Chinese footprints have been noticed in the cyber domain. Katoch and Datta (2013) reported that Chinese Special Operations Forces numbered 14,000 personnel; although Blasko (2015) states that the number is now closer 20,000 to 30,000 personnel (or approximately 1% of the PLA).[11] The Chinese SF have been participating in the SF competitions being conducted in West Asia (Jordan) and Central Asia (Kazakhstan). Participation in such competitions gives the Chinese SF the opportunity to observe and learn from other nations' SF capabilities as also to measure their capabilities with respect to others.

India

India was a late entrant (1966) to the SF domain. Field Marshal Slim, in his book, *Defeat into Victory*, was particularly scathing about the SF in general and Maj General Wingate and his body of troops in particular. Such views possibly conditioned the thoughts of generations of officers. The SF were seen as an upstart clamouring for quality manpower and resources at the expense of all others. SF thought has taken a long time to start getting acceptance inside the Army. It has yet to have wider acceptability in the rank and file of higher leadership, the published doctrines for SF employment notwithstanding. Campaigns continue to be the purview of single service HQ/Regional Army Commands and SF continue to be seen as a supporting enabler to conventional forces. The Indian SF has limited covert and soft-skill capabilities. Air, maritime, ISR support is on case-by-case basis. The lack of specialist weapons, equipment, and training infrastructure has hampered their effectiveness. The Indian SF manning policies and pay-structure is unique. The support personnel in SF units draw the same SF pay as the sabre teams. Intelligence Support Operation and Covert Operations are seen as the turf of Intelligence Agencies. A recent attempt by one of the COAS to create a unit to undertake covert operations ran into controversy, and led to the disbanding of the unit by his successor. In short, the Indian SF needs reorganisation and restructuring to meet the 21st century challenges.

Some of the other countries with competent SF are Israel, Jordan, Pakistan, Vietnam and France.[12] Jordanian SF is known to have been the most successful in infiltrating Islamist groups in West Asia, the Gulf, and Afghanistan. Recently, some of the Scandinavian countries have been adding Centres of Excellence on Hybrid Warfare.

Present Organisation and Structure of Indian SF

Under the Ministry of Defence, the Indian Army has nine SF units of four sabre teams each. In India's Regimental System, these are part of the Parachute Regiment. Operationally, these units are under different Army Regional Commands/Corps. Their primary role is to provide tactical/ operational support to the Army. They are also employed in counter-insurgency, anti-terror operations and trans-LC/IB actions. The Parachute Regiment Training Centre provides the manpower after basic training. The units also accept volunteers from the rest of the Army. The imparting of basic special skills is done inside the units, while advanced training of special skills is carried out in the Special Forces Training School. The Indian Navy has two units of Marine Commandos (MARCOS) under respective fleets (Eastern and Western). Their role is to support fleet operations including beachhead operations. The skill training of MARCOS is carried out either in the unit or in the diving school.

Under the Home Ministry, there are two units of Special Action Groups in the National Security Guard (NSG). These units are manned by the Indian Army personnel on deputation. They specialise in intervention roles which includes aircraft and buildings. They have better access to advanced weapons and are trained at the NSG Centre.

Under the Cabinet Secretariat, there is a Special Group and an Aviation Research Centre manned by Indian Armed Forces personnel on deputation (and also some retirees). The Special Group is trained to carry out special tasks.

Drawbacks in the Present Structure

The following points follow from the above:

- Indian SF capabilities are split in separate threads and are located in separate boxes.
- The SF capabilities are located in the defensive/reactive domain. NSG capabilities are reactive.
- The orientation of Armed Forces' SF capabilities is for conventional conflict. There are limited covert/unconventional capabilities. India needs SF capabilities not only for conventional war but also for the proxy war (no war, no peace scenario) being waged against her.

Lessons from Indian Experience of Countering Proxy War

India has done little to aggressively counter proxy war. Most of India's response has been in the diplomatic domain. The focus or the call after every attack has been to be more vigilant, but in defensive and primarily reactive mode.[13] Counter-terrorism in India is in the charter of the Home Ministry as part of Internal Security. Law and order continues to be a state subject. Counter-terror actions in India consist of the intelligence standing watch, the police pursuing the criminal aspect and the Armed Forces standing by, ready to respond. Adversaries waging proxy war pick the location and time to start a hostile act for the counter-terror forces to react. The neighbour waging the terror war faced occasional trans-border actions, which, till recently, were mostly kept confidential, and may be for some very valid reasons. The fact that India appeared incapable of finding and capturing terrorists and at times, had been forced to release captured terrorists, and that too, due to terror actions such as hijacking of Indian aircraft, reinforces the perception the terrorist is invincible. India did not take the right of self-defence actively and go after the perpetrators of terror. Domestically, strong anti-terror laws and actions have become a political issue being touted as detrimental to a community and the political fortunes of political entities.

Geopolitics is founded on two assumptions. First, a community's location defines the community. Second, the political system, particularly the leader, is trapped in that reality. Rulers are forged through the community's culture and constrained by reality. As the nation seeks aggressive response to terror against India, political leaders may be constrained to address the reality. Recent terror acts have evoked intense anger across India. Indian media has added to the fervour. Has the time come for the Indian polity to takes steps to address this menace of proxy war? Reorganising the Indian SF could be one such credible step, driven by the people of the nation.

One of the key challenges for India has been the reluctance of the decision-makers to approve application of force in spite of grave provocation. The argument was that a full-scale war with our neighbour would cause a setback to India's impressive economic growth. The attack on the Indian Parliament and 26/11 are a few among many such examples. Reorganised SF could provide India the options of countering the proxy war without waging a full-scale conventional war. The exercise of reorganising SF is over three decades old. It first faced internal resistance within the Army. Once approved in the eighties, it failed to evolve due to multiple reasons. Over the last decade, it had been under consideration. It may have been approved in some form recently.

Creation of non-state actors in India's Area of Interest starting from the early eighties ought to have been a clear warning that they would be employed against India. Seeking the isolation of a nation in the 21st century is incorrect and is unlikely to succeed. There have been occasional muscular responses by India against the proxy war. One such response was made during the late nineties when terrorists in Doda targeted Hindu marriage processions. It needs to be noted that post such action, no such incident has taken place in J&K.

It seems that the national anger and aspiration among the masses once again seek forceful action. Recently, in response to an act of proxy war, India responded with air-power. Application of air power very nearly caused the escalatory ladder to spin out of control. It is therefore, imperative that the Armed Forces quickly develop capabilities, which provide better escalatory control and can be provided to the decision-makers, if needed. Application of such capabilities efficiently and effectively shall require organisations, besides structures.

Recommended Tasks, Capabilities, Organisation and Structure for Indian SF

> *"SF needs educated consumers, political and military patrons, who understand what SF should or should not be asked to do ... SF particularly needs protection from fantasies". Indian system of employment of force has been, not surprisingly, bereft of SF thought. Between regimental system of Arms/Services and Regional Commands/Corps etc.*

SF has emerged as one of the viable tools for asymmetric response in hybrid warfare. Special Forces missions are of politico-military nature and therefore there is a need to integrate political authority in the decision-making cycle. Direct missions employing kinetic force in foreign countries require a sign-off from the political leadership. Integration of SF with national intelligence agencies would help in weaponising the intelligence on real time basis. India's requirement for SF including their role, capabilities and op imperatives are unique. Acknowledging the same in the Unified Commanders' Conference (July 2017), Defence Secretary, Sanjay Mitra, announced that Special Operations Division (SOD) would "soon" become reality. According to media, SOD will collate Special Forces of the Army, Navy and IAF, for supporting offensive and defensive operations. Thus, some of the revised roles and orientation of Indian SF ought to include the following:

- Counter Proxy war
- Psychological and physical dislocation of the adversary
- Recce and Surveillance
- Surgical operations—destroy adversary's nerve centre, command and control infrastructure, communication/early warning set-up
- Facilitate theatre-level degradation in conventional conflict
- Rescue operations

Employment Capabilities

Indian SF need optimisation of their covert capabilities, unconventional direct action tasks, recce, surveillance and target designation, precision surgical operations, hostage rescue skill-set, post-strike damage assessment, info operations, and capabilities of supporting allies through civil affairs. Covert capabilities would be adversary-specific. It requires area-specific cultural and language skills as base. These are best left in the classified domain. These could include specialised intelligence tasks. India, like all other nations, possesses external intelligence capabilities (both human and technical) as well as covert capabilities. Conflicts having extended to multiple domains, covert capabilities now need to be supplemented with a flexible sword arm in all domains. Target neutralisation and training friendly groups in multi-domain conflicts could be some of the tasks which can be flagged in the open domain. Civil affairs give SF the opportunity to create a database and gain knowledge. Paramilitary Forces (PMF) have been deployed for the security of Indian missions in Afghanistan and now, Iraq. Deploying SF on such missions would have provided long-term benefits to the nation. Support for conventional operations needs tri-service integration and jointness. The SF tasks would also include the following:

- Special reconnaissance conducted in a clandestine or covert manner to collect or verify info.
- Direct actions to target, designate, seize, destroy, capture, exploit, recover or damage targets.
- Facilitate theatre-level degradation during conventional operations.

- Counter-terrorism tasks to neutralise terrorists and their network.
- Unconventional warfare.
- Sensitive Site Exploitation towards neutralising terrorist and their network.
- Security assistance towards capacity-building of allies' military.
- Hostage rescue (would also need covert capability).
- Information support operations.
- Counter WMD operations.

Type of Tasks

Present Indian SF organisations have single horizontal structures. They are raised, trained, manned and equipped for conventional conflict and limited counter-terror operations. The units are able to adopt and mutate to take on the counter proxy war due to their inherent flexibility, superior training and high level of motivation. Intelligence Support Operations are a subject for the classified domain. Given the threats being faced by India and the employment of non-state actors operating with the support of the state in India's neighbourhood, it is imperative that the top end of trained manpower is harnessed for intelligence support operations and covert/unconventional tasks. There could be different routes for selecting and training such manpower. One such way is to allow intelligence agencies to select, train and employ personnel for intelligence operation. India faces a proxy war being waged from across its borders; there is a need for more militaristic capabilities for intelligence support operation and covert/unconventional operations.

Covert and unconventional tasks are different from intelligence support operations. Covert, unconventional tasks require a high degree of preparation, coordination and application, such as rescue operation. SF has a pool of trained manpower which can be evaluated and up-skilled for covert and unconventional operations. It will also lead to greater cooperation between intelligence apparatus and SF, simultaneously reinforcing trust between them. It would lead to a quicker response-time against proxy strikes. Thus, after training and laid-down stint of basic and advance experience, the select persons in the pool can be up-skilled. The selection of SF personnel would be based on their orientation and capabilities. There is need for providing the SF non-kinetic capabilities too. Indian SF need to be able to undertake four types of tasks. These are as follows:

- Intelligence support operations
- Covert and unconventional operations (Tier 1)
- Support conventional operations (Tier 2)
- Civil affairs and information operations

Structure

Current Indian SF are in the Army, the Navy, the MHA, and the Cabinet Secretariat. Navy provides the manpower for Naval SF. For the rest, the Indian Army provides the manpower. In case the SF need to undertake envisaged tasks to combat proxy war, there is a need for realignment of current structures to help undertake the same. At present, Indian SF operate largely in a single domain. The selection and training is decentralised. The skill-set, standards, etc., vary from unit to unit and for valid reasons such as terrain. There is a need to integrate these units horizontally more intimately and for the four verticals listed in the previous paragraph to be created. In order to achieve that and have a functional set-up, there is a need for a centre of excellence to do the thinking, a structure at the national level, and a structure at the tri-service level. Ideally, such changes in a democracy must be brought in through a legislative process. However, the way the Indian democracy and polity function, may be far-fetched idea. Therefore, changes through executive action may be the only viable option. The structures of the Armed Forces are hierarchical universally. While framing SF organisation, it would be imperative to flatten the structures on need basis.

- **At the National Level:** The emphasis ought to be on shaping the environment in the area of national interest and hone the capabilities towards the same. A structure which possesses the ability to integrate the aspects of political decision-making, control over the escalation threshold, integration of national intelligence apparatus, diplomatic implications, ability to manage crisis and fallout is required. General VP Malik in his book *India's Military Conflicts and Diplomacy: An Inside View of Decision Making*, says, "Continuous control of the escalatory ladder will require much closer political oversight and politico-civil-military interaction." The structure must have the authority to approve directions and decisions on the scope of application of SF. It ought to have its own secretariat. One of the major challenges would be how to weaponise the intelligence inputs in keeping with the OODA loop of proxy war. Intelligence agencies world over are notorious for deterring encroachment on their perceived turf. One of the suggested options is to provide the trained manpower to execute Intelligence Support Operations. Skilled SF manpower can be provided to this structure, which can advise the decision-makers. Ideally, such a structure should be chaired by the point-person responsible for providing single-point advice on national defence to the head of the political executive of the nation. However, a number of matured democracies have also kept them under civilian control. In India, the current government has created a few new structures. One of these structures that have representation of most of the stake-holders listed above, including the three Chiefs, could be assigned this responsibility. It is imperative that the body assigned this responsibility does not become a political tool. Parliamentary control in a democracy is exercised through financial control. The control is exercised through the respective ministries. There are multiple models for addressing this aspect. In the US, the Congress has provided a separate budget to SF. In the UK, it is through the Defence Ministry. In a few other countries, it is through the Intelligence Budget. In India, the Ministry of Defence may be a workable option with financial powers over the SF provided to the Headquarters of the Integrated Defence Services (HQ IDS), with a classified post-audit and not a pre-audit, so that the speed of execution is not impeded.

- **At the Tri-Services Level:** The focus would be on executing the decision taken at the national level as also to support military operations. It ought to be managed by a Tri-Service organisation. Nuts and bolts decisions and their execution towards integration, manning policies, acquisition of weapons and equipment, training, budgeting, laying down standards, developing the advice for national structure, creating a Centre of Excellence on SF, control over the training and testing institution(s), testing of manpower and earmarking of personnel for different verticals, research and planning ahead, and continuous monitoring ought to be undertaken at this level. Some of the important activities which HQ IDS may need to work on are:
  - Framing of manning policies
  - Earmarking of budget

- Fast tracking of procurement process
- Creating/upgrading and integrating training institutions
- Identifying training requirements and setting standards
- Creating training infrastructure
- Executing testing and evaluation
- Identifying air/maritime assets for insertion/support/extraction
- Measures for providing fire support
- Creation of integrated secure communication infrastructure
- Creation of administrative infrastructure
- Logistic support, particularly during operations

Organogram

A line diagram for one such an organisation is given in Figure 8.3.

Restructuring

The raising of the first Commando Unit in 1966 was of six companies as this was the organisation of an Infantry Battalion at that time. The Unit was divided in two and hence, both the Units got three companies each. For a long time, this was the basic structure of a Commando/SF unit. When a number of airborne units were converted to SF units, a sizeable manpower of the airborne unit became available. This manpower was added to the SF units. Reorganisation of the SF units was carried out to form fourth sabre team. It provided additional punch and flexibility to the SF unit.

The Way Ahead

- The SF of the Army and the Navy need to be brought under the newly raised SF Division. The unit undertaking Intelligence Support Operation may continue to operate under the Cabinet Secretariat.
- All manpower to this unit, henceforth, may be provided from the SF units of the Army and the Navy after due evaluation process. The infantry units of the Indian Army currently provide the manpower to Special Group (SG).
- There is also a need for an SF unit to undertake covert and unconventional direct action tasks. A joint SF unit may undertake these tasks. Reorganising an existing unit or raising a new unit

could do this. The manpower for this unit too would come from existing SF units. These units would need dedicated support of air and maritime assets, both for training and operations.

The manpower would be required to create Tier-1 structure for undertaking covert and unconventional operations, info operations and civil affairs organisation, enhance training establishment, Centre for Excellence, testing and evaluation organisation for personnel, weapons, equipment and communication, secretariat at the national level and staff at the theatre level. What are the options for obtaining the said manpower? It can either be sanctioned as additional increments or alternatively, can be re-appropriated from within the SF units. It is unlikely that the government would provide additional manpower for the same. One of the options could be suppressing the fourth sub-unit in some of the SF units temporarily for validating the change for a few years.

Centre of Excellence and SF Training School

The nation needs a Centre of Excellence on SF. It can be either collocated with SF Training School or could be a part of INDU. Both have their advantages and disadvantages. The Centre needs to be located away from prying eyes, yet quick access and connectivity is imperative. It should have infrastructure for theoretical training, while the practical training shall be carried out at the Training School. Evaluation of skills, SF-specific leadership and theatre/adversary-specific preparation (to include counter-terror), etc., could be undertaken at the Centre. The Centre would need wings for information operation, civil affairs and sensitive site exploitation. Currently, no institution provides training in such fields. The Centre could also be the repository for all types of SF research. Testing and evaluation could also be undertaken at the Centre. The testing and evaluation process would have to be transparent yet classified. Trial and evaluation of weapons and equipment, doctrine & tactics, organisations and structures evaluation are some of the other tasks, which may be undertaken at the Centre. For economy of effort, the Centre must be a joint organisation. The Centre would also need to prepare and conduct customised programme to train decision-makers to help understand the implications of different decisions.

Manning

SF shall continue to be an all-volunteer force. All entrants would join Tier 2. Tier 2 shall be the feeder for Tier 1. Tier 1 shall support Intelligence Support Apparatus. The manpower for Civil Affairs and Info Operations could be provided directly from Tier 2. The debate over Permanent versus fixed tenure never ends in the SF fraternity. It would be safe to say that at the end of the debate, the decision must serve the best interests of the organisation. The current tenure of three years in NSG and SG is not in organisational interests. It also is detrimental to organisational memory. There has to be a provision to retain personnel for a longer duration, as in SF units. Financial remunerations, retention in SF and incentives must be based on SF skills. SF should seek and provide cross-attachment for unique skills on deputation and protect the career interest of the SF personnel.

Organisation of SF Unit

The current organisation of the SF unit and SF sub-unit would need review to be able to meet the emerging scenarios. The organisation of different SF units may require customisation depending upon tasking. Standard organisation of SF units may be detrimental for customised tasking. The lowest level (squad) currently comprises three buddy pairs. Is there a case for making it to four buddy pairs so that it can be split into two buddy pairs each, thereby providing more flexibility in application?

Equipping

The procurement process would need modification to meet the needs of the SF. Empowered committee route is one such option. A specialist wing in the Training School would need to identify the needs and sources for the same. The Wing would need to work with Defence Research and Development Organisation (DRDO) and industries to develop capacity and capabilities. SF would need to maintain a variety of resources in storage for multiple options. Customised communication equipment and decision-making tools would need to be developed within the nation. Based on the organisational configuration, the equipping of each SF unit would require customisation.

Training

The role and mission-specific training would need to be developed covering the complete range of operations. It would be imperative to fix standards. The current set of standards would need to be reviewed to fix standards for Tier 1, civil affairs and Info operations. The current joint training for insertion, extraction, designation, fire support, logistics, etc., would need to be evolved. Currently, these are specific to the Army, the Navy and the Air Force. Linguistic, cultural and behavioural skill-training is imperative along with theatre-specific training. Covert trainers and trainees may need to be deployed abroad for reconnaissance and gaining experience. One such method is to send SF operatives on international flights as sky marshals. The US sends its SF personnel on study leave to regions of interest for language training. Indian SF would need to come up with more innovative ways to access their areas of interest. There is a need for a joint doctrine on fighting proxy war. Unpredictability needs to be built into the training curriculum. Perception management is imperative for fighting the future conflicts. Along with cyber, info operations would provide the SF with non-kinetic tools to supplement the kinetic capabilities.

Support

The SF missions may need fire support in case of emergency, aerial/maritime support for insertion/extraction/casualty evacuation. Assets for such activities would need to be earmarked on priority call basis. They would need to train together to create affiliation as well as confidence.

Communications

Communication is the key to application. It would provide the span of control for command. It ought to be the first part of equipment which needs to be addressed and indigenised. Secrecy and security would be the key feature.

Conclusion

The military mind is more accustomed to operating in the physical domain and obtaining tangible results. Asymmetric warfare, as a concept, creates a dichotomy and dilemma. India has faced this dilemma of proxy war being waged through hybrid means. These threats are here to stay. A study of our past wars as well as on-going conflicts in the world indicates that the component of asymmetry and hybridity is increasing in the conflict zones. Non-state actors fought the recent West Asia conflict against ISIS on both the sides, with sizable support from very unlikely state partners.

The recent victory ceremony over ISIS had a country-flag and a flag of a non-state actor.

It is learnt that orders for raising of an SF division have been issued. Indian Air Force and Indian Navy have agreed to provide officers but no manpower in the ranks. Apparently, the SF Division shall have a single SF unit under it. It may be a reluctant first step and possibly there shall be more to follow. The paper above gives one such road-map. The Feb 2019 terror attack in Pulwama, including a number of them over the last three decades, executed/abetted from across the border, has evoked a sense of frustration amongst the citizens of the country for the reluctance to effectively punish the perpetrator of the proxy war. There is a feeling that it may have dawned upon the political executive that India's enemies would not be deterred until they feel the heat. Conventional capabilities have not proven to be adequate deterrents. The Indian state has been reluctant to go down the path of elaborate covert and unconventional means. It has stuck to traditional, national power path. As the warfare is moving more and more into the asymmetric and unconventional domain, India needs to acquire tools to punish the perpetrators of such threats. USA has already come up with the doctrine for multi-domain warfare, largely catering for Russia and China. SF is one such tool. It is imperative that India moves to acquire the same. Acquisition of capacities and capabilities along with demonstrated 'will' to employ them, may offer to be one of the components of the deterrent.

Application of SF in international domain has consequences. Indian diplomacy would need to think of rational issues to justify the same. The diplomacy also has to be ready to deal with the fallout of the same. Kanti Bajpai, in his article titled 'Be Civil with the Military' states, "While we worry that the military might stray across into civil spheres, there is a growing sense that the balance has been damaged by the civilians. Civilians have not sufficiently involved the military in the issues where military advice and involvement is proper and vital." Restructuring of SF for fighting proxy war is one such glaring example.[14]

Secrecy is the paramount weapon for application of SF. The US officially denies the existence of Delta Force. There is virtually zero published materials on Chinese SF. Israeli SF were training both the parties of the conflict on the same base and the trainers never gave away their organisational affiliation. Anonymity is one of the greatest assets of the SF. It is not, therefore, necessary to have such conversations in totally open domains. Yet, informed conversation in the open domain helps mature decision-making in a democracy.

One of the key criticisms faced while writing an ideas document about the Indian Armed Forces is that what is being sought is too radical. The proxy war being waged against India is born out of radical ideas. Response to the proxy war will emerge from radical and unconventional thoughts. Creeping ideas and linear thinking is unlikely to provide India the necessary solutions. It is for India to decide the type and quality of SF it needs. It is said that it is imperative to speak softly but carry a big hammer. SF would be the hammer for the nation in the next decade and beyond. **In the end, the first principle of Special Forces needs to be reiterated**—SF are precious assets that take time, efforts and investments to develop.

NOTES

1 Archive.defense.gov (2011). *Defense.gov Secretary of Defense Speech: United States Military Academy (West Point, NY)*. [online] Available at: http://archive.defense.gov/speeches/speech.aspx?speechid=1539. Accessed on 9 Mar. 2019.

2 Conversation with officer present at the meeting.

3 Kiras, J. (n.d.). *Special operations warfare*. [online] Encyclopedia Britannica. Available at: https://www.britannica.com/topic/special-operations-warfare. Accessed on 9 Mar. 2019.

4 GOV.UK. (2018). *Global Strategic Trends*. [online] Available at: https://www.gov.uk/government/publications/global-strategic-trends. Accessed on 26 Jan. 2019.

5 Egorov, B. (2018). *5 legendary Russian special forces units*. [online] Rbth.com. Available at: https://www.rbth.com/science-and-tech/329610-5-legendary-russian-special-forces. Accessed on 22 Mar. 2019.

6 Cavanaugh, D. (2016). *Moscow's Alpha Group Is One of the World's Most Vicious Commando Teams*. [online] Warisboring.com. Available at: https://warisboring.com/moscows-alpha-group-is-one-of-the-worlds-most-vicious-commando-teams/ Accessed on 3 Mar. 2019.

7 English.Chinamil.com.cn. (2015). *Chinese airborne troops win glory in int'l special forces competition*. [online] Available at: http://english.chinamil.com.cn/news-channels/china-military-news/2015-07/10/content_6581621.htm. Accessed on 12 Mar. 2019].

8 Chinese Military Review. (2013). *Chinese Special Operation Team Wins First Position At International Special Forces Contest*. [online] Available at: http://chinesemilitaryreview.blogspot.com/2013/03/chinese-special-operations-forces-sof.html. Accessed on 12 Mar. 2019].

9 Blasko, D. (2015). *Chinese Special Operations Forces: Not Like "Back at Bragg"*. [online] War on the Rocks. Available at: https://warontherocks.com/2015/01/chinese-special-operations-forces-not-like-back-at-bragg/ Accessed on 13 Mar. 2019.

10 Majumdar, D. (2019). *China's Special Forces Units Are Getting Ready for War*. [online]

The National Interest. Available at: https://nationalinterest.org/blog/buzz/chinas-special-forces-units-are-getting-ready-war-26051. Accessed on 13 Mar. 2019.

11 Boot Camp & Military Fitness Institute. (2019). *An Overview of Chinese Elite & Special Forces*. [online] Available at: https://bootcampmilitaryfitnessinstitute.com/elite-special-forces/chinese-elite-special-forces/an-overview-of-chinese-elite-special-forces/ Accessed on 14 Mar. 2019.

12 Business Insider. (n.d.). *KASOTC offers courses to teach soldiers how to use vehicles in special operations..* [online] Available at: https://www.businessinsider.in/Step-inside-Jordans-special-forces-training-center-which-is-carved-out-of-a-mountain-and-has-everything-the-most-elite-soldiers-in-the-world-need/KASOTC-offers-courses-to-teach-soldiers-how-to-use-vehicles-in-special-operations-/slideshow/63373161.cms. Accessed on 20 Mar. 2019.

13 Scahill, J. (2011). *JSOC: The Black Ops Force That Took Down Bin Laden*. [online] The Nation. Available at: https://www.thenation.com/article/jsoc-black-ops-force-took-down-bin-laden. Accessed on 12 Mar. 2019.

14 Bajpai, K. (2010). *Be Civil With The Military - Times of India*. [online] The Times of India. Available at: https://timesofindia.indiatimes.com/edit-page/Be-Civil-With-The-Military/articleshow/5648165.cms. Accessed on 23 Mar. 2019.

9

Future of Airborne Operations as Relevant to the Indian Construct

Colonel Anuraag Singh Rawat

ABSTRACT

Airborne forces have come a long way from 1758, when Benjamin Franklin thought of using balloons to insert troops, to being today's elite forces which can swiftly respond to any fast developing contingencies and achieve disproportionate success.

Future Land Warfare is going to be heavily impacted by the rapid advances in technology and is not going to be restricted to a conventional form as we know it today. The future of Airborne operations, in the last few years has been debated in the US, UK, Russian armies, to name a few, however each country has recognised the strategic advantages accrued by their Airborne forces, and thus continued to keep them, albeit with certain modifications. Against this backdrop the future of Airborne Operations in the Indian construct is examined with specific reference to their feasibility in conventional operations and in operations other than War.

Introduction

Airborne Forces the world over are considered *'crème de la crème'* among the elite forces and are second to none. They carry this aura justifiably so, since whenever we talk of achieving shock or surprise in the battlefield, employing vertical envelopment, achieving simultaneity of operations, it all conjures up images of the maroon berated men of the Airborne Forces. *"Airborne operations consist of the movement and delivery by air, into an objective area, of combat forces and their administrative support, for the execution of tactical and strategic missions"*.[1] These would essentially be joint operations and are conducted by Army combat forces while the Air Force flies them in. The men and their weapons and stores may be air dropped using parachute or may be air landed using existing landing facilities.

During the First World War in 1917, Winston Churchill was credited with having first proposed the creation of an airborne force to assault behind the German lines. However, the first modern operation planning dates to late 1918, which involved dropping elements of the US 1st Division behind German lines near Metz. The operation was planned for February 1919 but the war ended before such an attack could be seriously planned. WWII witnessed the creation of dedicated division-sized formations for airborne assaults and most modern armies have since maintained the capability of conducting airborne operations.

Future Land Warfare is going to be heavily impacted by the rapid advances in technology and is not going to be restricted to a conventional form as we know it today. Much of this has been written in the preceding chapters and against this backdrop what would Airborne operations in future metamorphose into? Would they be even possible to be conducted in the era of enhanced Air Defence capability and increased battlefield transparency especially in the Indian context? Would the cost-benefit analysis support launch of these operations especially in an increasingly risk averse environment? For the purpose of putting a timeline and in consonance with the rest of the book when future airborne operations are being discussed a window of 10-15 years in the future is being looked at and heliborne operations are not being discussed.

Historical Perspective

Benjamin Franklin, one of the founding fathers of the United States is credited with being amongst the first people who thought of inserting troops using the aerial medium. In a letter dated 16 Jan 1784, he suggested using 5000 balloons with two men in each of them and wrote, "*...where is the Prince who can afford so to cover his country with troops for its defence, as that ten thousand men descending from the clouds, might not in many places do an infinite deal of mischief...*".[2] While the thought was revolutionary, not much was done on the same and during the First World War no major operations using parachutists as we know them today were undertaken, though planning near the end of the war was carried out by the United States (US) Army.

The period between the two World Wars saw a lot of interest and advances in use of Airborne Forces and the first true paratroop drop was carried out by Italy in 1927 using a concept of static line jump, which opened the door for mass jumps.[3] The Italians initially and subsequently the Russians were the leaders in developing the concept of Airborne Forces. In a demonstration near Moscow, in August 1933, the Russians parachuted 46 soldiers and a small 1.7 ton T-27 Armoured car[4] and by 1936 had significantly enhanced the capability and capacity of their Airborne Forces. Germany too realized the potential of the Airborne Forces and started training and raising them in the 1936–37 period. In fact German Airborne Forces took part in the Army manoeuvres of "Autumn 1937 wherein 14 demolition squads were dropped at night to target the railway lines and communications and they were highly successfull."[5]

The British took to raising Airborne Forces only in June 1940 after Winston Churchill issued his famous instruction to General Sir Hastings Ismay, his Chief of Staff in the War Cabinet Secretariat, where he talked about raising a corps of at least 5000 parachute troops. These instructions commenced the process that brought about the birth of the British airborne movement and things moved very rapidly from then on. The first men of No. 2 Commando Battalion arrived at Ringway on 8 July by which time the basic Landing School structure was being put in place and in November 1940, No.2 Commando was renamed the 11th Special Air Service. The expansion of the Airborne Forces continued with the 1st Parachute Brigade being formed in September 1941 and on 31 October 1941 the 1st Airborne Division, consisting of the 1st Parachute Brigade and the newly formed, glider-borne 1st Air landing Brigade was raised.[6]

The United States of America (USA), amongst the major Armies of the world, were one of the slowest off the starter block, as far as raising of Airborne forces go. Though in June 1940[7] a test platoon of paratroopers, was formed and a Provisional Parachute Group headquarters at Fort Benning was established in March 1941. It was only in July 1942 that the Army Ground Forces ordered the activation of two airborne divisions to be done not later than 15 August 1942.[8] This resulted in the 82 and 101 Divisions being renamed as Airborne and they formed the nucleus of the US Airborne forces. The Indian Airborne story commenced in June 1941. The War Office (in England) approved the raising of a Parachute Brigade in India.[9] The first airborne troops to be used in battle in WWII were the elite German *Fallschirmjäger*, during the invasion of Denmark and Norway in April 1940, however these were restricted to a small number (platoon and company strength) being used to seize key installations and choke points.[10] The subsequent invasion of Holland in May 1940, by many historians is considered as the first actual use of Airborne Forces since these forces were used, very effectively, in large numbers for the first time.[11] As part of operations the Germans dropped small packets of paratroopers to capture the important bridges that led directly across Holland and into the heart of the country thus clearing the way for the 10th Panzer Division, which effectively breached the defences.[12] The capture of Crete by the Germans in May 1941 standouts for being the first major operation in which the initial attacks were only by Airborne forces, however the Germans due to a combination of reasons including underestimating the enemy strength and resistance offered by the Allied troops, suffered very heavy casualties and nearly failed. While the capture of Crete clearly demonstrated to the Allied Forces the utility and effectiveness of the Airborne Forces, Germany after its Crete experience never used them in the airborne role in any large numbers.[13]

The Allied forces initially were not too successful in the use of Airborne forces in Algeria and Sicily during WWII. *Operation Torch,* which envisaged a quick seizure of Algeria and dash to Tunisia in November 1942, incorporated the use of US Airborne forces as a vital part of the plan and though the troops captured their objectives, they could not hold onto them. In Sicily (July 1943) division strength Airborne troops were used by the Allied Forces, in combination with Amphibious forces. "A combination of darkness, strong crosswinds and crew inexperience resulted in paratroopers from the initial missions being scattered along 50 miles of coast."[14] Two days later, a friendly fire also took a heavy toll on aircraft carrying the Airborne troops. However, despite the dispersed presence of the Airborne troops, they managed to create confusion and fear amongst the enemy and thus helped in making the operation in Sicily a success.

The success of the Airborne forces in June 1944, during the *Normandy Landings* completely vindicated the faith placed on them. The three Divisions Airborne drops of British and American Forces, was instrumental in protecting the beach head operations by delaying German reinforcements from counterattacking the landing forces, helped in the breakout by capturing the choke points and spread chaos and confusion by disrupting communications.[15] Emboldened by the success of the Airborne Forces during Normandy Landings, in September 1944, the largest airborne operation was mounted by the Allied Forces, called *Operation Market Garden*, to create a foothold on the Rhine and seize a direct route into northern Germany. The airborne part of the operation was undertaken by the First Allied Airborne Army with the land operation by the 2nd Army. The parachute drops and glider landings were accurate and heavily concentrated and thus the bulk of the airlift was an outstanding success. However despite a good start, the operation was a failure due to the spreading of the Airborne landings over more than one day, slowness of the Armour to establish linkup, inclement weather conditions during the resupply period, poorly chosen landing sites and faulty intelligence which resulted in the paratroopers landing in an area of the German Armoured formations. These and other challenges resulted in high Allied casualties as well as failure to meet the objectives of *Operation Market Garden*.[16]

Post Market Garden, only one major Airborne operation, *Operation Varsity* (March 1945) was attempted by the Allied Forces and it tried to rectify the problems identified in Operation Market Garden. This operation entailed a quick concentration of Airborne Forces across the Rhine, to break the enemy resistance by securing crossing places and linking up with the ground forces. The drops to achieve mass and concentration were the largest single lift Airborne operations of the war, and were not too far in depth, thus enabling a quick link up. Overall the operation was a success though many question the need of the same, since Gen Patton's Division managed to cross the Rhine further south relatively easily and post-operation analysis of the enemy suggested that success may have been achieved without employing Airborne troops.[17]

The Airborne concept was validated in battle by both the Axis and Allied forces during the course of WWII and a brief study of them reveals *the difficulties involved in their planning and execution and a requirement for extremely high levels of jointmanship*. The difference between success and failure was often minuscule, with a lot being left to luck especially during the transportation and landing phases despite the best of efforts to achieve air superiority and provide adequate covering fire for these initial phases. The casualties in successful operations were high and in the unsuccessful ones they skyrocketed. However despite these challenges the Airborne operations when successful gave out of proportion dividends and this saw all the major armies supplementing their Airborne Forces during WWII and they continued to maintain them post that, albeit with some modifications and cuts.

Post WWII, Airborne operations involving multiple Division landings have not taken place. However various countries, especially USA, have on occasion used Airborne Forces usually in battalion or lesser strengths, with varying degrees of success. The US used Airborne troops twice during the Korean War, once in Vietnam and in the invasion of Grenada (October 1983) and Panama (December 1989). They also dropped Rangers onto the Kandahar airfield (October 2001) and during *Operation Iraqi Freedom*, elements of the American 75 Ranger Regiment dropped onto an airfield in Northern Iraq and subsequently they parachuted elements of the 173rd Airborne Brigade onto an Iraqi airfield. British and French paratroopers and commandos landed on key points along the Suez Canal (November 1956) after Egypt's move to nationalize the strategic waterway and though militarily a success, it was a diplomatic and political disaster for Britain and France.[18] More successfully in January 2013, French airborne forces were dropped into Mali, near the city of Timbuktu, to drive away Islamic militants.[19]

In India post partition the Airborne Division was disbanded. Indian Airborne Forces have been used twice post-Independence and both times have come out with flying colours.[20] On 11 December 1971, they were airdropped at *Tangail* to capture Poongli Bridge on the Jamuna River which cut off the Pakistani 93rd Brigade which was retreating from the north to Dhaka. The drop and subsequent tasks including link up were carried out at minimal cost and thus the operation was a huge success, especially in the strategic domain. The unit subsequently was the first to enter Dhaka on 16 December 1971.[21] The Brigade in November 1988 launched *Operation Cactus* in Maldives in response to a coup attempt to topple the government. The Airborne troops took off less than 16 hours after the Maldivian President's request for assistance.[22] They travelled 2500 kilometres; air landed at Male and got the situation under control in less than seven hours. It was a swift surgical operation which was executed with copybook precision.[23]

Though sparingly used post WWII, the Airborne forces are *regarded as elite forces which can swiftly respond to any fast developing contingencies* and *achieve disproportionate success.* Their *concept of employment has thus evolved over a period of time, with reduced strength and more precise insertion* being favoured.

Future Operating Challenges

An airborne force is most vulnerable till it meets *terra firma* and bulk of the casualties occur while transiting to the place of drop and, after deplaning before command and control has been achieved. This has historically been an operational challenge and will continue to only intensify in the times to come with a greater impact due to technology, space based assets, increasing transparency and greater potency of weapon systems.

Airborne forces in the future are likely to get targeted from their mounting base, as real time surveillance using a plethora of platforms including satellites and UAVs would be able to track the movement of the forces and anti-access measures would be put into place. These measures could involve cyber assets taking down the control network at the airports, to long range Surface to Surface Missiles targeting the force/ planes/airport. Thus by using a combination of capabilities and assets the force would be targeted at the mounting base(s) to prevent the operation from being launched.

Area Air Defence systems like the Patriot System and the S-400 missile defence systems, developed by the United States and Russia respectively, are becoming more and more automated and effective and impact the medium/high altitude defence systems. The S-400 system which is being procured can simultaneously engage 80 targets up to a range of 400 kms and systems like these, with every upgradation, are going to be even more resistant to electronic countermeasures and difficult to penetrate thus impinging on the survivability of an airborne force. In the future, suppressing or destroying this medium/high-altitude threat could be a time-consuming and resource-intensive effort with no surety of success in a given timeframe.

Army Air Defence (AAD) and man-portable air defence systems (MANPADS, shoulder-fired missiles) are the low altitude threats and the next class of air defences that can affect airborne operations. They are generally available in much larger numbers, being cheaper vis a vis SAM systems and they are usually optically directed. Thus, due to their passive nature, they are more difficult to detect before they commence their engagement. The accuracy, lethalness and proliferation of these weapon systems are on the rise, with fourth generation MANPADS already in service in various armies of the world. When operating against Non State actors sophisticated Air Defence systems may not be available however

AAA and MANPADS would usually be available in good numbers. This would lead to their neutralisation being that much more difficult.

Air defence thus presents a multifaceted challenge to airborne operations requiring a multitude of countermeasures. The *increase in Air Defences means in future their suppression is going to be more effort intensive and with lesser chance of success.*

Transformational Trends: Meeting Future Challenges

The future of Airborne operations, in the last few years has been debated in the US, United Kingdom (UK), Russian armies, to name a few. However, each country has recognised the strategic advantages accrued by their Airborne forces, and thus has continued to keep them, albeit with certain modifications. UK has undergone a major reorganisation as part of Army plan 2020[24] which is further being built on in the Joint Force 2025[25] vision, and the 16 Air Assault Brigade in an airborne roles available as a rapid reaction force. The Brigade with two Parachute and two Airborne battalions along with the supporting Arms and services components is part of the Air manoeuvre force available to it. UK as per their doctrine on Land Operations looks at its Air manoeuvre force as a 'specialist' type of light force. They exploit the mobility of aircraft to provide reach and speed. Air manoeuvre forces include attack, support and reconnaissance helicopters, air assault and airborne infantry with organic combat support and combat service support."[26] However, one school of thought tends to believe that airborne operations are doctrinally neglected by including the concept within the wider air manoeuvre doctrine and this does not allow exploitation of the airborne capability to the fullest.

As per United Kingdom's National Security Strategy and Strategic Defence and Security Review 2015 four challenges driving its security priorities include threats from terrorism, state based threats, cyber threats and erosion of rule-based international order.[27] Airborne operations are an important and integral response to nearly all contingencies arising from these challenges. However, the two main restrictions of the UK airborne forces, i.e. a lack of mobility and armoured support, especially in the initial phases of operations are aspects that still need to be resolved.

The Russian Airborne Forces (VDV) is one of the biggest Airborne Forces in the world today and have been expanding and evolving in the last decade. As per inputs they consist of two parachute divisions, two air assault divisions, four independent brigades, along with a separate

Spetsnaz brigade, and a number of support and training units.[28] The independent brigades consist of a mix of parachute and air assault battalions and the Russian Airborne Forces are an arm of the Armed Forces separate from the Land Forces like Aerospace or Strategic Missile Forces. They have thus been given a very elitist status and are usually the first to be employed in any externally developing situation.

Russian Airborne Forces have for long been used as elite motor rifle units thus their conceptual employment faces a challenge. In addition, reports indicate that despite having such a large Airborne Force, its air assets have a lift capacity to drop less than a division at a time.[29] In all probability to resolve some of these challenges Russia has been experimenting with its Airborne Forces and it tried out few of these during the exercise Vostok 2018. The two air assault divisions are likely to have an increased force structure and heavier equipment including tanks and air defences, while the parachute divisions would still train to perform the more strategic air assault mission, and the independent brigades would conduct heliborne operation.[30] Russian Armed Forces have a large helicopter component and this diversification would reduce the load on the fixed wing airlift requirement while also increasing the air mobility component of the force and offer it various options at varying operational depth.

The US Army has two divisions, i.e. the 82 Airborne Divisions and the 101 Airborne Division as part of the XVIII Airborne Corps that cater for the airborne requirements. The Airborne Divisions serve as the core of the United States Global Response Force, and its quick reaction capability ensures speedy deployment worldwide from the continental United States via transport aircraft. Post reorganisation the 101st has shifted from airplanes to helicopters as the primary method of delivering troops into combat, while the 82nd continues to be air dropped/air landed for operations. During the transition of the US Army into a force comprising of modular Brigade Combat Teams (BCT), the 82nd Airborne Division also transitioned from a division-based structure to one based around modular brigade combat teams. Each BCT, as currently organised, has a reconnaissance squadron and an artillery battalion, as well as engineers and other key enablers at the brigade level in addition to the airborne infantry units.[31]

The US Airborne Forces in recent times seem to lack tactical battlefield mobility and light armour capability. These impinge on their employment and survivability in operations. Rand in one of its studies has identified the same and recommended the use of Light Armored Vehicle, second generation (LAV-II), family of vehicles.[32] These vehicles are being used by the Marines and their trials by the Airborne forces have been reported and, in October 2018 the US Army reactivated an armoured company for the 82nd Airborne, equipped with the LAV-25A2, thus indicating it is moving to address issues of tactical mobility and light armour capability.[33]

China too has substantial airborne forces comprising three Airborne Divisions as part of the 15th Airborne Corps. However, the modernisation in China's armed forces has impacted the airborne forces too. The command structure has been made flatter with the division headquarters being taken out and the operational brigades coming under the corps headquarter directly.[34] The US Secretary Of Defense Annual Report to Congress: Military and Security Developments Involving the People's Republic of China[35] says that the People's Liberation Army (PLA) Airborne Corps [formerly the People's Liberation Army Air Force (PLAAF) 15th Airborne Corps] has reorganised its previous units into nine brigades consisting of six airborne infantry brigades, a special operations brigade, an aviation brigade, and a support brigade. This was done with an aim to create a responsive and streamlined airborne corps capable of air-delivering modular combat units—including aerial drop of mechanised infantry forces. Two helicopter-based air assault infantry brigades have also been formed, with subsequent plans to equip these brigades with both transport and assault helicopters.

A brief look at the various major armies in the world clearly brings out the strategic importance associated with the Airborne Forces and them still being considered a force multiplier and an essential component of the Armed Forces. The Airborne Forces are being *structurally altered/ modified to generate a faster response* and are *modernising* their equipment to meet *the emerging challenges* and be prepared to react to future operational requirements. *Better and more protected battle field mobility, stronger manoeuvring capability, flatter and more responsive command structures, leveraging technology for achieving better battle field transparency, command, control and communication and increased use of helicopters* are some of the common aspects being implemented for enhancement of the combat potential of the airborne forces.

Indian Construct

In the next 15 years India would be an undisputed regional power and by the middle of the century would want to be a power to reckon, on the global stage. Disputed territorial issues in the Eastern and Western borders are not likely to have been resolved in the next 10-15 years, though economic considerations may prevent the situation from exacerbating on the Northern front. However the China–Pakistan nexus and impact of China Pakistan Economic Corridor (CPEC) would ensure that the border issue on the Western Front is kept active using a combination of hybrid measures.

Keeping present capabilities, trajectory of reforms and modernisation in mind, it is expected that India's edge over Pakistan in conventional operations would be maintained, while China is likely to improve its overall capabilities using a combination of technology infusion and restructuring to transform for its role as a global power. Indian Armed Forces while primarily being prepared to respond to the challenges on the Western and Northern fronts in the near future would be expected increasingly to have the capability to play a greater role in the immediate and extended neighbourhood. The Navy is building its capabilities to be blue water Navy while the Air force after acquiring the 'C' series of aircrafts and air to air refuellers has improved its strategic lift and long strike capability. The Army's airborne force is one such force that can rapidly respond to contingencies occurring at our borders or extended neighbourhood and put boots on ground. The Air Force has a fleet of AN32, IL-76, C17 and C130 aircrafts which are available for the airborne force. Post the induction of the aircrafts, the strategic lift capability of the Air Force has witnessed a quantum increase and given a boost to the conduct of airborne operations.

In case of conventional operations in our Western or Northern front enemy's air defence is going to play a major role in deciding about the employment of airborne forces. Linked to the air defence is the length of the airborne stream, i.e. the number of planes being used to transport the airborne forces and the nose to tail distance covered by them. During WWII the airborne stream used to stretch for hundreds of kilometres and would seem to go on forever. Survivability of such a stream in today's air defence environment is very suspect and effective suppression of enemy air defence (SEAD) using a combination of kinetic and non-kinetic measures can never be foolproof. In addition where Man Portable Air

Defence Systems (MANPADS) are involved then these measures are not at all effective.

Crystal Gazing—Airborne Operations in India

What tasks can airborne forces in India be used for in the future? Can they be used in conventional operations by India against near/over-parity adversaries? Are there tasks where they could be employed to give out of proportion success? Airborne forces provide rapid operational deterrence that impacts the best laid out adversarial plans and they have the unique capability of delivering a combined arms force. This force can be inserted almost anywhere and are light enough to move quickly. When we look for strategic tasks and places for employment for the airborne force, their employment on our Western Front can be almost anywhere. Though dense development and urbanisation has restricted some areas in the developed sector, they have conversely raised the strategic significance and sensitivity of those places, thus increasing their importance as targets.

The High Altitude Area (HAA) on our Northern Front poses no hindrance for airborne operations since altitude of Indian airfields permit effective use of the aircrafts for airborne operations. Moreover the terrain configuration to the North of the Line of Actual Control (LAC) lends itself to airborne operations with no dearth of areas for dropping zones. Depth of operations unlike those in plains and deserts are likely to be limited, to facilitate speedy link up with ground forces and thus reduce the danger to the airborne stream. In addition precision aerial delivery systems can be used to ensure that delivery of stores is carried out in an accurate manner especially in a high altitude terrain.

While the coming years will see an increase in the potency of air defence systems. Their counter measures are also likely to see a proportionate rise. Thus SEAD operations will continue to be pivotal for launch of airborne operations. However, for the threat to be minimised, the length of the airborne stream needs to be shortened thus reducing their exposure level. The advent of the IL 76 and lately the C130 have helped in reducing the length of an airborne stream tremendously. Firstly these planes have a capacity to carry many more paratroopers, thus reducing the number of planes required. Secondly the avionics permit more precision flying further reducing the length of the stream. In addition, if multiple dropping zones are used the airborne stream can come down drastically, thus increasing the chances of success.

Another method in the future could be the use of combat free fall (CFF) technique by the airborne force to increase surprise and decrease the time spent by the airborne stream in enemy territory. For every 1000 feet vertical height the paratrooper can go 1000 feet in the horizontal plane and thus if the force jumps at 20,000 feet it can be inserted minimum 15-17 kilometres inside, wind conditions remaining favourable. Conflicts in the future are going to be short, intense and the offensives, due to terrain and force friction, may not be aimed at achieving too much depth. Thus the CFF technique for insertion of the airborne force may be a potent way to negate the gaps in SEAD and be able to execute airborne operations despite a dense air defence cover. However all paratroopers are not qualified for a CFF jump and specialised training and equipment is required for the same. A nearly similar insertion could also be carried out using new technology parachutes like the RAM Air Static Line Canopy parachutes and this would lessen the specialised training required for CFF. So a combination of tactical, technical and equipment upgrades can still ensure that an airborne force is utilised against near/over-parity adversaries with telling effect. However one has to train, equip and plan accordingly and most of all think out of the box.

With India's growing economic might and stature it would also be expected to be able to help in places away from our borders. Airborne forces are an ideal force for reacting to any *Time Urgent Response Contingencies* or *Out Of Area Contingencies*. Airborne forces maintain a very high state of readiness and are ready to deploy at a very short notice and thus have the capability to deliver a large force in a short time over long distances and if required, rapidly intervene in an unstable region or country. These forces can move quickly, act as a deterrent, deploy rapidly and lastly being a strategic asset their employment reflects the intent of the nation. The increasing threat posed by terrorism, extremism and the associated instability makes it imperative that such a force is available to a country like India. The successful execution of *Operation Cactus* in Maldives by the Indian airborne forces is a testament to the fact that they can be effectively used to diffuse security threats to our assets/interests in littoral/sea-based nations.

India has a total coastline of 7516.6 kms, more than 1200 islands and an Exclusive Economic Zone (EEZ) of approximately 23 lakh km^2.[36] It dominates the main Sea Lines of Communications passing through the Indian Ocean Region (IOR). Case in point being the Andaman Nicobar islands which dominate the Malacca straits, which has nearly 100,000 merchant vessels carrying $3 trillion worth of cargo passing through it each year, including much of China's oil supplies and trade.[37] The sensitivity and growing importance of the island territories cannot be over emphasised for India in the coming days. Airborne forces can be effectively employed for defence of own island territories and offshore assets. Their high readiness status, capability to move large distances in a short time and ability to be inserted into the battlefield through a multitude of methods makes them unique for these tasks.

West Asia and Afghanistan are turbulent hotspots of terrorism and the balance of South and South East Asia is being slowly impacted by the spectre of terrorism. Small island nations in the Indian Ocean too have a fragile security apparatus. India as an emerging power in the region would be looked at as having the capability to be a security provider and must have the capability in the future for carrying out operations outside our national boundary to pursue a mandated politico–military objective. In addition we have a very large expatriate population in West Asia and the onus of ensuring their safety in moments of crisis also falls on the country. Airborne forces are ideally suited for any such quick intervention as airborne operations make any spot on the globe accessible and it is the fastest way to get a substantial force on ground. The Indian armed forces since Independence have had a large role in Human Assistance and Disaster Relief (HADR) operations both at home and abroad. They have been at the core of the relief operations on which subsequent effort and assistance has built up being the first responders.

Airborne operations in the future, in India, are thus going to *cover the entire spectrum from conventional operations to military operations other than war*. However due to *India's role as a security provider in the regional context airborne forces in future are thus more likely to be required for operations other than conventional operations.*

Modernising: The Way Forward

Airborne forces offer the government the strategic ability to respond in a multitude of situations ranging from conventional to Grey Zone options as they are best suited for tasks requiring high readiness support. Keeping in mind India's growing stature and aspirations at the regional and world stage, enhanced airborne capabilities could also offer the decision makers options to stabilise potential conflict situations more quickly and prevent them from escalating out of control. While near/over peer conflict increases the risk to an airborne force this can be mitigated by series of measures including joint operational design and the integration of technology to suppress the enemy's air defence system.

Thus there is no doubt that *Indian airborne forces* in the future will continue to *serve as the pivot of its strategic response capability* and could be employed for a gamut of tasks. As future conflicts are going to be seamlessly connected, unconventional and asymmetric in nature with hybridity in operations dominating, we have to have a force which can respond at a moment's notice and be honed to fight in such an environment. The airborne forces thus are going to be an *effective instrument in our preemptive as well as response strategy* and they have to be trained and equipped for the same. Their *roles in the future may also thus be more in the Grey Zone conflict domain than the conventional one, not for the lack of capability but for the want of opportunity*. However, to be effectively employed in a high attrition, technologically dominant battlefield the airborne forces would have to also evolve and be better supported.

Airborne forces the world over are trying to increase their tactical mobility as well as have better protection in the battle field by using armoured carriers. The US is experimenting with the US Marines LAV-25[38] armed with 25 mm automatic cannons, while the Russian and Chinese airborne forces already have armoured fighting vehicles. These vehicles provide protected mobility and increase the firepower available with the airborne forces. They also ensure that the airborne force can be dropped further away from the objective, as they now have better mobility, thus increasing the element of surprise as well giving an option to have a DZ in an area which being further from the objective may be more secure and less protected by ground troops and air defence.

However, conversely, the increase in vehicles would naturally increase the lift requirement thus requiring additional air effort, which would already be stretched. Even if the air effort was available, it would mean increasing the length of the airborne stream and thus correspondingly increase the exposure. When we look at the expanded role envisaged for the Indian airborne forces in the future, involving operations in conventional wars to actions against hybrid forces along our borders or further away, then the flexibility to employ airborne forces has greater manoeuverability and staying power stands to logic. To cope with the future challenges better mobility vehicles with some armour protection in sufficient numbers are thus a preferable option and could be conceptually further validated. While some options exist in the present inventory, the Infantry Combat Vehicle (ICV) being one, a wheeled version would be a better option. In addition the airborne force must have better high mobility vehicles which can be air dropped, in place of the existing four wheeled vehicles, which are standard issue for the balance of the army.

Airborne forces require specialised training and equipment especially to meet the future hybrid challenges. They need to think out of the box and have a non-conventional combat ethos to deal with the emerging challenges, which must get reflected in their training. Airborne forces should have the capability to conduct mass combat free falls thus enabling them to be inserted by being dropped far away from the Dropping Zone (DZ). They thus, must have the requisite equipment in sufficient numbers as well as be able to raise their own training standards and be in a position to insert a sizeable force by CFF. The training would also incorporate drops at multiple DZs thus helping in reducing the length of the airborne stream.

Technological advances in parachute development for men and material drops needs to be kept abreast with and be inducted in service for the airborne forces. The RAM Air Static Line Canopy parachutes have a high glide ratio, which allows the parachutist to travel more. They are more precise and assist in softer landings and the systems associated with them will ensure less dispersion of airborne forces and accurate landings. These parachutes can also be an alternative to the CFF insertion especially since training a person for CFF requires a lot of time, equipment, effort and of course money. By jumping at altitudes similar to the CFF force but using a static line RAM Air Canopy parachute, the airborne force can be inserted 15-20 kms away from the point where they exit the aircraft.

Similarly for accurate delivery of logistic loads the Guided Precision Aerial Delivery System (GPADS)[39] is a revolutionary concept. The system's guidance, navigation and control software analyses its environment in real time, ensuring accurate payload delivery as per the inputs fed into the global positioning system (GPS). With an ability to travel 25 kms or more based on the environmental conditions and height of drop, and ability to land within 150 meters of a designated location by continuously adjusting for wind conditions, these systems are only becoming more accurate with time. The long-distance capability of systems like the GPADS increases safety for the aircrew as well as the airborne forces by keeping a large vertical and horizontal separation and future load delivery would have to be completely based on such devices.

However technological advances cannot be limited to just these and airborne forces need to be totally integrated with the developments in Intelligence, Surveillance and Reconnaissance (ISR) capabilities, countering adversaries air defence and indirect fires to name a few. Airborne forces need to be treated at par to Special Forces in terms of equipment procurement since lack of investment in technology will ensure that airborne forces rapidly lose their inherent ability and edge to combat the growing myriad challenges they would be employed to deal with.

The strategic lift capability of the Air force has improved tremendously over a period of time. However the present capability needs to be further augmented to support the envisaged airborne missions of the future. In addition equipment dropping capabilities of the aircraft and the current equipment being utilised or likely to be bought needs to be factored in while selecting aircrafts to be utilised for the airborne forces. After all the US and Russian planes are built to support the heavy drops of their own military equipment and the same needs to be factored in while selecting strategic lift aircrafts in the future.

Conclusion

The role and efficacy of the employment of airborne forces in today's environment is often a hotly discussed topic. Their employment in conventional conflicts conjures in the mind photographs and movies of World War II which showed streams of aircrafts stretching for hundreds of kilometres going past a point for more than an hour and the havoc wrecked on them by the enemy air force and air defence. Juxtapose that scenario to today's sophisticated air defence system which tracks and engages multiple aircrafts nearly 400 kms away and airborne operations seem a 'No-Go'! The primary arguments against an airborne force stem from the high cost of maintaining them, to the existing threat level against an airborne stream and thus an envisaged high attrition rate. Last but not the least is often the capability or lack of it to lift the complete airborne force and move it for insertion. All these reasons coupled together along with the constantly shrinking budgets due to economic constraints cause the axe in any major reorganisation to fall on airborne forces and thus the constant debate about their usefulness in the future operational environment rages on.

Future conflicts for India would be distinguished by operating in a zone of ambiguity or Grey Zone and will thus be a blend of conventional and unconventional. This hybridity of operations would be prevalent across multiple domains and vary from non-contact to contact warfare. In addition the Indian Armed Forces will have to be prepared to take part in military operations other than war which would include HADR, Internal Security (IS) Duties and Out of Area Contingency tasks, including assistance to friendly foreign countries and assistance in non-combatant evacuation procedures. Therefore it is imperative for the Army to be prepared for the multi-faceted security challenges that lie ahead and airborne forces form a cornerstone in its future response strategy.

Airborne forces are a national asset with airlift capability being available as an *instrument of force and thus power projection*. Airborne forces in the future, in addition to being used in an innovative manner in conventional conflicts, will play a major role in hybrid warfare and our strategy for countering the same. Furthermore the availability of these forces is a deterrent as they demonstrate the force capability to project anywhere in the region/world at a short notice. *India* in the future would *face a multitude of challenges which would require a rapid and decisive response*. The airborne forces can lead the immediate response being an extremely high readiness force capable of easily moving great distances in a very short time frame. They are an invaluable force multiplier for Future Land Warfare.

NOTES

1 Airborne Operations, FM 57-30, Department of Field Manual US Army. Ch 1, Sec 1, para 1a, p. 3.

2 From Benjamin Franklin to Ingenuous, 16 January 1784, National Archives available at https://founders.archives.gov/documents/Franklin/01-41-02-0310, accessed on 17 May 2019.

3 Robert Jackson, "Bailing Out", Pen and Sword Military, South Yorkshire, England, 2006, p. 35.

4 Ibid., p. 37.

5 Ibid., p. 38.

6 Origin of the British Airborne Forces, http://www.pegasusarchive.org/origins1.htm, accessed on 15 May 2019.

7 Leonard Rapport and Arthur Northwood J, ".Rendezvous With Destiny: A History Of the 101st Airborne Division", Pickle Partners Publishing, November 2015, p. 15.

8 Ibid., pp.16–19.
9 Maj Gen Afsir Karim, AVSM (retd), "The Story of the Indian Airborne Troops", Lancer International, New Delhi, 1993, pp. 1–4.
10 Airborne Operations in World War II, https://www.globalsecurity.org/ military/ ops/ airborne1.html , accessed on 14 May 2019.
11 Army Pamphlet No 20-232, "Historical Study: Airborne Operations, A German Appraisal", Department of the Army, Washington 25, D. C, October 1951, p. 17.
12 Airborne Operations in World War II, https://www.globalsecurity.org/ military/ ops/ airborne1.htmtl , accessed on 14 May 2019.
13 Peter D Antill, "Crete 1941: Germany's Lightening Airborne Assault", Osprey Publishing Limited, New York, USA, 2005.
14 Airborne Operations in World War II, https://www.globalsecurity.org/ military/ ops/ airborne1 .htmtl, accessed on 14 May 2019.
15 Antony Beevor, "D-Day: The Battle for Normandy", Viking, New York USA, 2009.
16 Stephen Badsy, "Arnhem 44: Operation Market Garden", Bloomsbury. London, UK, 1993.
17 Matthew J. Seelinger, "Operation VARSITY: The Last Airborne Deployment of World War II", 20 January 2015, https://armyhistory.org/operation-varsity-the-last-airborne-deployment-of-world-war-ii/, accessed on 18 May 2019.
18 "Hitting the Silk – 15 Airborne Operations Carried Out Since World War Two", 25 March 2016, https://militaryhistorynow.com/2016/03/25/hitting-the-silk-15-airborne-operations-carried-out-since-world-war-two/, accessed on 07 May 2019.
19 Fergus Kelly, "Mali: More than 100 French troops parachute into Menaka", 27 September 2018, https://thedefensepost.com/2018/09/27/france-troops-parachute-menaka-mali/, accessed on 17 May 2019.
20 Maj Gen Afsir Karim, AVSM (retd), "The Story of the Indian Airborne Troops", pp. 121–22.
21 Ibid., pp. 184–201.
22 Vishnu Gopinath, "Operation Cactus: The Day India Saved the Maldives", 06 Feb 2018, https://www.the quint.com/news/india/operation-cactus-maldives-crisis-should-india-intervene-again, accessed on 16 May 2019.
23 Maj Gen Afsir Karim, AVSM (retd), "The Story of the Indian Airborne Troops", pp. 202–235.
24 House of Commons Defence Committee, Future Army 2020, Ninth Report of Session 2013–14, p. 21, https://publications.parliament.uk/pa/cm201314/ cmselect/cmdfence /576/576.pdf, accessed on 28 March 2019.
25 National Security Strategy and Strategic Defence and Security Review 2015, pp. 28-29, https://assets.publishing.service.gov.uk/government/uploads/system/ uploads/attachment_data/file/555607/2015_Strategic_Defence_and_ Security_ Review.pdf, accessed on 11 May 2019.
26 "Land Operations", Land Warfare Development Centre, Army Doctrine Publication AC 71940, pp. 7-6, para 7-10(b), https://assets.publishing.service. gov.uk/government/uploads/ system/ uploads/attachment_data/file/605298/ Army_Field_Manual__ AFM__A5_Master_ADP_ Interactive_Gov_Web.pdf, accessed on 14 May 2019.

27 National Security Strategy and Strategic Defence and Security Review 2015, https://assets.publishing.service.gov.uk/government/uploads/system/uploads/attachment_data/file/555607/2015_Strategic_Defence_and_Security_Review.pdf, accessed on 11 May 2019, pp. 28-29.

28 Michael Peck, "Russia's Military Has a Problem: Too Many Paratroopers, Not Enough Transport Planes", 01 October 2018, https://nationalinterest.org/blog/buzz/russias-military-has-problem-too-many-paratroopers-not-enough-transport-planes-32337, accessed on 15 May 2019.

29 Ibid.

30 Michael Kofman, "Rethinking the Structure and Role of Russia's Airborne Forces", CCW Russia Brief, Issue 4, January 2019, https://static1.squarespace.com/static/55faab67e4b09141053471 94/t/5c506ed6032be4e6cda7cb3c/1548775127852/Russia+Brief+4.pdf, accessed on 11 April 2019.

31 John Gordon IV, Agnes Gereben Schaefer, David A. Shlapak, Caroline Baxter, Scott Boston, Michael McGee, Todd Nichols, Elizabeth Tencza, "Enhanced Army Airborne Forces, A New Joint Operational Capability", RAND Corporation, Santa Monica, Calif, pp. 11-12.

32 Ibid., p. XVIII.

33 Todd South, "The Army is upgrading for 'great-power competition,' and it just reactivated an airborne unit that packs an armored punch", dated 30 October 2018, https://www.businessinsider.com/us-army-82nd-airborne-reactivates-armored-vehicle-unit-2018-10?IR=T, accessed on 17 April 2019.

34 Lt Gen Prakash Katoch, "China's Airborne Capability – Honed and Ready" 11 October 2017, http://www.indiandefencereview .com/news/chinas-airborne-capability-honed-and-ready/, Indian Defence Review, accessed on 22 May 2019.

35 Annual Report to Congress: Military and Security Developments Involving the People's Republic of China 2018, 16 May 2018, pp 97,116,123, https://media.defense.gov/2018/Aug/16/2001955282/-1/-1/1/2018-CHINA-MILITARY-POWER-REPORT.PDF, accessed on 24 May 2019.

35 Indian Air Force Transport Aircraft, http://indianairforce.nic.in/content/transport-aircraft, accessed on 28 May 2019.

36 Niti Ayog, "Incredible Islands of India", 10 August 2018, pp. 6, https://niti.gov.in/writereaddata/files/document_publication/IslandsDev.pdf, accessed on 28 May 2019.

37 Ajai Shukla, "New naval base in Andamans boosts military posture in Indian Ocean", dated 26 January 2019, https://www.business-standard.com/article/defence/new-naval-base-in-andamans-boosts-military-posture-in-indian-ocean-119012501573_1.html, accessed on 01 June 2019.

38 Gilberto Villahermosa, "Marine LAVs For the 82nd Airborne Division", 03 November 2018, https://www.counterfactmagazine.com/library/2018/10/10/title-template-rmf77, accessed on 16 May 2019.

39 Guided Precision Aerial Delivery System, https://airborne-sys.com/product/firefly-military-cargo-delivery-parachute/, accessed on 17 May 2019.

10

China Looks through the 'Goldwater-Nichols' Prism: Theatre Commands and its Implications for India

Dr. Amrita Jash

"Once a country's military lags behind, its national security will be fatally threatened. I often read historic materials about modern China, and when I see how lagging behind leaves a country vulnerable to attack, I feel deep pain in my heart!"

– Xi Jinping[1]

ABSTRACT

Under Xi Jinping's dictum of 'building a strong military', China has witnessed the most extensive restructuring of its national defence establishment. Of which, the key military reform has been the transition from the Military Regions to that of adopting a Theatre Command structure. What calls for this transition is the quest to make the People's Liberation Army (PLA) an effective combat force operating under an integrated joint command and control structure. With this restructuring, China has streamlined the command structure with the primary aim to prevent bottlenecks in communication and causing greater centralisation of the military authority. In this perspective, with 'jointness' as the key, the query lies in understanding China's drive towards transformation into a Theatre Command structure. In view of this, the paper seeks to examine three key aspects: First, what prompted China to turn towards "jointness"? Second, what are the key aspects of China's Theatre Command Structure? And third, what are the implications for India?

Xi Jinping and China's Road to Military Reform

In his speech at the 19th National Congress of the Communist Party of China (CPC), held in October 2017, Chinese President Xi Jinping noted that China has "initiated a new stage in strengthening and revitalising the armed forces".[2] Xi categorically stated that:

> *"Historic breakthroughs have been made in reforming national defence and the armed forces: a new military structure has been established with the Central Military Commission exercising overall leadership, the theatre commands responsible for military operations, and the services focusing on developing capabilities. This represents a revolutionary restructuring of the organization and the services of the people's armed forces".*[3]

The above statement by Xi reflects China's resolve to adapt the military for the new era under new conditions by making structural, organisational and other adjustments to China's Armed Forces. With Chinese Dream being the core of national strategy, PLA's core missions are aimed at fulfilling two centenary goals: first, by 2035, PLA's modernisation to be "basically completed" and; second, by the mid-21st century (2050) PLA to be "fully transformed into world-class forces" driven by the logic that "a military is built to fight".[4] However, the foundation to these key objectives was laid in November 2013, at the Third Plenum of the 18th Central Committee of the CPC that called for "deepening national defence and military reform". As the communiqué emphasised on the:

> *"Objective of building a line of strong armies for this Party under new circumstances, [...] build a modern military force system with Chinese characteristics. We must deepen military structural and personnel allocation adjustment and reform, move adjustment and reform of military policies and institutions forward, and promote the integrated and deep development of the military and the people".*[5]

As noted, it was the first time in history a CPC plenary session had adopted "independent" defence and military reforms.[6] Undertaking the "largest scale military reform since the 1950s", the key characteristic has been streamlining PLA's structure and functioning it under the authority of the Central Military Commission[7] to achieve unification of PLA's operational and administrative command under CMC.[8] Of which, one of the key reforms undertaken is the transitioning of the PLA from the seven Military Regions (MRs) to that of five Theatre Commands (TCs) on 1 February 2016[9]—with an objective to execute joint operations with enhanced combat effectiveness. This reform towards improving the 'joint operation command authority under the CMC' also suggested that changes to the four general departments had been imminent[10]—with 15 new agencies consisting of departments, commissions and offices, as noted in Figures 10.1 and 10.2.

The key objective behind creation of the TCs is mainly two-fold: first, to centralise PLA decision-making in the hands of the CMC and second, to build a joint battle system and strengthening joint command structure. Thereby ensuring jointness and integration at all levels. Wherein, the CMC and its subsidiary departments will provide overall management, the theatres will focus on operations, and the services will manage force building (军委管总、战区主战、军种主建).[13] Under this new operational (war fighting) formula, the chain of command runs from the CMC to the TCs down to the units, while the administrative chain runs from the CMC to the service headquarters and then to the units.[14] This distribution of order separates the combat commanding function from the construction and management functions, by putting the focus of joint operational command on the TCs, and making the Services responsible for troop construction and management.[15] This is similar to the US system where the theatre Commanders are integrated and joint.

These benchmarks thereby, point at the continuum of change that the PLA has been witnessing under China's quest to implement the 16th Five-Year Plan (2016-2020) to ensure that the set targets and tasks are fulfilled as scheduled. More importantly, the success of which will pave the path for the formulation of the 14th Five-Year Plan for military development. In this perspective, the chapter seeks to examine the organisational reform of the PLA from the point of building a joint operational structure. In doing so, the chapter examines three key questions: first, what does the PLA seek to achieve under its newly formed 'Theatre Command' framework and why? Second, how does it plan to achieve it?; Third, how does this restructuring impact India?

China's Perception of the Changing Strategic Environment and PLA's Military Thinking

Owing to 'building a strong army and advancing the goal of modernisation of national defence and the military, Xi Jinping in his 19th National Congress speech categorically stated:

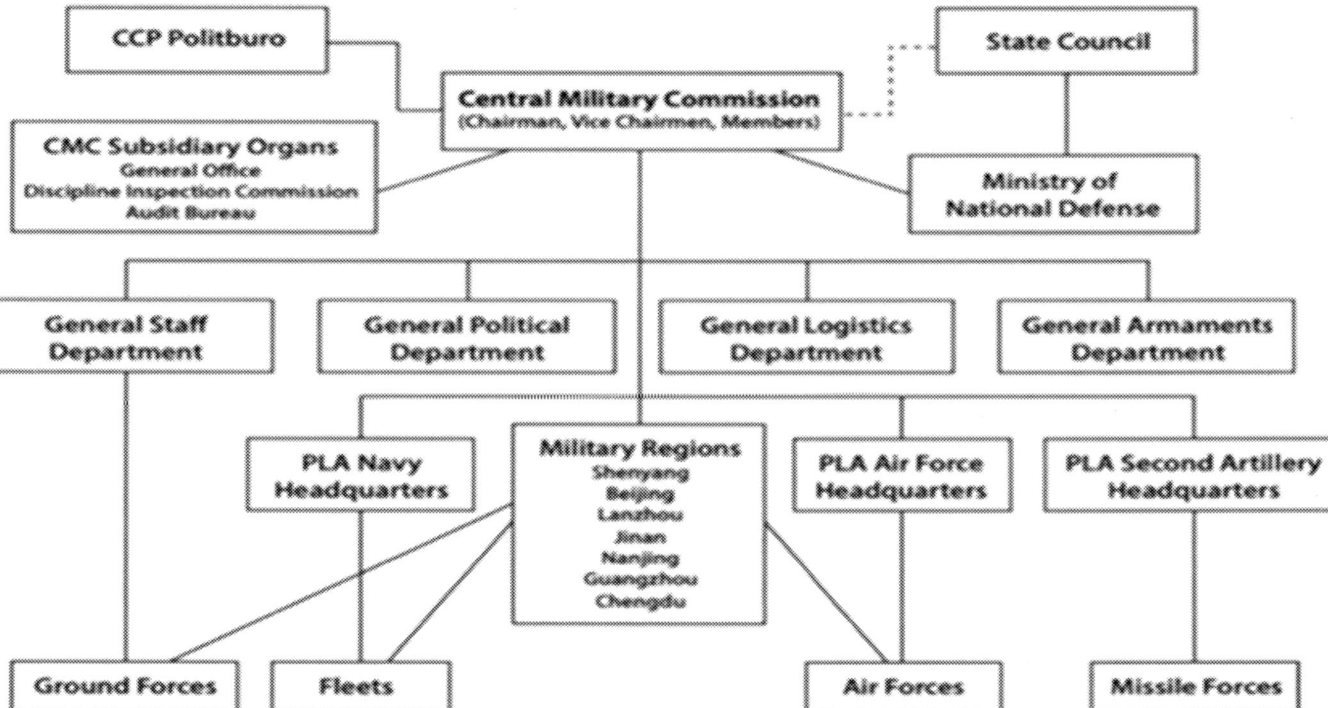

Figure 10.1: PLA Organisational Structure Before Reforms

Source: Adapted from Philip C. Saunders and Joel Wuthnow (2016).[11]

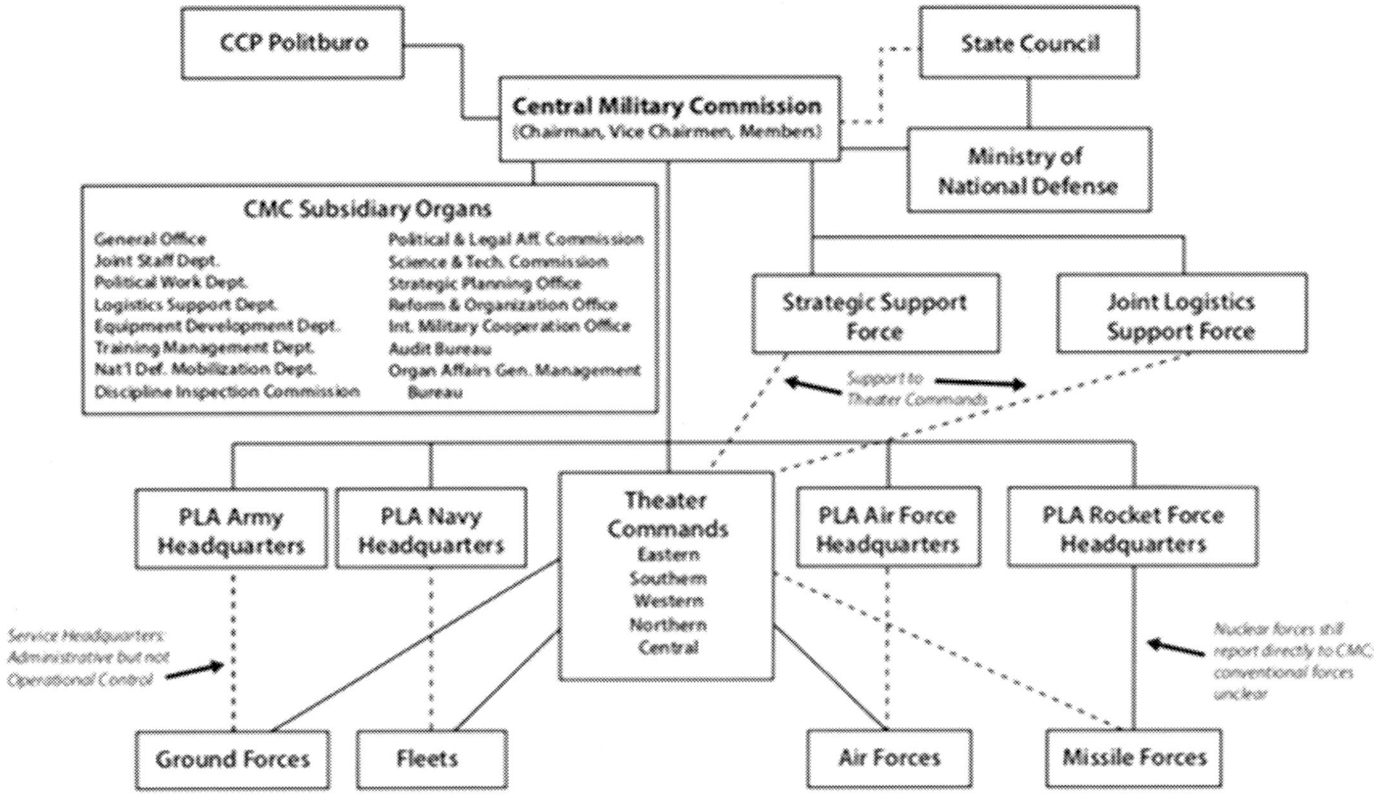

Figure 10.2: The New PLA Organisational Structure After Reforms

Source: Adapted from Philip C. Saunders and Joel Wuthnow (2016).[12]

> *"Confronted with profound changes in our [China's] national security environment and responding to the demands of the day for a strong country with a strong military, we must fully implement the Party's thinking on strengthening the military for the new era and the military strategy for new conditions, build a powerful and modernised army, navy, air force, rocket force, and strategic support force, develop strong and efficient joint operations commanding institutions for theatre commands, and create a modern combat system with distinctive Chinese characteristics".*[16]

Given these changes in the strategic environment, China seeks to build a 'strong PLA' that can 'fight and win'. This quest towards building a 'strong military' is driven by China's perception of its security environment, which in Xi's views is faced with *"Three Trends"* (三个前所未有, *sange qiansuo weiyou)* and *"Three Major Dangers"* (三个危险, *sange weixian*).[17] Wherein, the "Three Trends" exemplify the external environment, the international situation that is constantly changing and new opportunities and challenges that are continually emerging, while the "Three Major Dangers" are that of China being "invaded, toppled and separated".[18]

In this perspective, China's contingencies are mainly three-fold:[19] first, the Taiwan challenge, wherein, PLA's combat readiness seeks to prepare itself for a contingency to unify Taiwan with China by force, while simultaneously "deterring, delaying, or denying" any third-party intervention on Taiwan's behalf.[20] Second, securing sovereignty given imminent contingencies related to the territorial and maritime disputes in the South China Sea, Diaoyu Islands in the East China Sea and the unresolved boundary dispute with India.[21] Finally, domestic security challenges from 'separatist and extremist forces'—East Turkistan independence in Xinjiang and "Tibet independence" forces have become a serious challenge to China's internal security.[22] A new dimension has also been added by the recent mass civilian demonstrations in Hong Kong which is posing a challenge to the Chinese authorities.

What is noteworthy is that although China perceives that in "the foreseeable future, a world war is unlikely, and the international situation is expected to remain generally peaceful", however, China's key challenges stem from concerns of "new threats from hegemonism, power politics and neo-interventionism", whereby "the world still faces both immediate and potential threats of local wars".[23] Adding to China's core security concerns over "Taiwan independence", "East Turkestan independence" and "Tibet independence" as noted above, the 2015 White Paper on *China's Military Strategy* categorically mentions the imminent security challenges to China are posited by: US re-balancing strategy and its military presence and military alliances in Asia; Japan's increasing militarist posture; some offshore neighbours (Vietnam) taking provocative actions and reinforcing their military presence on China's reefs and islands; external countries (India) meddling in South China Sea affairs and constant close-in air and sea surveillance and reconnaissance against China.[24]

In view of this, the scope of PLA's role in protecting China's evolving national security interests are manifold. Being the first ever, 2015 White Paper in clarifying PLA's role in protecting China's evolving national security interests highlighted eight "strategic tasks" or types of missions that the PLA must be ready to execute.[25] They are as follows: (a) to deal with a wide range of emergencies and military threats, and effectively safeguard the sovereignty and security of China's territorial land, air and sea; (b) to resolutely safeguard the unification of the motherland; (c) to safeguard China's security and interests in new domains; (d) to safeguard the security of China's overseas interests; (e) to maintain strategic deterrence and carry out nuclear counterattack; (f) participate in regional and international security cooperation and maintain regional and world peace; (g) to strengthen efforts in operations against infiltration, separatism and terrorism so as to maintain China's political security and social stability; and (h) to perform such tasks as emergency rescue and disaster relief, rights and interests protection, guard duties, and support for national economic and social development.[26] In addition, in recent times, as noted in the 2017 White Paper highlighted the increasing need for PLA is to be able to conduct expeditionary operations and other activities to defend and secure growing Chinese national interests overseas from "destabilising and uncertain factors".[27] That is, making the PLA to become a strong, combat-effective armed force capable of winning regional conflicts by employing integrated, real-time command and control networks.[28] These aspects have been further iterated in the White Paper issued recently in 2019.

In view of the above, to quell the risks of these contingencies, China's quest for military preparedness is driven by a two-fold perspective: first, the core objective is to "win informationised local wars" (信息化條件下的局部戰), which acts as the basic point to call for combat readiness; second, such advanced capabilities are aimed at increasing the PLA's ability to carry out joint operations on a modern high-tech battlefield.[29] The priority lies in modernising the PLA's command, control, communications, computers, information, intelligence, surveillance, and reconnaissance (C4I2SR) system as a response to trends in modern warfare, wherein the emphasis is on "importance of rapid decision-making and information sharing and processing".[30] Thus, with 'integrated joint operations' (一体化联合作战) as the benchmark, the mission of the Chinese military is at the foremost, to deter many types of threats to China's sovereignty and territory, and, if deterrence fails, to win informationised local wars, which is considered to be the most likely form of combat the PLA will face in the future.[31]

In addition, to its core task of preparing to conduct combat operations, the Chinese military doctrine contends that PLA may also be required to perform non-traditional security tasks, known as "military operations other than war" (MOOTW).[32] Thereby, the core objective of China's modernisation, as the 2013 edition of *The Science of Military Strategy*, published by PLA's Academy of Military Science is that China must comprehensively prepare for the "threat of war" and make "preparations to contain ... [or win] war".[33] Wherein, the types of warfare that China is likely to face in the future, as *The Science of Military Strategy* notes are four-fold: (1) a "relatively large-scale high-intensity anti-separatist war" that would centre on Taiwan; (2) a "medium-scale, low to medium-intensity self-defence and counterattack operation" along the periphery that could involve encroachments or threats to PRC maritime claims; (3) a "small-scale, low-intensity anti-terrorist, stability maintenance" operation to protect internal stability and Chinese citizens in China and abroad; and (4) a large-scale ground invasion which is seen to be of remote possibility.[34]

PLA's *'Jointness'* under the command of *"CMC-TC-Troops"* Structure

In this process of reform, on 1 February 2016, China abolished the pre-existing seven military regions (Shenyang, Beijing, Jinan, Nanjing, Guangzhou, Chengdu, and Lanzhou) and replaced it by five newly created Theatre Commands (战区)—Eastern, Southern, Western, Northern and Central Theatres, as outlined in Figure 10.3.

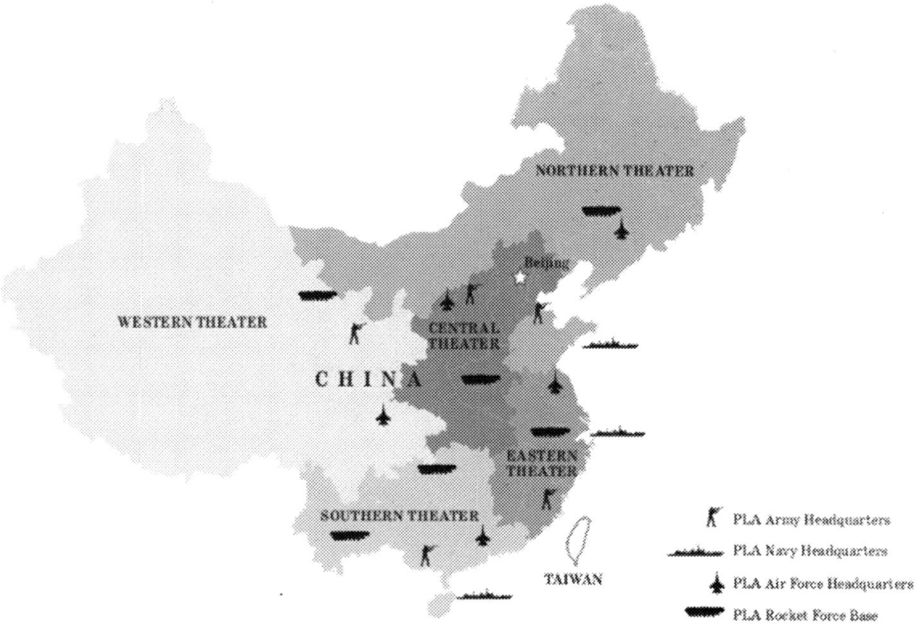

Figure 10.3: China's Theatre Commands

Source: USCC 2018 Annual Report.[35]

This new framework has replaced the pre-existing "CMC-four general departments-military region/branch-troops" four-layer structure with a "CMC-Theatre Commands-troops" three-layer structure in order to strengthen powers of the five TCs.[36] Wherein, the CMC would provide "general management", the TCs would focus on "operations", and the military services would manage "force building".[37] In view of this, against the erstwhile MR, TCs function as a joint operational command, with the ability to quickly shift to commanding status in wartime without setting up a temporary commanding system as that of the MRs. Likewise, as noted, each theatre command has Army and Air Force components and three coastal commands have a Navy component. Unlike the MRs, theatres have subordinate units drawn from the individual services.[38] Further, each TC has key focus areas as outlined in the order of protocol in Table 10.1.

As Table 10.1 suggests, the very distribution of the command structure exemplifies that China's vision of reorganisation is not just guided by

Table 10.1: The Operational Focus and Structure of Theatre Commands

Theatre Command	*Former Military Region*	*Leadership*	*Focus Areas*
Eastern Theatre Command	Nanjing Military Region	Theatre Commander: *Liu Yuejun* Political Commissar: *Zheng Weiping*	• Preventing Taiwan independence • Compelling Taiwan unification • Countering any foreign intervention during a Taiwan conflict • Defending maritime sovereignty claims in the East China Sea
Southern Theatre Command	Guangzhou Military Region	Theatre Commander: *Wang Jiaocheng* Political Commissar: *Wei Liang*	• Defending maritime sovereignty claims and China's sea lines of control in the South China Sea • Defence along the border with Vietnam
Western Theatre Command	Chengdu and Lanzhou Military Regions	Theatre Commander: *Zhao Zongqi* Political Commissar: *Zhu Fuxi*	• Combating domestic extremism and terrorism in Xinjiang Uyghur Autonomous Region and Tibet Autonomous Region • Addressing an Indian border dispute contingency • Guard against infiltration by Central Asian extremist and terrorist groups
Northern Theatre Command	Shenyang Military Region plus Inner Mongolia and Shandong provinces	Theatre Commander: *Song Puxuan* Political Commissar: *Chu Yimin*	• Stabilising the Korean Peninsula and conducting border stability operations associated with a North Korean contingency • May share responsibility for contingencies involving Japan with the Eastern theatre • Likely be responsible for northern border contingencies involving Mongolia and Russia
Central Theatre Command	Beijing and Jinan Military Regions	Theatre Commander: *Han Weiguo* Political Commissar: *Yin Fanglong*	• Conducting capital defence operations during any contingency involving another theatre's area of responsibility • Responsible for responding to domestic emergencies

Source: Prepared by the Author with reference to USCC 2016 Annual Report[39] and Ministry of National Defence of the PRC.[40]

geography but most importantly, the threats and challenges it encounters in each quarter, both internal and external.[41] This is also witnessed in China's capabilities in the TCs.

In Chinese perspective, "integrated joint operations" (一体化联合作战) is the key concept that forms the foundation of PLA's thinking on joint operations.[42] Wherein, the PLA textbook *Science of Campaigns* defines *integrated joint operations* as "using integrated methods and information technology, blending an operational system from all services and arms and other types of armed strengths with operational units to form an integrated whole".[43] In doing so, the ultimate objective is to seize control of the "three superiorities" (information, air and sea superiority), controlling the battlefield, and destroying the enemy's operational system.[44] PLA's evolving framework for integrated joint operations is the key driving force behind two key concepts: non-contact warfare (非接触作战) and target-centric warfare (标中心战)[45]—driven by "the guiding ideology of comprehensive supremacy, precision strike, and destruction of systems". The other key ideas that drive PLA's modernisation objectives are: "informatisation" (信息化) and "system-of-systems operations" (体系作战).[46]

Owing to this conceptual framework of seeking jointness, Xi has called for building a "joint battle command system with Chinese characteristics" —a system that is "absolutely loyal, resourceful in fighting, efficient in commanding and courageous and capable of winning wars" and be "efficient and active in both peace and war".[47] Such military primacy lies in enhancing the training of joint operations and command in order to win the initiative in future wars, more specifically, to "meet the needs of fighting and winning an informationised war".[48] This refers to the evolving nature of modern warfare featuring greater emphasis on cyber and space operations, and on long-range precision-strike systems, which would need China to improve its ability to conduct high-end joint operations in multiple domains, including by establishing a permanent joint command and control (C2) mechanism.[49] To note, in the aftermath of US operations in former Yugoslavia, PLA's training for future wars was based on the notion of "three attacks, three defences" (三打三防), which called for attacking with precision-guided munitions, cruise missiles, and attack helicopters while defending against electronic warfare, stealth aircraft, and ISR.[50]

Role of the Theatre Commands: Be Combat Ready to undertake 'Strategic Tasks'

What calls for China's such a combat ready attitude is growing concerns over the People's Liberation Army's (PLA) "peace disease" and the lack of ability to fight and win a modern campaign. Highlighting this issue, *People's Liberation Army Daily* in an editorial stated: "Peace disease has been a common symptom in our military for decades" [...] "If we do not make up our mind to eliminate those evils, we must pay a heavy cost in the event of a war" and that "we can only stop a war if we are able to fight".[51] This very statement reflects China's current dilemma. What caused this 'peace disease' is China's long-standing inexperience in war-fighting given the last war it fought was in 1979 against Vietnam.[52] This 'gap' therefore, has necessitated the need for the PLA to become combat ready to fight modern warfare. Calling this shortcoming as PLA's "Five Incapables", Xi identifies it as: the inability of some PLA leaders to effectively judge the military situation and understand their orders, make operational decisions, direct troops in combat, and handle unforeseen battlefield developments.[53]

Accordingly, China has upscaled its training to prepare PLA troops for future, as witnessed in the activities in the Zhurihe Combined Tactics Training Base in Inner Mongolia—PLA's largest and most advanced training base that involves two units—red and blue units.[54] Wherein, the red unit is comprised of PLA troops from different regions, while the blue force is called the 195th Mechanised Infantry Brigade is China's first professional simulation opposition force brigade, which came into being in 2014.[55] Adapting it to PLA's new command structure, in July 2016, at Zhurihe, troops from the five TCs conducted a large-scale drill with an aim to boost their "trans-regional" capabilities—exemplifying the combat mission of the TCs.[56]

The rationale behind making itself combat ready is that China's growing military muscle does not guarantee it an absolute win unless it trains itself in combat readiness, thus, making the stakes higher than ever. More importantly, this restructuring towards 'jointness' further clarifies China's significant departure from Deng Xiaoping's dictum of "Keeping a low profile". For the theatre commands exemplify China's confidence and military preparedness towards fighting future wars. It is pertinent to note that currently all the theatre commanders are from the Army and for these aspects to be translated to ground the Navy and Air Force have to be given their appropriate share.

Western Theatre Command and Tibet Military Command: Implications for India

Out of the five TCs, the Western Theatre Command (WTC) is the most expansive. Its jurisdiction includes Sichuan, Tibet, Gansu, Ningxia, Qinghai, Xinjiang and Chongqing. It is mainly responsible for maintaining security along China's border with India supporting the People's Armed Police Force (PAPF) to maintain domestic stability in Tibet and Xinjiang.

In view of this, WTC holds direct implications for India given the unresolved boundary problem. For India-China relations in the twenty-first century is still weighed down by the fixed contours of the protracted border issue which resulted from the 1962 war. The testimony to it lies in the 2017 Doklam stand-off, a territorial stint of China reciprocated by India's strong resistance, which resulted into a 73 days stand-off between New Delhi and Beijing. It remains indisputable that the Doklam crisis hit India-China relations to the lowest ever since the 1962 war adding new dimension to the protracted boundary conflict.

What makes it different? The past episodes of Chinese incursions/ transgressions witnessed in areas such as Daulat Beg Oldie, Depsang, Chumar, Trig Heights, Pangong Tso Lake and others in the western sector, to that of Asaphila, Samdurongchu, Changtze and others in Arunachal Pradesh did not result in any kind of military activity between India and China. However, with Doklam, the existing status-quo at the border took a significant departure thereby, further extending the scope of India-China boundary dispute. It was first time ever that India and China got involved in a military stand-off in a terrain that falls beyond their disputed boundary and also involved a third party—Bhutan.

The agreed peace between the two governments resulted into a thaw. As on August 2017, Indian Ministry of External Affairs issued a statement that "expeditious disengagement of border personnel at the face-off site at Doklam has been agreed to and is ongoing".[57] To which, Beijing responded by stating that it "will continue to exercise its sovereign rights and preserve its territorial sovereignty in accordance with historical border agreements".[58] This suggests that a temporary thaw does not call for a permanent peace at the border between India and China. To argue so as Doklam stand-off acted as a test case that saw both New Delhi and Beijing test each other's resolve—calling for a new pattern in securing their respective territorial claims. Wherein, war seems to be outlawed but such episodes might become a routine phenomenon. This makes it imperative to understand the dispute and the contingencies involved.[59] Wherein, the contingency lies in the possibility of mountain warfare in the future between India and China.

What makes it so? The undemarcated border acts as a potent point of friction between India and China. This is further justified by three key factors: first, the 21 rounds of border talks have failed to reach a resolution; second, the increasing instability as witnessed in episodes of friction in areas such as Daulat Beg Oldi, Trig Heights, Pangong Tso Lake, Chumar, Demchok, Samarlungpa in the western sector and, in Arunachal Pradesh at Asaphila, Migyitun, Samdurongchu, Changtze and Fish Tails; and third, the increasing military build-up by the two countries along the border has resulted into a heightened security dilemma. Adding to these complexities, the Doklam stand-off has further raised the risks of escalation of an unwarranted confrontation between the two countries.

Given this contingency, the WTC becomes important for India given it is responsible for warfare at the border area with India. Wherein, the Tibet Military Command (TMC), which is part of the WTC and looks after the security along China's border with India, holds special relevance to India. Specially, in the aftermath of elevations of TMC's status, the strategic implications are more significant. That is, in May 2018, TMC was elevated to a level higher with respect to other provincial military commands,[60] as was raised up in authority by placing it under the direct jurisdiction of PLA ground forces. While the other 28 provincial military commands were put under the control of the newly established National Defense Mobilisation Department.[61] The other exceptions being the Beijing Weifang District,[62] and the Xinjiang Military Command, which unlike TMC are yet not under the jurisdiction of the PLA Army.

This reform signifies two important implications:[63] first, the amalgamation of the provincial military commands under one Department has diminished their importance. And second, most importantly, the elevation of TMC's political rank and bringing it under the PLA Army clarifies its exceptional status as well as its greater role in PLA's joint operations to conduct combat missions.[64] In this regard, the operational structure of TMC within the Command and Control framework of CMC can be understood from Figure 10.4.

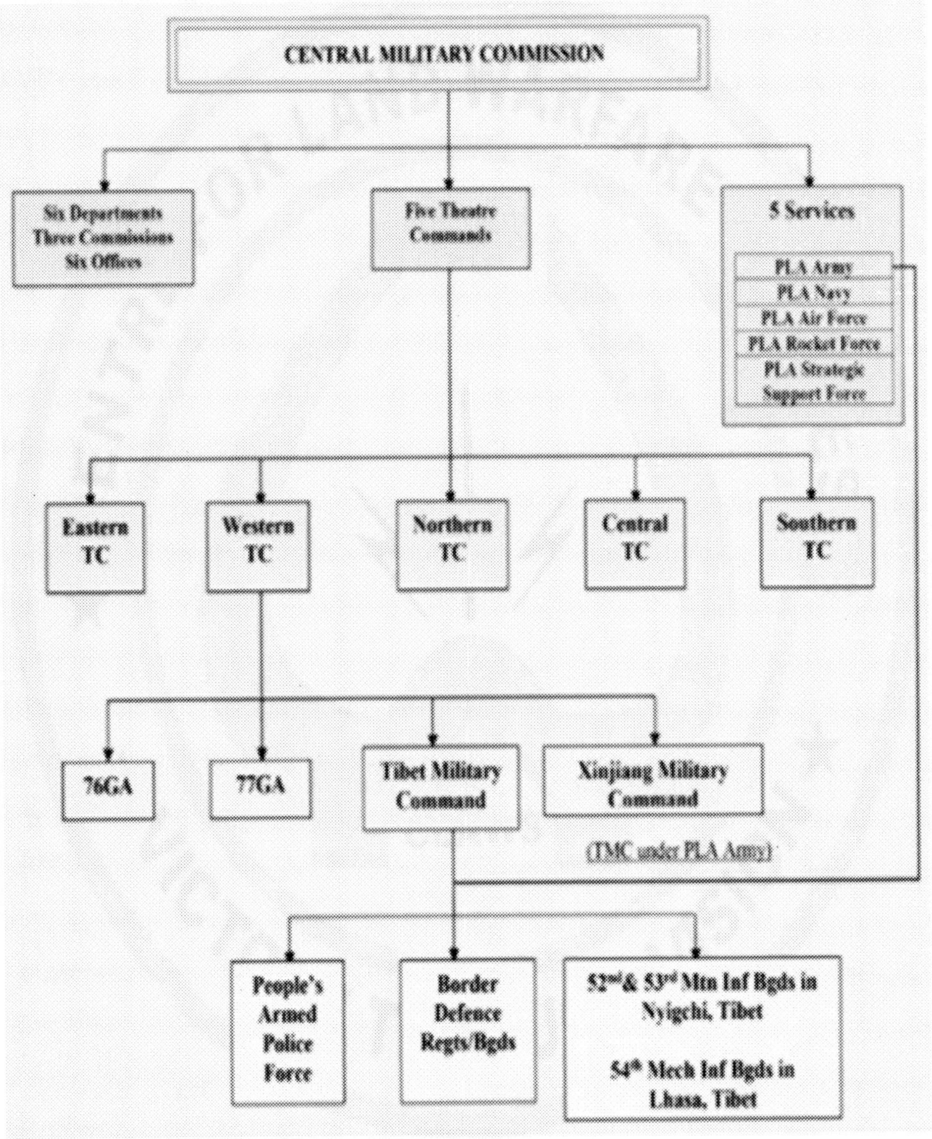

Figure 10.4: Structure of Tibet Military Command within the C2 structure of the CMC

Source: Adapted from Amrita Jash (2019).[65]

Besides the elevated political status of TMC, China has also revamped its military activities that exemplify its core concentration on combat missions. This can be assessed from the key developments in terms of new military equipment deployment, infrastructure build up and military activities taking place in Tibet that significantly contribute to the enhancement of the combat capability of the TMC.

This includes the following:[66] First, in December 2018, a new "Type 15 lightweight Tank" has been commissioned by PLA Ground Forces.[67] What makes it significant in China's combat missions are its three key features:[68] It is pertinent to note that unlike PLA's other main battle tanks such as Type 99 and Type 96, Type 15 is significantly lighter with about 32 to 35 tonnes weight. Next, in terms of firepower, Type 15 uses a new 105 mm tank gun, which is superior to Type 88a tank and Type 59D tank. It is equipped with Type 94, 105-mm tank gun capable of firing armour-piercing rounds and gun launched missiles. Finally, the Type 15 tank is mainly meant for rugged and mountainous terrain of the Himalayan region[69] as believed it can "outperform" other Chinese tanks in combat operations in plateau areas like Tibet and can be quickly deployed in Tibet "if border dispute reoccurs".[70] This implies the significance of Type 15 to operate in the high-altitude combat missions in Tibet, in case of any possible outbreak between India and China.

Secondly, in January 2019, the PLA Ground Forces in TMC has been equipped with new vehicle-mounted howitzers, which as Chinese analysts speculate to be the "PLC-181 vehicle mounted howitzer".[71] The howitzer has a 52-caliber cannon with a range of over 50 kms and shoots laser-guided and satellite-guided projectiles, Further, it is reported that it will significantly "boost the high-altitude combat capability of the PLA in Tibet".[72] It is pertinent to note, the howitzer was used in an artillery brigade in Tibet during the 2017 Doklam stand-off between China and India.[73] In addition, China has also unveiled a 10-tonne Z-20 medium lift helicopter to be deployed in the Tibetan Plateau and the mountains in Qinghai, where it will have to operate 4,000 meters above ground.[74]

Thirdly, China has also stepped up its infrastructure build up in Tibet as witnessed in terms of upgraded roads, railways and air bases.[75] To note, there are 14 airbases in the Lanzhou and Chengdu regions with key bases in Hoping, Bangda, Shiquanhe, Bayixincun and Kongka; and two airfields in Lhasa and an additional four are soon to be operational.[76] While China has constructed 96,000 km of roads in Tibet by 2018, with over 4,000 km of highways added a year since 2012,[77] which include the 409-kilometre Lhasa-Nyingchi Highway (north of Arunachal Pradesh) commissioned in 2017 and a 135 km Yaán-Kangding expressway, making it the second expressway from Sichuan to connect to Tibet after the

National Highway 318 which links up with Lhasa.[78] In addition, apart from the Gormud to Lhasa railway line commissioned in 2006, China also began construction of the 435 km Lhasa-Nyingchi railway line, to be completed by 2021. Further in 2019, China plans to launch a 1,700 km Sichuan-Tibet railway connecting through areas bordering Arunachal Pradesh which is likely to be completed by 2026.[79]

It is of interest to note that PLA is active in undertaking drills in WTC as witnessed in the 2017 armoured brigade military drill in Tibet. This was undertaken at 5,100 metres above sea level for the first time and included the PLA's most advanced battle tank, the Type 96B—aimed at testing "full combat readiness".[80] In 2018, PLA conducted a military drill in the Tibet Autonomous Region to test their logistics and armament support capabilities and most importantly, to test military-civil integration.[81] It was the first logistics exercise in the region since the Doklam stand-off and as reported was aimed to "realise the country's goal of building a strong military in the new era".[82] Besides, China has also cited the need to strengthen the control of airspace over the mountainous region. Calling it an urgent need to deal with any current threat from India, China has been strengthening the 3.5-generation fighter jets or even stationing more advanced fighters in the WTC and as reported will continue to do so.[83]

PLA's such military preparedness in the WTC is driven by Xi Jinping's core objective that calls for: the armed forces' ability to respond quickly and effectively to contingencies, asking them to upgrade capability of joint operations, foster new combat forces, and improve military training under operational conditions.[84] These developments thereby, clearly reflect China's intention as well as increasing ability to effectively intervene in any sector in the Himalayas, thus raising significant security concerns for India. This further makes it imperative for India to revise its own combat effectiveness against China.

Conclusion

Given the increasing uncertainty of the strategic environment, PLA's intentions lie in acting responsive rather than reactive. Military preparedness aims at responding to situations in a multiple domain sphere. In this perspective, the establishment of Theatre Commands by China is an important step forward in actualising its goal to fight a contingency at multiple and critical domains. Most importantly, the theatre commands provide traction to China's quest for 'jointness' to undertake strategic missions both inside and outside China. The key objective is to execute combat operations to fight and win in order to secure its expanding national interest given the importance of integrating operational and support activities across multiple theatres in future conflicts. Since the TC structure is still at its nascent stage, the challenge for China's armed forces remains in terms of training the personnel's at all levels to achieve the optimum coordination with the new structure in order to undertake integrated joint operations. To fill this gap, China has upscaled the combat training activities as well as frequent upgradation of its equipment to fight future wars. However, shortcomings still remain in terms of integration and planning, which act as the nodal factor to achieve success. It is important to note that China's military preparedness under its Theatre Command structure does reflect its sincerity towards building a joint war fighting mechanism. However, since it is still at its evolutionary phase, it will be too soon to reach any conclusion on how it qualifies for PLA's effectiveness in fighting future warfare.

Despite the shortcomings, the TC structure does hold significant relevance, especially for India given the unresolved territorial dispute. With the heightened security dilemma and the rising political and economic clout of both India and China, a compromising attitude is incorrect, thus, leaving less room for settlement of the boundary issue. With such an uncertainty attached, the possibility of a future military conflict cannot be completely ruled out. Moreover, with TMC's expanding role within the WTC and its elevated status further adds to the propensity. For rather than undertaking a limited role under the National Defense Mobilisation Department, TMC's role is much pronounced in terms of undertaking joint operations. Wherein, the future possibilities entail undertaking combat missions and cross-regional operations calling for a significant concern for India. More specifically, in their territorial quest, the Himalayan border between India and China is possibly, the only area where a high-altitude war can take place in future. Accordingly it is necessary for India to expertise its own command and control structure to quell an unwarranted Chinese misadventure.

NOTES

1 Quoted in Xinhuanet, "Building a strong army through reform," March 16, 2016, http://www.xinhuanet.com//mil/2016-03/16/c_128804009.htm, accessed on May 02, 2019.

2 Xi Jinping (2017), "Secure a Decisive Victory in Building a Moderately Prosperous Society in All Respects and Strive for the Great Success of Socialism with Chinese Characteristics for a New Era," Delivered at the 19th National Congress of the Communist Party of China, October 18, 2017, p. 5, http://www.xinhuanet.com/english/download/Xi_Jinping's_report_at_19th_CPC_National_Congress.pdf, accessed on April 02, 2019.

3 Ibid.

4 Xi, n. 2, p. 48.

5 "Communiqué of the Third Plenary Session of the 18th Central Committee of the Communist Party of China," China.org.cn, January 15, 2014, http://www.china.org.cn/china/third_plenary_session/2014-01/15/content_31203056.htm, accessed on May 04, 2019.

6 Xinhuanet, n. 1.

7 Xi, n. 2, p. 48.

8 You Ji, "Xi Jinping and PLA Transformation through Reforms," RSIS Working Paper No. 313, May 21, 2018, p. 2, https://www.rsis.edu.sg/wp-content/uploads/2018/05/WP313.pdf, accessed on May 05, 2019.

9 Zhang Tao, "Army adjustment and establishment completed in five Theater Commands," China Military Online, February 04, 2016, http://english.chinamil.com.cn/news-channels/china-military-news/2016-02/04/content_6890499.htm, accessed on May 05, 2019.

10 The other reforms entailed: First, the four semi-autonomous general departments (responsible for operations, political work, logistics, and armaments/equipment) were disbanded and replaced by 15 functional departments, commissions, and offices within the CMC. Second, separate national- and theater-level ground force headquarters were established for the first time. Previously, the general departments served primarily as PLA army headquarters and only secondarily as a joint headquarters, while the seven MRs were overwhelmingly focused on ground force affairs. Third, both a Strategic Support Force (SSF)—responsible for consolidating operations in the information domain, including space, cyber, and electronic warfare and a Joint Logistics Support Force (JLSF) were created. And fourth, the responsibilities of key PLA components were adjusted so that TCs would concentrate on combat preparations and the service headquarters, which had previously led peacetime operations, would focus on what in the U.S. military are called "organize, train, and equip" missions. See, Joel Wuthnow and Phillip C. Saunders, "Chinese Military Reforms in the Age of Xi Jinping: Drivers, Challenges, and Implications," China Strategic Perspectives 10, March 2017, pp. 4-5, https://ndupress.ndu.edu/Portals/68/Documents/stratperspective/china/ChinaPerspectives-10.pdf?ver=2017-03-21-152018-430, accessed on May 05, 2019.

11 Phillip C. Saunders and Joel Wuthnow, "China's Goldwater-Nichols? Assessing PLA Organizational Reforms," Strategic Forum: National Defense University, April 2016, p. 2, https://inss.ndu.edu/Portals/68/Documents/stratforum/SF-294.pdf, accessed on May 26, 2019.

12 Ibid., p. 3.

13 Ibid., p. 3.

14 Blasko, n. 7, p. 688.
15 Zhang, n. 14.
16 Xi, n. 2, pp. 47-48.
17 Sun Jianguo, "Upholding the Chinese Approach to National Security", China Institute of International Studies, June 11, 2015, http://www.ciis.org.cn/english/2015-06/11/content_7983173.htm, accessed on May 26, 2019.
18 Ibid.
19 Amrita Jash, "Xi Jinping's World-Class Military: Not Only Fights, But Also Wins Wars," Indian Defence Review, Jan-Mar 2019, Vol. 34, Issue. 1, pp. 48-49.
20 Office of the Secretary of Defense, "Annual Report to Congress: Military and Security Developments involving the People's Republic of China 2018," May 16, 2018, p. 10, https://media.defense.gov/2018/Aug/16/2001955282/-1/-1/1/2018-CHINA-MILITARY-POWER-REPORT.PDF, accessed on May 27, 2019.
21 Jash, n. 25.
22 Ibid.
23 The State Council of the People's Republic of China, "China's Military Strategy", May 27, 2015, http://english.gov.cn/archive/white_paper/2015/05/27/content_281475115610833.htm, accessed on April 20, 2019.
24 Ibid.
25 The State Council of the People's Republic of China, n. 29.
26 Ibid.
27 Office of the Secretary of Defense, n. 26, p. 7.
28 Ibid.
29 Jash, n. 25, p. 48.
30 Defense Intelligence Agency, "China Military Power: Modernizing a Force to Fight and Win," 2019, https://www.dia.mil/Portals/27/Documents/News/Military%20Power%20Publications/China_Military_ Power_ FINAL_ 5MB_20190103.pdf, accessed on June 07, 2019.
31 Blasko, n. 7, p. 687.
32 Ibid.
33 2018 Report to Congress of the U.S.-China Economic and Security Review Commission (Washington: U.S. Government Publishing Office, 2018), p. 210. Available on the internet at https://insidecybersecurity.com/sites/insidecybersecurity.com/files/documents/2018/nov/cs2018_0480.pdf, accessed on June 3, 2019.
34 Cited in Mark R. Cozad, Chinese Contingency Planning for Regional Hotspot, (Santa Monica, CA: RAND Corporation, 2017), p. 10.
35 2018 Report to Congress, n. 41, p. 216.
36 Yasuyuki Suigura, "The Joint Operation Structure of the Chinese People's Liberation Army with Focus on the Reorganization of the Chain of Command and Control under the Xi Jinping Administration," NIDS Journal of Defence and Security, Vol. 18, p. 17.
37 Ibid. p. 16.
38 Saunders and Joel Wuthnow, n. 16, p. 3.
39 2016 Report to Congress of the U.S.-China Economic and Security Review Commission (Washington: U.S. Government Publishing Office, 2016), p. 206.

Available on the internet at https://www.uscc.gov/sites/default/files/annual_reports/2016%20Annual%20Report%20to%20Congress.pdf, accessed on June 4, 2019.

40 Ministry of National Defense of the People's Republic of China, "Theater Commands," http://eng.mod.gov.cn/theater-commands/index.htm, accessed on June 4, 2019.

41 Amrita Jash, "Tibet Military Command: People's Liberation Army's Combat Role in High-Altitude," Issue Brief, No. 181, May 2019, Centre for Land Warfare Studies, p. 2.

42 Edmund J. Burke et al., Assessing the Training and Operational Proficiency of China's Aerospace Forces: Selections from the Inaugural Conference of the China Aerospace Studies Institute (CASI) (Santa Monica, CA: RAND Corporation, 2016), p. 37.

43 Ibid.

44 Ibid.

45 Ibid., pp. 36-37.

46 Ibid., p. 37.

47 2016 Report to Congress, n. 51.

48 Ibid.

49 Saunders and Joel Wuthnow, n. 16, p. 7.

50 Burke et al., n. 57, p. 35.

51 Ibid.

52 Till now, China has fought only on four episodes: in 1950-53 against US and UN forces in the Korean War, in 1962 against India, in 1969 against Soviet Union and in 1979 against Vietnam.

53 2018 Report to Congress, n. 41, p. 209.

54 Amrita Jash, "Can't be Called a 'Paper Tiger', China Gears its 'Combat Readiness'," CLAWS Focus, No. 1957, Centre for Land Warfare Studies, December 19, 2018, http://www.claws.in/1957/can%E2%80%99t-be-called-a-%E2%80%98paper-tiger%E2%80%99-china-gears-its-%E2%80%98combat-readiness%E2%80%99-dr-amrita-jash.html, accessed on June 4, 2019.

55 Ibid.

56 Yao Jianing, "Chinese army begins large-scale drill," China Military Online, July 16, 2016, http://eng.chinamil.com.cn/view/2016-07/16/content_7176139.htm, accessed on June 05, 2019.

57 Ministry of External Affairs, Government of India, "Press Statement on Doklam disengagement understanding," August 28, 2017, https://mea.gov.in/press-releases.htm?dtl/28893/Press_Statement_on_Doklam_disengagement_understanding, accessed on June 10, 2019.

58 Quoted by Sanjeev Miglani and Ben Blanchard, "India and China agree to end border standoff," Reuters, August 28, 2017, https://www.reuters.com/article/us-india-china/india-and-china-agree-to-end-border-standoff-idUSKCN1B80II, accessed on June 10, 2019.

59 The 4,050 kilometer boundary shared between India and China is divided in three sectors: western sector, middle sector and eastern sector. Out of the three, the clash of territorial claims lie at mainly two sectors: first, the western sector, which involves Aksai China, the northeastern section of Ladakh second, the

eastern sector which lies in Arunachal Pradesh. While the middle sector that runs along the watershed of Ladakh to Nepal where Indian states of Himachal Pradesh and Uttarakhand touch base with Tibet—remains comparatively free of tension.

60 The provincial military region/command is a military-level organisation set up by the PLA in all provinces, autonomous regions and municipalities directly under the Central Government. It leads a number of military divisions and a certain number of troops and is responsible for the military work in the province where the military is located. The main tasks are to lead reserve forces, militia, military service and mobilization. Earlier to the 2016 military reform, provinces had been led by the seven military regions.

61 National Defense Mobilisation Department looks at conscription, military sources for military forces, and guidance reserve forces such as militia and reserve forces.

62 The Beijing Weifang district is assigned to the Central Theatre Command. It is under the dual leadership of the former Beijing Military Region and the Beijing Municipal Party Committee and Government. Its main task is to be responsible for military security, garrison duty, anti-terrorism and stability in the Beijing area, carry out militia, military service and mobilisation work, maintain the military discipline of the capital, and assist local maintenance of public security.

63 Jash, n. 53, p. 4.

64 Ibid.

65 Ibid. p. 3.

66 Ibid. p. 4-5.

67 Yang Yi, "China's type 15 lightweight tank commissioned," Xinhuanet, December 27, 2018, http://www.xinhuanet.com/english/2018-12/27/c_137702935.htm, accessed on June 11, 2019.

68 Jash, n. 53, p. 4.

69 Ibid.

70 Ibid.

71 Chen Zhuo, "Mobile howitzers help Tibet border defense," China Military Online, 08 January 08, 2019, http://english.chinamil.com.cn/view/2019-01/08/content_9398635.htm, accessed on June 11, 2019.

72 Ibid.

73 Liu Caiyu and Ji Yuqiao, "Mobile howitzers help Tibet border defense," Global Times, January 07, 2019, http://www.globaltimes.cn/content/1134945.shtmln, accessed on June 11, 2019.

74 Jash, n. 53, p. 5.

75 Ibid.

76 Ibid.

77 Srikanth Kondapalli (2019), "Is India ready? China steps up military build-up in Tibet as America passes law of Reciprocal Access", *Financial Express*, 14 January 2019, URL: https://www.financialexpress.com/defence/is-india-ready-china-steps-up-military-build-up-in-tibet-as-america-passes-law-of-reciprocal-access/1443394/ (Accessed on 08 March 2019).

78 Ibid.

79 Jash, n. 53, p. 5.

80 "PLA armoured brigade holds 'high altitude drill' in Tibet with most advanced tank," Tibet Environmental Watch, July 21, 2017, http://tew.org/pla-armoured-brigade-holds-high-altitude-drill-in-tibet-with-most-advanced-tank/, accessed on June 11, 2019.

81 Yao Jianing, "PLA holds high-altitude drill on plateau in Tibet," China Military Online, June 29, 2018, http://eng.chinamil.com.cn/view/2018-06/29/content_8074859.htm, accessed on June 11, 2019.

82 Ibid.

83 "Citing threat from India, China Stations 3.5 Gen Fighter Jets in Tibet," Tibetan Review, February 21, 2018, http://www.tibetanreview.net/citing-threat-from-india-china-stations-3-5-gen-fighter-jets-in-tibet/, accessed on June 11, 2019.

84 Chengcheng, "Xi orders armed forces to enhance combat readiness", Xinhuanet, January 04, 2019, http://www.xinhuanet.com/english/2019-01/04/c_137720169.htm, accessed on June 11, 2019.

11

Need to Revamp the Indian Armed Forces for the Future

Lieutenant General (Dr.) Rakesh Sharma

"Victory smiles upon those who anticipate the changes in the character of war, not upon those who wait to adapt themselves after the changes occur."

– **Giulio Douhet**

ABSTRACT

The world of warfare is changing rapidly, and it can be predicted with confidence that futuristic operational environment will be more contested, more lethal, and more complex. Future portends that asymmetric battlefield tactics will cumulate with conventional warfare, which includes cyber, social, economic, and psychological strategies that may not necessarily involve physical combat or destruction–and armed forces direct involvement. The accelerating speed of technological development is profoundly changing the nature and character of warfare. In the Indian context, future of land warfare seeks readiness to face a focused threat posed by military forces below or above the threshold of open warfare and nonmilitary means across the full range of the threat spectrum. There are momentous changes afoot in the realms of warfare. Warfare will always have a future; the all-important question is the typology that it would follow. Wars in the future may be without extreme violence, aggression, destruction, and mortality, and yet cause enough suffering to achieve political success.

The Indian Armed Forces need major innovations in military technology—as a driver of newer concepts in military doctrine and strategy, refashioning organisational structures and re-envisage human resource policies. An overhaul in the Indian Armed Forces is an inevitability, better still before the next war.

SETTING THE STAGE

Chanakya many centuries ago had argued to 'prepare for war', not for 'deterrence', to win wars. The last six centuries have witnessed extensive transformation in warfare. Of these the last 150 years, have been most profound, sequentially with mechanisation, communications and data processing influencing every noteworthy aspect of warfare. If the internal combustion engine transformed transportation making journeys that took weeks or months, later took days or hours, it had obvious effects on warfare. Swords, muskets, machine guns, artillery, tanks, airplanes, and rockets have all had their day on the evolution chain of weaponry. How did the art and science of warfare advance since the Berlin Wall came down in 1989? Certainly, US-led forces won swift and, for Americans and their allies, all but bloodless victories over Iraq in 1991 and 2003, Yugoslavia in 1999 and Taliban in Afghanistan in 2001. In 2003, in contrast, precision guidance assisted as much as 70 per cent of the aerial firepower directed against Iraqi forces and other targets. However, in each of those cases the opponent as a regular military opponent was very feeble and it was easy to subjugate the enemy. It has been argued that the strategic narrative of the post-Cold War period, to the present day and well beyond, is a process of transition from Industrial Age Warfare to a new chapter shaped and driven by the technologies of the Information Age.

Warfare is not what it used to be. The world of warfare is changing rapidly, and it can be predicted with confidence that futuristic operational environment will be more contested, more lethal, and more complex. Asymmetric battlefield tactics cumulate with conventional warfare, which includes cyber, social, economic, and psychological strategies that may not necessarily involve physical combat or destruction–and armed forces direct involvement. Rapid military modernisation in the neighbourhood, proliferation of advance capabilities, including long range precision vectors, Information Warfare and use of Artificial Intelligence all necessitate an armed forces overhaul.

What will be the consequences of this military transformation and as future is envisaged? Conventional warfare had continued to exhibit a strong defensive bias based upon firepower, with the propensity to entrench and go underground, especially in Indian concept of war fighting. In the plains and the deserts mechanised offensive operations based on strike and pivot corps take prominence cumulated with the defensive bias. Wars of attrition are to bleed the enemy to surrender. Such wars of attrition are getting scarce, as are mass armies and massed operations are becoming obsolete, along with the concept of total war. Obviously, interstate wars with the kind of mobilisation of 1939–45, or even in 1991 Iraq War are passé.

By definition, if wars are broadly armed, violent hostilities between states, governments and insurgents, then by implication wars entail some degree of confrontation using weapons and other military technology by armed forces employing military tactics and operational art within a broad military strategy. War has a general characterisation of extreme violence, aggression, destruction, and mortality. Carl von Clausewitz on the study of war and warfare had opined that it *"is meant to educate the mind of the future commander, or, more accurately, to guide him in his self-education, not to accompany him to the battlefield; just as a wise teacher guides and stimulates a young man's intellectual development, but is careful not to lead him by the hand for the rest of his life."*

The saying goes that best teacher of war, is war! The Indian context is not different. The organisation by its emphasis on Blitzkrieg and excessive reliance on linear defences may remain underprepared for the next war. The failure to acknowledge the uncertain future and security environment may indeed lead to excessive reliance on the warmth of status quo or even misguided innovations. Accordingly, an overhaul in the Indian Armed Forces is an inevitability, better still before the next war. The accelerating speed of technological development is profoundly changing nature and character of warfare. The Indian Armed Forces need major innovations in military technology—as a driver of newer concepts in military doctrine and strategy, refashioning organisational structures and re-envisage human resource policies. This is the central theme of this chapter, based upon the underlying analysis of the likely adversarial behaviour, and the typology of wars that would ensue. It centres on the utility of information, information warfare, and information in war; the operational framework and battlefield geometry by which military forces are employed; and posits, that a new conceptual construct is required to improve contemporary and more importantly future warfare.

THE PROSPECTIVE GEO-STRATEGIC CONTEXT

Consideration of the prospective geo-strategic environment is imperative in contemplation of the futuristic armed forces, its strategy for mid and long term and the national, joint and services organisational structures.

India currently is placed in adversarial strategic environment, which mandates a strong and effective military force to ensure the territorial integrity and sovereignty and address internal turmoil. India aspires to become a five trillion dollar economy in five years or so, with which will also come in extra-territorial responsibilities, which too necessitates that she will have to quickly build up and consolidate military strength and choose options wisely in order to play the key role of regional balancer and stabiliser marking out its geostrategic perimeter. Undeniably, India will be a leading power in the foreseeable future. However, India is a nation that has unsettled borders, and is also incessantly deployed in countering infiltration and terrorism, and left wing extremism. The context of change hence has to perforce visionary and far-reaching implications.

China and Pakistan—Future Adversaries?

China has nearly reached the pinnacle as a global power with global aspirations, and desires to re-obtain its primacy of previous times. Indeed, China is spreading its wings. Contemplating China's future course is 'an exercise in frustration.'[1] With a pending intransigent boundary dispute, it is mandatory to explore how the relationship with China will unfold. Indeed with a focus on 2050, becoming a Responsible Great Power is imperative for the nation. In President Xi Jinping's Report to the Party Congress in 2017, China as a 'strong power' or 'great power' was repeated twenty-six times. A key statement in the Nineteenth Party Congress was that 'China will continue to play the role of a responsible power'.. Would the responsible great power imply that the boundary dispute or any perceived geo-political challenge that a rising India may project, would be a thing of the past?

Chinese military strategy documents highlight the direction for a People's Liberation Army's (PLA) capability to win wars, deter potential adversaries, and secure Chinese national interests. There is a stress on the importance of the maritime and information domains, offensive air operations, long-distance mobility operations, and space and cyber operations. Informatisation has pre-eminence in PLA's conceptual premise. In a well-planned manner, China is transiting from restructuring, exercising, deadly long range nuclear missiles and expanding its blue-water navy, to potent space and cyber warfare-capabilities. The proposed 64 billion dollar China-Pakistan Economic Corridor and the expanding Belt and Road Initiative clearly exhibits China's ambitious outlook. China will have a modern military capable of modern war in near future. India can ill-afford to ignore China's increasing economic and military might, its assiduous strategic bases in Indian Ocean Rim Nations, lack of progress in the Sino-Indian border talks, and close economic and military affiliations with Pakistan. China might prefer to seem a status quo responsible power that supports largely the ongoing world order. However, it is portraying revisionism to promote and shape an environment favourable to its ambitions. With increasing comprehensive national power and global presence, stronger possibility exists of a threat to India manifesting from China in mid and long term. We have misunderstood China in the past and there is a danger that we continue to misunderstand China in the future if we don't comprehend the underpinnings of Chinese behaviour today.[2]

For Pakistan, a nation having taken birth without a clear identity, and with its inability to create and nurture one subsequently, maintaining integrity itself is an onerous task. Pakistan suffers from crisis of identity, and an omnipresent threat of Balkanisation. Its internal financial state is precarious, and is under immense pressure from the FATF and the Bretton Woods Institutions. Animosity with India and Islam lends Pakistan credence of identity, which is its bedrock to retaining itself as a nation-state. It also allows the Pakistan Army its continual position of eminence in the society. The geo-strategic location of the nation, grave asymmetries in development among the provinces and the extraordinary role that Army has played, compounds the anxieties on the state of Pakistan presently and in the future. Its current poor economic state and attempts to seek soft loans adds fuel to fire. Pakistan, defines its security in tangible terms—as military capability to thwart a military threat from India. The twin pillars of the India-centric security perception are building national military capability with the objective of challenging India's military might and providing for an effective defence, and searching for military-oriented alignments, which can assist primarily in dealing with New Delhi.[3] It is also obvious to any discerning analyst, that any comprehensive strategic transition to a more benign thinking in Pakistan in the foreseeable future is unlikely and would keep India embroiled in combating an intransigent Pakistan Army on the Line of Control, the International Border, and in proxy war in the hinterland. This kind of hybrid war will give Pakistan distinct advantages. It will remain a low-cost option, and ties down the rise of India's rise as a major power.

Pakistan's intransigence to support terrorist organisations and proxy war in J&K is hence well evident. In matters of China-Pakistan collusion, Pakistan has already upgraded its security calculus with China through the China-Pakistan Economic Corridor (CPEC), a 15-year plan starting 2015, that is to be completed by 2030. The collusive nuclear warhead-ballistic missile-military hardware nexus between China and Pakistan, described by both as an 'all-weather friendship', has grown to menacing proportions. Pakistan has long been a difficult and disruptive neighbour to Afghanistan, hoping to limit India's influence there, and cultivating radical groups within Afghanistan as proxies. It has augmented Afghanistan's instability by providing intelligence, weapons, and protection to the Afghan Taliban and the Haqqani network.[4] It is obvious that the anti-Indian-ness will remain the DNA of the Pakistan Army—which virtually controls the polity of the nation, is unlikely to be done away with, in the foreseeable future.

With collusive support from China, Pakistan is also a testing ground for Chinese latest technology, in the next conflict or even in peacetime. It would employ a combination of different types of warfare, conventional, insurgent, terrorist, Information Warfare (IW)—a concoction of military and non-military, kinetic and non-kinetic. Hence any great socio-political change in Pakistan that would lead to attitudinal change with India may not happen without attendant internal upheaval and instability; it would remain elusive. Pakistan therefore will remain an adversary in perpetuity, as can be gleaned from analysis, and hence does require hard power considerations.

Maritime Frontier

Indian Ocean's major sea lines of communication connect West Asia with Europe, East Asia, Africa and the Americas. More than 80 per cent of world's sea-borne oil trade transits through Indian Ocean (40 per cent through Strait of Hormuuz; 35 per cent through Strait of Malacca to the West Coast of USA, SE Asia nations, Japan, China, Australia) making it a lifeline of international trade and economy. It also has the world's industrial hub to its east in Asia, while to its west lies world's largest concentration of oil reserves (80 per cent) within the Persian Gulf region. China's rise and increasing assertiveness is correspondingly enhancing its power, resource, and market access. Construction of strategic infrastructure assets in the IOR by China from where it can access resupply and general refit for its naval patrol vessels within the IOR; port facilities in Gwadar (Pakistan), Hambantota (Sri Lanka), Chittagong (Bangladesh) and Kyaukphyu (Myanmar), as well as increasing Chinese maritime ties with Maldives, Seychelles and Mauritius, all point towards Chinese intent at projecting power as it seeks to protect its maritime interests, and has thus created a contiguous naval profile through the IOR. It is also reported that China is persuading Thailand to build the Kra Isthmus Canal as a solution to the Malacca dilemma. China has modernised its Navy, thus expanding its blue-water navy capabilities to the IOR. Of the China's military modernisation, it has been stated that the goal is to provide China with the ability to fight high-intensity short duration 'informationized' regional wars with an emphasis on 'maritime military struggle', which means the ability to fight 'in a complex electromagnetic environment' at greater distances from the mainland than the PLA has planned in the past.[5] All these activities are portent of a heightened maritime arms race within the IOR and beyond. India continues to be the dominant naval power in the Indian Ocean Region, with vast responsibilities due to the extensive maritime trade, the island territories, vast coastline and geo-political ambitions.

Insurgencies and Terrorism

Indian Armed Forces have been and will remain to be committed extensively in internal security, in combating terrorism and insurgencies. It is true that Indian security forces are much stronger than the irregulars in combat. The armed forces have advantages in numbers, equipment, training and discipline. However the terrorists and insurgents, some of the global variety like the ISIS, wage an asymmetric warfare that favours them. However, it can well be foreseen that future is of Hybrid warfare that will be a combination of asymmetric, regular or conventional, irregular and terrorism as tactics. Hybrid warfare blurs the distinction between war and peace. Hence in Indian context, future of land warfare seeks readiness to face a focused threat posed by military forces below or above the threshold of open warfare and nonmilitary means across the full range of the threat spectrum.

In sum, hence one can call geo-strategic environment of the future as it pertains to India, is not a gloomy picture, with the nation destined to achieve greater heights. However, geo-strategic concerns and anxieties remain, and have to be planned for. "In theory, foreign policy determines military strategy...Reality is rarely so simple."[6] Foreign and Security Strategy will be the offshoot of all-encompassing National Security Strategy. To be prepared for eventualities, it is understandable that future war fighting will be a national endeavour. Land warfare strategy is therefore but one (though major) component of the national power, as Future Wars will be largely Information Age wars. Formal declaration of war in future will be meaningless—we might as well be in the throes of an undeclared war—with resort to plausible deniability!

TECHNOLOGY—THE DRIVER OF FUTURE WARFARE AND MILITARY STRATEGIES

Warfare has always remained evolutionary. If ever there was a time to get serious about the ongoing revolution in military affairs, it is now. Technology is placing warfare on a decisive threshold to transit into new modernity, and to forecast new war-fighting strategies. In future wars, machines will make life-and-death engagement decisions, even without reliance on human interface. Top Militaries around the world are sprinting to have robotic vehicles, mostly armed, and many autonomous, in maritime, aerial or land warfare. Added to it is the rise of artificial intelligence (AI), which is called the "next industrial revolution."

The truth is the ongoing revolution in military technology demands a revolution in strategic thinking. Future battlefields will be brutal upon forces arrayed of the very large, expensive and heavily manned systems variety, when swarms of intelligent, autonomous and near incognito machines will provide devastating effects of greater enormity than witnessed ever before. Artificial intelligence and other emerging technologies will change the way war is fought. With the plethora of sensors of a very wide variety functional in the world, and increasingly increasing in coverage and intensity, warfare will get progressively difficult. Success in future warfare will require a different kind of military, one built around large numbers of small, inexpensive, expendable, and highly autonomous systems.

This great transition in warfare can be ascribed to the newer technologies of the Information age. For decades, there has been a race to newer technologies. Today this race for these newer technologies has become a sprint, and this sprint of technologies has been trending decisively in favour of incognito offence. In land warfare in future, especially in plains and deserts, large manoeuvre by ponderous formations and deep thrusts will be rendered difficult, in an era of hybrid warfare that includes militias, guerrillas, terror groups, precision projectiles and information warfare. To envision the necessities to revamp the armed forces, it is imperative to focus on most significant aspects of the technological transition, largely as they relate to the northern neighbour.

Information Warfare (IW), Artificial Intelligence (AI) and Cyber Warfare

Information warfare constitutes the foundation of the People's Liberation Army's (PLA) doctrine of winning wars what it calls "informationized wars." Information warfare "relies upon networked information systems and informationized weapons, fighting on air, land, sea, space, and in the electromagnetic spectrum." The underlying philosophy at the core of the concept is that of Observe, Orient, Decide and Act (OODA) cycle, that describes the stages involved in initiating any military manoeuvre at all levels of warfare (tactical, operational and strategic). The OODA loop is meant to achieve higher operational tempo in an event of war by synergising engagement among multiple nodes of operations into a collective effort and direct them toward a common goal. In this context, advances in computing speeds and capacity will greatly affect the OODA loop. Today the role of technology is changing from supporting to fully participating with humans in each step of the process. In 2047 technology will be able to reduce the time to complete the OODA loop to micro or nanoseconds. Air Force strategist John Boyd, originator of the OODA loop, described the objective: 'Collapse adversary's system into confusion and disorder by causing him to over and under react to activity that appears simultaneously menacing as well as ambiguous, chaotic, or misleading'.[7]

AI can take many forms, but it essentially comprises algorithms capable of processing and learning from vast amounts of data and then taking decisions autonomously or semi-autonomously. AI is used in many weapons systems, in the tangible world as well as in cyber space. Cyber warriors use AI to process large volumes of data to help detect attacks against critical infrastructures. By 2025, soldiers would interpret information faster and more quickly recognise threats like a vehicle-borne improvised explosive device, or potential danger zones from aerial war zone images. Artificial intelligence and machine learning make decisions about what to attack, who to attack, when to attack. In their cyber war against the West, some foreign powers have been using artificial-intelligence-based applications to sow discord, spread disinformation, polarise society, attack critical infrastructure, including health systems, smart grids and nuclear power plants, and generally disrupt society, especially in NATO countries. Some foreign powers use AI in the automated reconnaissance of foreign networks, extraction of actionable intelligence, and subversion of adversaries' decision-making processes. The rapid advances in AI has enmeshed with cyber security, with the former being used to break through traditional cyber security systems.[8] In field of Artificial Intelligence China is at a par with the United States.

The People's Liberation Army Strategic Support Force (SSF) was established in December 2015, responsible for cyberspace and electronic warfare vital to its capabilities to win wars. The SSF integrates the PLA's information warfare capabilities, enabling the coordinated pursuit of electronic countermeasures, cyber operations, and psychological warfare missions. The C4I2SR capabilities enable the PLA to effectively conduct joint operations and successfully prosecute "system vs. system" warfare, which it characterises as essential to winning modern wars. China is attempting to utilise AI to direct high technology weapons capabilities, especially in cyber and EW domains, and leveraging Big Data and Machine Learning for 'cognitive EW'. The latter provides the ability to aircraft and other weapon systems to enter the war zone, fathom the electronic threats and develop and employ countermeasures.

The oncoming fifth generation (5G) of mobile technologies will increase the speed of data transfer and improve bandwidth over existing fourth generation (4G) technologies, in turn enabling new military and commercial applications. China and the Chinese firm Huawei is in the forefront of this revolution. 5G technologies are expected to support interconnected or autonomous devices, such as smart homes, self-driving vehicles, precision agriculture systems, industrial machinery, and advanced robotics. 5G technologies have potential military applications for autonomous vehicles, command, control, communications and computers (C4), information, intelligence, surveillance and reconnaissance (I2SR) systems—which would each benefit from improved data rates and lower latency (time delay). While each of these applications could increase military effectiveness, there are concerns over data security, particularly passing sensitive information like intelligence or operational requirements over commercial systems.[9] It is of interest to note that China is ahead of the United States in the field of 5G networks.

Lethal Autonomous Weapon Systems (LAWS)

A serious oncoming trend is LAWS which are weapon systems that "once activated, can *select and engage* targets without further human intervention". As an example Russian base and Russian Naval CSS point in the city of Tartus in Syria successfully warded off a terrorist attack with massed application of Ten assault drones unmanned aerial vehicles (UAVs) in the night of 5th–6th January, 2018. The reality is that drone swarms represent a large step, toward a future in which conflict and violence, which will be available to established armies or terrorists alike. Similar attack took place on Saudi oil facilities on September 14, 2019. The much publicised Swarm tactics are still at a nascent stage, but in time will become a major force multiplier. These weapons will be able to search for, decide to engage, and engage targets on their own and no human can intervene. The more that militaries rely on the electromagnetic spectrum for communications and sensing targets, the more vital it will be to win the invisible electronic war of jamming, spoofing, and deception fought through the electromagnetic spectrum.

Russell (Dr Stuart Russell is a pioneering researcher in Artificial Intelligence) described these lethal drones used en masse as a kind of "weapon of mass destruction. You can make small, lethal quadcopters an inch in diameter and pack several million of them into a truck and launch them with relatively simple software and they don't have to be particularly effective. If 25 percent of them reach a target, that's plenty." Used in this way, even small autonomous weapons could devastate a population.[10] AI can be used for offensive and defensive purposes; it can take many forms, but essentially AI comprises algorithms capable of processing and learning from vast amounts of data and then taking decisions autonomously or semi-autonomously. In 2025, AI would be used in many weapons systems, in the tangible world as well as in cyberspace. Tactical battle space development—AI is used in autonomous vehicles in reconnaissance and offensive and defensive roles, e.g., killer vehicles, access denial systems like smart mines or automated systems that respond to attack.[11]

In 2017, China announced its plans to become the world leader in Artificial Intelligence (AI) by 2030. As US and China compete to innovate in this domain, the relative trajectories of their advances will have an impact on future military balance. The People's Liberation Army (PLA) is benefiting in a big way due to scientific advances in China. The military dimension of China's rise in AI has remained opaque. The PLA intends to take full advantage of this technological upsurge. The Centre for New American Security (CNAS) has released a report which claims that China is challenging the US and will have world's best armed forces before 2049.[12]

Precision Projectiles and Hypersonic Weapons

China is focusing on the delivery of precision strike munitions via individual projectiles (such as cruise and ballistic missiles) rather than the platform-based strike forces (such as aircraft, ships, and submarines). Growing in size throughout this transformation, the Chinese missile force now consists of about 100,000 personnel. PLA Rocket Force doctrine calls for a range of deterrence, compellence, and coercive operations. The missions of a conventional missile strike campaign could include "launching firepower strikes against important targets in the enemy's campaign and strategic deep areas." Potential targets of such strikes would include command centres, communication hubs, radar stations, guided missile locations, air force and naval facilities, transport and logistical facilities, fuel depots, electrical power centres, and aircraft carrier strike groups. In all, Chinese military writings on conventional missile campaigns stress the importance of surprise and suggest a preference for pre-emptive strikes." Pre-emptive missile strikes to initiate active hostilities could be consistent with China's claimed overall military strategy of "active defense, rendering the equivalent of a 'strategic first shot' ".[13]

China currently fields about 1,200 conventionally armed short-range ballistic missiles (SRBMs, 300-1000 km range), 200 to 300 conventional medium-range ballistic missiles (MRBMs, 1000 to 3000 km), an indeterminate number of conventional intermediate-range ballistic missiles (IRBMs, 3000-5,500 km), and 200-300 ground launched cruise missiles (GLCMs, 1500+ km). An initial wave of ballistic missiles would neutralise air defences and command centres also crater the runways of military air bases, trapping aircraft on the ground. These initial paralysing ballistic missile salvos could then be followed by waves of cruise missiles and aircraft targeting hardened aircraft shelters, aircraft parked in the open, and fuel handling and maintenance facilities. Flechette submunitions likely would be used against missile launchers, parked aircraft, fuel tanks, vehicles, air defence weapons, and ships in port. Penetrating munitions would be used against airfield runways, aircraft shelters, and semi-underground fuel tanks. China's military is developing powerful lasers and electromagnetic rail guns for use in a future "light war" involving space-based attacks on satellites. [14]

Space Wars

Satellites have been called "infrastructure of infrastructure," enabling our television, internet, telecommunications, energy, trade, and financial networks to function. Every nation's satellites face increasing threats, starting with killer debris in the vast supersonic junkyards circling the earth. Satellites are also vulnerable to a wide array of intentional threats, such as killer satellites. Other nations have learned how to attack the global commons of space. "New threats to commercial and military uses of space are emerging, while increasing digital connectivity of all aspects of life, business, government, and military creates significant vulnerabilities. During conflict, attacks against our critical defence, government, and economic infrastructure must be anticipated."[15]

In 2017, it was estimated that China spent almost $11 billion on space, across its civil and military programs. China's has a burgeoning space program, including developing space launch vehicles, satellites, and related items. Military space activities are run through the People's Liberation Army (PLA). China has proven its kinetic physical counter space capabilities several times with a range of direct-ascent ASAT systems and conventional midcourse missile interceptors that could potentially be used as an ASAT. In a conflict, China also could be capable of striking an adversary's satellite ground stations with ballistic missiles, cruise missiles, or long-range strike aircraft. China can also pose a threat to space systems through its ability to attack the ground stations that control them with conventional forces. China's military is developing powerful lasers and electromagnetic rail guns for use in a future "light war" involving space-based attacks on satellites.

In 2018, the US Director of National Intelligence stated that China is making advances in directed-energy technology that can "blind or damage sensitive space-based optical sensors, such as those used for remote sensing or missile defense. In 2019, there was a similar claim, stating "China is pursuing laser weapons to disrupt, degrade, or damage satellites and their sensors and possibly already has a limited capability to employ laser systems against satellite sensors." Moreover, Chinese military and technical writings often refer to directed energy as a key technology in a successful counter space strategy. In June 2018, the South China Morning Post reported that China had made significant progress on ionospheric radar, located on the island of Hainan. Such radar could disrupt signals from satellites, cutting off communications or access to satellite networks for those operating in the area. China has highly advanced cyber capabilities, a majority of which are run by the SSF in conjunction with its counter space operations. Chinese hacks against secure government networks to steal personal information and technical data are well known, but the country's efforts to attack and infiltrate space systems have received relatively less attention. Additionally, recent activities demonstrate that China is proliferating its electronic and cyber capabilities.[16]

In sum, China's leader Xi Jinping says his "Chinese Dream" includes a "dream of strong armed forces". Organisational reforms may be less eye-catching than missiles that fly at Mach 5, unmanned cargo planes and electronically powered superguns.[17] Mr Xi's principal aim is to increase "jointness" ... (which) refers to ability of different services—army, navy and air force—to cooperate on the battlefield quickly and seamlessly.[18] Modern precision munitions, niche technological solutions, and first-echelon forces will indeed result in lethality unseen on the battlefield in decades and projected in today's news reports and defence papers. The mode of utilisation of the modern technologies and weaponry in future warfare is still in too nascent as stage to predict or envision. Suffice it to say that war prosecution conventionally across borders, with attrition or decimation of force or capture of disputed territories, may be overtaken by the revolution in military technologies underway. It is obvious that the heady concoction of IW, AI, cyber and electronic warfare and LAWS, can be devastating, without placing military forces in harm's way.

THE ARMED FORCES AT CROSSROADS AND VISION FORWARD

Military historians have penned elaborate treatises analyzing last wars. Military History abounds with carefully planned campaigns having gone awry—like the Maginot Line of 1939, or the Operation Barbarossa of 1941. Historically a large number of military strategies failed on the altar of actual wars. The upgrades in the military strategy and technology (especially in artificial intelligence, robotics and the like)—in our neighbourhood, are happening in leaps and bounds that would make military history provide poor lessons. As argued earlier, transformation of threats—from conventional to non-conventional, diffusion of power—

from state to Non-State Actors; shifting demographics, public attitudes and perceptions; rapid advances in technology and a fluctuating global economy are some of the contours of the future security environment. It is therefore axiomatic to assert that the 21st century security environment will be defined by uncertainty. These factors will directly and indirectly affect the resourcing, structuring and decision-making in both, the internal and external strategic security environment.

Indian Armed Forces are at serious crossroads, indeed, have remained at the threshold of many a decade of delayed transformation! It isn't that the Armed forces have not carefully planned war-fighting strategy—though it has been largely internal bereft of focused guidance or with knowledge of the polity. The war-fighting strategy, which excessively relies on strategy of the past, and not of the oncoming information warfare—hybrid warfare, may not be able to demonstrate intellectual curiosity, a willingness to adapt, freedom to experiment, or a culture ready for innovation that is imperative for the future.

The Inevitability of Change

The envisaged geo-strategic environment exhibits volatility, complexity and challenges of ambiguity, where conventional will co-exist with non-conventional, State and Non-State adversaries will act as one. Assuredly there will be intense demographic pressures, driven by aspirations of better standards of living. The effect of the sprint in military technologies and the collusive nature of the neighbourhood adversaries will compel India to adopt asymmetrical methods. In future conflicts, the adversaries will increasingly gain access to multi-domains of warfare. It is likely that the adversaries will offset our dominance in one domain by aggressively pushing in a domain that we have weakness in. This has become a feature of Chinese military strategy, which seeks to prevent its adversaries from achieving a dominant advantage in space, IW, AI, air, sea, and cyber operations. Next War will be a competition, one between adversaries, a contest of action and counteraction that concludes or changes based on the agency of competitors, and this competition unfolds in the domains accessible to each competitor: land, sea, air, space, and cyberspace. Dominating in war is not about dominating a domain. It is about dominating an enemy.

Futurists of warfare suffer from the same failures of imagination that frequently shackle their brethren in other professions: They over emphasise present trends and assume that their society's cultural norms will similarly bind adversaries.[19] Indeed the next fog of war may be so intense, that its sheer complexity might overwhelm, in case the operational premise is based upon fighting the last war, even if with some spick and span. It needs to be considered that a complex interaction between our perceptions of our neighbours beyond the border as well as the larger superpowers and their perceptions and assessment of our situation and our objectives. It is within this matrix of relationship that the specific goals of our military strategy will get structured. As time would pass, there will be obvious changes in infrastructure, terrain and weather—all of which will have material effect on warfare. It must hence be fathomed that current military planners and strategists face the Herculean challenge of envisioning a war or typology of a war which might be around the corner or may be many, many decades away, and adversaries that could be the same or much, much different!

While some military reformers and theorists continue to propose ways of war predicated on dominance of particular domains, most modern military thinking envisions future operations that are inherently joint. That remains a singularly most important shortfall in the Indian Armed Forces, and needs addressal in all gusto. Jointness will focus on the challenge of employing the armed forces in environments where operations are contested in multiple domains.

The failure to acknowledge that the uncertain future and security environment may indeed lead to misguided innovations. The organisation by virtue of its table-top and ground exercises (with limited equipment) of the Blitzkrieg kind, might be leading to a false bravado or over-confidence. Similar impudence might emanate from the excessive reliance on linear defences. The accelerating speed of technological development is profoundly changing the nature of warfare. The Army needs major innovations in inculcating military technology—as a driver of newer concepts in military doctrine and strategy. Or conversely the doctrine and military strategy precedes the plans for seeking select military technology. Either way, change in the armed forces is an inevitability, better still before the next war.

The Approach

Military-technological competition is inevitable. Uncertainty and unpredictability of the future wars apart, the selection of technologies must be to defend and to nullify to credible extent the adversaries' onslaught, and to be offensive enough to contribute to a convincing semblance of victory. Indeed, the costs of acquiring technologies in the wish list is astronomical. The speed at which the technologies become obsolescent and the budget available to plan these acquisitions are also significant issues. Many of these technologies—both for offence and defence, need induction in field units and formations, and most are for back-end military technical warriors. Intakes of such technologies have a material effect on doctrines and strategy, organisational structures, conduct of operations and training. The decision on intake of these technologies is critical to prepare for a futuristic war—mindful of the timeframe it entails. There is no doubt that there are powerful technologies—and ingenious applications of them in the physical and informational space—that portend changes to the future of conflict. In our neighbourhood the emerging technologies relative to fresh non-kinetic domains—cyber, information warfare and autonomous systems, dictate serious contemplation. Such non-kinetic means act as force multipliers to target the will of the nation by coercive shaping an adverse environment in the adversary's favour, leading to softening through exploitation of existing fissures and fault lines. However, it must be acknowledged that non-kinetic measures by themselves are not the ultimate recipe for victory. These are force multipliers, the effect of which would vary from target-to-target, and ultimate victory may require a mix of both kinetic and non-kinetic means.[20]

Indian Armed Forces culture which is excessively traditional and orthodox is adversative to strategic or operational innovation. Traditional organisation like the Army, are themselves silo-ed in distinct verticals that contest significant reforms, which invariably get jettisoned to bask in the warmth of status quo, or allow some isolated reforms. A successful Army innovation and transformation will be disruptive and turbulent, yet in finality create a capability based force. In this context, innovation would be germane to creating new ideas and knowledge base. Disruptive innovation would be one that radically changes the way in which the armed forces would operate. To succeed in the transformation, the armed forces will have to adopt to commercial/ civilian innovation models, like AI and predictive analytics.

Stephen Rosen, in *Winning the Next War,* offered a bottom-up framework for understanding military innovation based on intra-service competition and showed that higher levels of competition within service branches stimulate innovation. However, in own armed forces peacetime innovation would have to be top-down through intellectual, doctrinal, strategic and structural changes in response to their changing perception of the international security environment, inevitably of course with push and concurrence of civilian leadership. Understandably, hence this innovation and transition will be a slow process that would require clear plan, with detailed pathways for preparing the adaptation to the next era armed forces.

Preparing for a transition that might take a decade or so is an onerous responsibility, as it would necessitate resilience to withstand temporary setbacks and changes. It all would commence with a well-conceptualised vision, distilled from a basket of disparate ideas and imagination, articulated with a large-picture orientation of an immediate, mid-term and distant future. THE VISION should comprehensively summarise the strategic objectives and intentions. Further it must be conceptual in accepting the complexity of the future, yet encompass the acquisition of military-technologies that are a MUST to combat a technological war and the structures imperative to achieve the vision. The potency of the enunciated vision should be potent enough to stir imagination to build consensus internally and create imperatives to shape the political environment by effective communication. Creating the VISION itself will be an intensive process that would require a broad based intellectual debate, where points of view are impressed upon and substantiated or negated, reasoned and conclusions drawn there upon. In fact strategic leadership systemic is a void in the organisation—relying largely on on-the-job learning in a highly careerist environment. With the fluidity of environment a steady repertoire of visionary strategic leadership—irrespective of rank hierarchy or of uniformed/academic nature, is an imperative for the Armed Forces. It would be pertinent to note that the United States relied on John Boyd, Andy Marshall and numerous middle ranking officers to create this vision.

The ideal course hence would be initiating processes for evolving the VISION through the challenges of ambiguity, navigating through this challenge by drawing on the examples of the leading global powers assuming that those are the state of the art strategies, and extrapolate to own realities. The two imperative baskets of future military strategy and future military technology should then be followed by restructuring to implement the two, and not vice versa. The current strategies are outliving their utility, in an era where nuclear weapons are spoken off casually as weapons by the Western adversary; where the definition of war itself is contentious—with no-contact, proxy, undeclared, hybrid, being all typologies are war; and where regimes have changed or critically undermined elsewhere by information warfare alone in its manifestations.

Preparing for such a future, invariably will cause internal turbulence and instability especially in human-resource and career management policies and will settle down over a period of time. As military operations will become more complex with the rise in the number and variety of options available to commanders, future warriors must contend with computers and satellites in addition to bayonets and bullets, and to work with civilian warriors. The expansion of military activity beyond the air, sea, and land domains to space and cyberspace has broadened the community of war fighters to include computer scientists and astrophysicists.

The prospective wars in Indian subcontinent—whenever prosecuted, will be in multiple domains, some evident currently, and many off the horizon, under development or under wraps. These wars may or may not territorially relate and may emanate from geo-political rivalries; though territorial linkages may apparently exist, to obfuscate appreciation of intent. These may be wholly non-kinetic in nature, in modern warfare domains of information warfare, space and cyber space and electronic spectrum that may cripple critical infrastructure. Or in the fields of precision weaponry—ground or air delivered and autonomous systems that may be aimed to incapacitate critical and defensive infrastructure and forces. The likelihood of conventional force-on-force kinetic warfare would exist in parallel or even tangentially, and must require simultaneous catering for. And to top it, sub-conventional warfare has the permanence of threat, especially from the Western adversary. Whether these have independent disaggregated capabilities to seal a war to a belligerent adversary's favour and achieve political ends, cannot be fathomed. Hence an admixture of one or all—kinetic and non-kinetic—has the likelihood of manifesting itself, to assure of an end state that suffices for political success, and hence to be planned for. This would take time but definitely take place in the medium and long term.

Conclusion

In sum, there are momentous changes afoot in the realms of warfare. The warfare of the future may well target civilian infrastructure by even non-kinetic means, with the adversary relying on plausible deniability. The nation will demand reprisals, without even clarity on the adversary having employed covert non-kinetic means. Traditional domains of force-on-force would co-exist, and yet may have reduced salience. Technology like cyberspace has expanded the domain of warfare to arena unheard of a couple of decades or so earlier. Similar expansion of information warfare, precision weaponry and autonomous systems and many more will continue to expand to newer vistas. Indeed the Northern neighbour refers to information domination, 'winning informationised local war' and application of information technology in all aspects of war and defining military doctrine in terms of technology. It is obvious that the measure of victory in future wars will be successful paralysis over destruction! In the case of northern adversary, for political reasons, there is no aversion on undertaking 'strategic initiative', implying initiation of war.

The Indian Armed Forces are one of the most significant custodians of national security. However in crystallising thoughts and plans on future wars, time may not be on our side and India might already be the testing ground for military technologies, without even appreciating it. Indian Armed Forces in concert with the elements of national power need to work to eliminate the strategic and operational uncertainty, and step on the pedal. If the oncoming era is of back-end warfare—combat by programming computers, launching missiles or operating drone swarms ensconced thousands of miles away, in safe environments, then so be it! Assuredly, warfare has a future, the all-important question is the typology of warfare, and what it would take to accept it as inevitable, and assiduously work to acquire the capabilities. The Strategic conclusion is that technology has fundamentally transformed the character of war, and maybe its nature too, in a significant measure! Wars in the future may be without extreme violence, aggression, destruction, and mortality, and yet cause enough suffering to achieve political success. Threat of violent hostilities, however, may coexist.

Sir John Chipman heading the IISS had once famously stated that "...the world in the 20th Century lived tactically but in the 21st Century the world will have to live strategically". Obviously then, this 21st century security visualisation and technological environment is leading to the challenge of devising optimal strategies, to crafting visions, to assist in translating own 'audacious dreams and ideas' into reality.

> *"Inevitably, senior leaders, even the most effective, build a picture of what they think future war will look like and then confront combat realities that differ substantially from their assumptions."*
>
> **– Williamson Murray**

NOTES

1 Harvey Nelson, "The Future of Chinese State", in The Modern Chinese State (ed.) David Shambaugh (Cambridge, UK: Cambridge University Press, 2000), p. 216.

2 Harsh Pant, The China Challenge, in Harsh Pant Ed, China Ascendant Its Rise and Implications, Harper Collins Publishers, Noida, 2019, p. 5.

3 Ayesha Siddiqa, "Pakistan's Security Perspective: Problems of Linearity", in PR Kumarswamy, (ed.) Security Beyond Survival (Sage Publications, New Delhi, 2003), p. 169.

4 Vanda Felbab-Brown, Why Pakistan supports terrorist groups, and why the US finds it so hard to induce change January 5, 2018 accessed at https://www.brookings.edu/blog/order-from-chaos/2018/01/05/why-pakistan-supports-terrorist-groups-and-why-the-us-finds-it-so-hard-to-induce-change

5 Manoj Joshi, China's Military Modernisation and Its Implications, in Harsh Pant Ed, China Ascendant Its Rise and Implications, Harper Collins Publishers, Noida, 2019, p. 18.

6 Richard K Betts, Soldiers, Statesmen and Cold War Crises, Harvard University Press, 1997.

7 Paul Scharre, Army of None, Autonomous Weapons and the Future of War, WW Norton & Company, New York, 2018, p. 23.

8 Debasis Dash, Autonomy and Artificial Intelligence: The Future Ingredient of Area Denial Strategy in Land Warfare, Centre for Land Warfare Studies, New Delhi, 2018.

9 Maj Gen PK Mallick, 5G, Huawei and India, Vivekananda International Foundation, New Delhi, 2019, July 201.

10 Paul Scharre, Army of None, Autonomous Weapons and the Future of War, WW Norton & Company, New York, 2018, p. 70.

11 Paul Scharre, Army of None, Autonomous Weapons and the Future of War, WW Norton & Company, New York, 2018.

12 The Big Story: Artificial intelligence and PLA, The Takshashila PLA Insight, Issue No 7, June 14, 2019.

13 Michael S. Chase, PLA Rocket Force Modernisation and China's Military Reforms, Rand Corporation, California USA.

14 Michael S. Chase, PLA Rocket Force Modernisation and China's Military Reforms, Rand Corporation, California USA.

15 National Defense Strategy, United States Department of Defense 2018.

16 Todd Harrison, et al, Space Threat Assessment 2019, Center for Strategic & International Studies, Washington DC, April 2019.

17 China-Army dreamers, The Economist, Vol. 431, No. 9149, London, Jun 29th-Jul 05th, 2019, p. 25.

18 Ibid.

19 Seva Gunitsky, Aftershocks: Great Powers and Domestic Reforms of the Twentieth Century, Princeton University Press, 2017.

20 Prakash Katoch, Countering Pakistan's Belligerence: Non-Kinetic Measures, Scholar Warrior SPRING 2017, p. 11.

12

Logistics in the Future Battlefield

Lieutenant General Balbir Singh Sandhu

"The line between disorder and order lies in logistics..."

– **Sun Tzu**[1]

ABSTRACT

Logistics to support future conflicts in the Indian subcontinent needs to be dynamic, versatile, agile and tailor-made for different types of terrain, nature of operations and the type of formations taking part in the operations. The conflicts will range from insurgency in hinterland or Border States to conventional war with a nuclear backdrop. The future logistics system must be agile to integrate and deploy at short notice independently in a theatre. It must have the physical agility to integrate information and distribution resources besides the material handling assets. The logistic support providers must have the mental agility to forecast and provide round the clock logistic support in a fluid and fast changing operational scenario. Deployment and relocation of logistic echelons must be well thought out, to cope with the fluid operational situation. Relying on archaic procedures, time-consuming and uneconomical processes will surely not be able to deliver results in the future battlefield. India would rely on Integrated Logistics for the future. Ultimately, a system which is lean and based on the concept of 'Sense and Respond' with no duplication and high level of accountability both during peace and war, is the need for the future battlefield in the subcontinent. This chapter analyses these issues in details.

Introduction

It is extremely difficult for a military thinker to predict the contours of future battlefield due to infusion of latest technologies which are developing so fast that an earlier innovation becomes outdated even before its implémentation.[2] Moreover, the spectrum and range of warfare is growing at an unpredictable pace to include both kinetic and non-kinetic elements. In the Asian subcontinent, conflicts range from insurgency to conventional conflicts with a nuclear backdrop. Space is also an emerging area of conflict which cannot be ignored. As an emerging and pivotal power in Asia, India needs a comprehensive national security policy and preparedness to meet the future challenges in an extremely complex and volatile world order.

Logistics is inherent in defence preparedness of a country. It will not be out of place to state that during the period prior to outbreak of hostilities, logistics including infrastructure building, procurement of weapons and equipment play a much more important role than strategy and tactics. The logistics preparedness indicators act as major deterrent during the 'No War' situation whereas Strategy and tactics are key to success on outbreak of hostilities. In case the armed forces of a country are logistically well prepared in terms of equipment capability, serviceability and the levels of ammunition holding, besides the infrastructure to build up the same at a point of decision, it surely deters an adversary from attempting a misadventure especially in our context, where we have unsettled borders with two of our neighbours.

We also need to comprehend that we are up against two nuclear neighbours one of whom is an acknowledged economic giant and an almost emerged military superpower. Unfortunately for India, both Pakistan and China are so-called 'all-weather' friends and it serves their purpose to keep India embroiled in a reactive mode, handling sub-conventional security issues. It is in China's interest that India stays bogged down hyphenated with Pakistan and is unable to take major economic leaps. China does this by hedging Pakistan against India who is ever ready to oblige using its specialisation in sub conventional warfare. In return, China provides military, diplomatic and to an extent economic support to Pakistan. To counter this security environment, India must utilise all the elements at its disposal be it economic, diplomatic or strategic to safeguard her core values and sustain itself as an important player in the region.

Despite induction of high-tech weapon systems, our logistics and supply chain is structured to meet the requirements of basic weapon systems and equipment. The irony is that we cannot afford to ignore the basic supply chain requirements as they exist today, yet innovate to support the futuristic equipment. High tech equipment deployed in the field areas will need repair and maintenance support. This would require improvement of local resources and infrastructure which needs immediate attention. Some of our operational areas do not have basic facilities such as power and roads. We use generator sets for power which are big emitters of thermal and electronic signatures inviting enemy's precision strikes. There is a need for transformation and not just upgradation of logistics infrastructure and processes. To address these basic issues, there is a requirement for investment of time and funds. Such ventures need prompt decision making, availability of adequate funds and prompt implementation. We need to confess that delays are big stumbling blocks in achievement of such goals. There are endless committee reports, seminars briefs and parliamentary panel reports outlining what we need to do, but delayed decision making, lack of communication and coordination amongst various sections/departments of the state act as big impediments.

The standard supply chain of the armed forces must be commended for its reliability during the past wars since independence, yet, it is a known fact that the system, processes and the procedures are based on what we inherited at the time of independence from the colonial rulers. The system for sure has stood the test of time, hence need not be thrown out of the window but we need to realise that the British Army from whom the supply chain system was inherited, has transformed its systems and come a long way to make their supply chain in synchronisation, with present day realities. This chapter will look at the challenges that the current logistics system faces keeping in mind the emerging and the future battlefield scenario as also recommend the way forward.

Challenges

Tardy Procurement Processes. The period immediately after independence, due to hyper nationalism that existed at that time, defence procurement was extremely important, where actions of the then governments in respect of defence procurement were never questioned by the political opposition or the media probably due to blind faith and lack of information. With the dawn of an era information explosion and hyperactive media, a lot of details started coming out in public domain due to which people have started seeing 'Red' in every defence deal. As a result, the pendulum swung to the other extreme resulting in delays.

Defence Procurement Procedure (DPP) and Defence Procurement Manual (DPM) have resulted in minimising discretion and ensuring transparency to a great extent in capital and revenue procurement, however no manual can cover all contingencies so the spirit, trust and responsibility with which it is interpreted holds the key to successful procurement of critical weapons and equipment for the armed forces.

Lack of Accountability. Armed forces are the instrument of national power tasked to deliver the political objective. On the other hand the other agencies are not held accountable for delays which affect procurement. There is a need to expedite the entire process.

Multiple Logistics Services. At the Army Headquarters there are four directorates which look after logistics. Besides the policy being formulated by Directorate General of Operational Logistics (DGOL), procurement and maintenance involves Deputy Chief of Army Staff (P&S), Master General of Ordnance (MGO), Quarter Master General (QMG) and various directorates. Within each directorate, there is duplication. Spare parts for the vehicles are procured both by the Electronic and Mechanical Engineers (EME) as well as the Army Ordnance Corps (AOC). Similarly, a proposal regarding construction of a building goes to more than one branch of Army Headquarters. There is an urgent need to merge some directorates and prevent duplication and ultimately reach a single point logistics concept.

Changing Equipment Profile. Some of the modern weapon systems need storage in temperature controlled environment and similar conditions for their transportation for them to be effective in the battlefield. The terrain in the Indian context is so varied that there are areas with temperatures as high as 49 degrees centigrade in the deserts and sub-zero in the high-altitude areas. Storage and transportation of the modern weapon systems will need specialisation in terms of physical infrastructure and trained manpower for maintenance of such assets. Repair of such equipment in a field area will be another challenge especially on outbreak of hostilities when we can ill afford long down time. Such infrastructure and facilities will need heavy investments and that too for multiple contingencies. On the other hand, there may be non-kinetic weapon systems which will operate from areas located towards rear of the combat zone, thereby making logistic support much easier. A realistic and innovative approach to equipment maintenance is needed.

Synergy with Operational Plans. With high-intensity day and night operations, fluidity and flexibility of operations will be even more pronounced involving much larger distances in shorter time frame. To support such operations logistically would need extra redundancy, contingency stocking to cater for multiple options and much faster means to build up stocks in the thick of battle. Realism in operational training backed by actual logistic activities specially those related to drawl of ammunition during peace time will go a long way in ensuring success during actual operations. A realistic visualisation of the magnitude of logistic support that will be required for implementation of an operational plan needs to be logically calculated. Velocity will need to replace mass.

Supply Chain Procedures. Our reliance on age-old procedures of demand, processing at various levels and ultimate rejection or materialisation has taken a heavy toll of logistics efficiency. Use of technology in the logistics in the corporate sector has currently overshadowed the importance of transportation. Reliable and timely transportation is taken for granted. The clients currently demand real time tracking of the consignment and its likely time of delivery or the vacant space available in the warehouse where a consignment will be stored before retail despatch. As a result, it is often discussed whether logistics is a Transportation or Technology industry. Unfortunately, Armed Forces especially the Army has been reluctant in adopting technology for efficient functioning of its supply chain and logistics. One of the main reasons for slow absorption of technology is the need for security clearance. It has been observed that the Army generally wants the whole supply chain operation to ride over the army intranet whereas there is a need to provide interconnectivity between the vendors and the army units to ensure seamless interoperability resulting in efficiency. Software and equipment planned to be used for some of the army projects becomes obsolete before the project is finally launched, such is the pace of evolution of technology for which the government procurement procedures have no provisions to incorporate.

Integrating civil and military expenses. Maintaining standing armed forces is an extremely expensive proposition for any country. At the same time, to safeguard sovereignty and territorial integrity of a country, defence expenditure is the annual insurance instalment a country must pay. Consequently, there is a need to economise expenditure incurred on maintaining and equipping armed forces so that more funds are available for development related projects. Therefore, projects with strategic and development dividends need to be integrated from the inception stage at the highest level to serve the ends of national security. Competition with adversaries militarily without economic backing has proved to be disastrous in the case of erstwhile USSR. China has learnt her lessons right in which they advocate that all strategic projects must incorporate economic aspects and vice versa. Development of elaborate connectivity projects in Tibet Autonomous Region (TAR), be it aviation, railways or highways are touted as major tourism projects, whereas they serve the purpose of mobilisation and build-up of armed forces in Tibet as well. This is an apt example of synergising economy with strategy. Similarly, within the three armed forces, there are very elaborate logistic institutions which have been duplicated by each service and procedures which are at variance with each other including the documentation and the forms used for various processes. It is essential that the three services must have a common communication platform so that there is regular consultation and interaction. Integrations of logistics between the three services will for sure go a long way in cost savings through optimisation, avoid duplication and build foundation for joint manship.

Economy versus Assurance. It would always be desirable to achieve highest levels of economy because availability of resources for such expenditure are generally scarce. In the corporate world, concepts such as Third- or Fourth-party logistics are in vogue to cut costs and minimise inventory. Logistics are totally outsourced to a third party thereby leaving the concerned industry to concentrate all efforts on the core business. In fact, with introduction of GST the concept of warehousing has undergone a sea change. With latest technology to track consignments and minimum time taken to travel by the load carrying vehicles, the time duration for which stores are held in a warehouse has been minimised. These concepts lead to 'just in time' logistics which minimise warehousing and take risk in delivery due to reliable tracking technology and efficient transportation. By adopting these processes, it is aimed to achieve economy thus increasing the profit margins for the core business as also give a boost to specialisation in the logistics industry. Such concepts cannot be adopted across the board for the armed forces; however, a review can be done of the stock levels maintained at each echelon.

Stocking. Levels of stocks to be held at each level must be stipulated based on a detailed study of the terrain and the prevalent communications network in that theatre thereby calculating the lead time. Ultimately, there is a need to maintain highest levels of assurance at the tactical and operational levels. We may consider adopting a modified version of 'Distribution Based Logistics' in our Western Theatre which has been discussed subsequently. Another issue which merits attention is outsourcing. With industrial development, the armed forces must not perform non-core functions to achieve cost cutting and manpower optimisation which can be redeployed on combat duties. However, there is a need to be a judicious mix of outsourcing and in house support so that efficiency, reliability and security in the combat zone are not compromised.

Distribution Based Logistics (DBL) in the Future Battle Space

Concept of DBL was applied for logistics support during the Operation Iraqi Freedom (OIF) in which limited stocks were held at the theatre level to cater for periodic replenishment and minor disruptions.[3] Main stocks were held at Intermediate Support Base (ISB) in Kuwait. Reliance was on better communications systems to replenish the forward troops. A study carried out by Rand Corporation, post the war received mixed response from the field formations in which while some items like fuel were very well supplied but troops faced critical situations in respect of chilled water and spare parts for the equipment which had adverse effect on morale. In view of improved communications network on our Western front, such a concept with suitable modifications can be examined to be adopted. In fact, Modified Logistics Support System (MLSS)[4] currently in vogue at some formations where all links in the chain of maintenance are not being used is an apt innovation to adopt a tailor-made logistics system and shun the standard layout of the supply chain. Any system needs to evolve with time by infusing technology so that it is efficient and responsive. However, it needs to be kept in mind that no concept should be adopted blindly because an advanced army like the USA found it suitable because Indian Armed Forces operate in a challenging environment which no other western army operates in.

Future Battle Space. The requirements of logistics support ahead of the Corps Maintenance Area have changed dramatically. With large number of formations committed in Counter Insurgency Operations, the standard routine maintenance from a brigade logistic node is complex. There is a need to commit increased quantum of troops on protection duties for collection of meagre quantities of daily maintenance store in case we plan to follow the standard supply chain. Accordingly, the need for forward delivery by the vendors in small quantities is inescapable. This results in sacrificing economy of scales. On the other hand, logistics for deserts, plains, riverine terrain, mountains and high-altitude areas have totally diverse requirements which need different organisations, processes and equipment to meet the logistics challenges. Indian Army has introduced latest items of food stuff, including frozen foods and long shelf life dehydrated and tinned products which need suitable storage and handling parameters. Similarly, equipment in the forward areas now includes tanks and other heavy machinery which probably cannot be so easily evacuated and would need in situ repair. This will change standard repair and recovery chain. Evacuation of causalities will require much quicker response though there are likely to be more specialised immediate care available in the forward areas.

The future battlefield will have surveillance system which can look deep inside and locate logistic installations. Standard concept of camouflage and concealment may no longer be effective. There will be long range precision weapon systems which can target these installations probably at the commencement of hostilities making the entire logistic system dysfunctional. It was experienced during the Kargil conflict that the ammunition dump and the other operational logistics installation were the first to be targeted. Threat to lines of communication from irregulars and Fedayeen kind of attacks is a reality which will be a big challenge. Earlier, such threats to the axis of maintenance was visualised primarily during mobile offensive operations. In the security situation prevailing in the subcontinent with transnational reach of insurgent groups, the threat to lines of communication even in the hinterland is a possibility. Therefore, a much better coordination between the armed forces and civil administration will be a necessity and continuous assessment by the intelligence agencies of such a threat both during peace and war is a must. Logistic installations may become the centre of gravity of the enemy in order to incapacitate launch of major offensive operations by a stronger adversary.

One aspect which invariably is taken for granted is space. This can be critical especially for the offensive formations which must be prepared for multiple options till the last moment. Any advance planning or coordination can lead to compromising the offensive plans. Therefore, a logistic grid which has the capacity to accommodate logistic elements of the strike formations in addition to the pivot formation elements must be established for sustained operations. A balance between the concept of 'hook on' and integral elements to provide intimate logistic support must be ensured. Army must barter unused land chunks for substantial land banks keeping in mind the likely operational options where infrastructure can be created to be useful during the operations.

Besides the logistics and maintenance challenges emanating from the battlefield environment, an active media looking for stories may be a big challenge especially when handling sensitive issues like causalities evacuation or move forward of material. While there will be a concrete media policy in place and access to operational areas will be regulated, logistic echelons are more likely to be accessible to the media. An awareness and education of the personnel involved in logistics will go a long way in preventing an embarrassment to the armed forces because any lapse would make an interesting story in the present era of an overcrowded media community who are guided more by sensationalism than a spirit of responsible nationalism.

Way Ahead

Logistics to support future conflicts in the subcontinent need to be dynamic, versatile, agile and tailor made for different types of terrain, nature of operations and the type of formations taking part in the operations. The conflicts will range from insurgency in hinterland or Border States to conventional war with a nuclear backdrop. The future logistics system must be agile to integrate and deploy at short notice independently in a theatre. It must have the physical agility to integrate information and distribution resources besides the material handling assets. The logistic support providers must have the mental agility to forecast and provide round the clock logistic support in a fluid and fast changing operational scenario. Deployment and relocation of logistic echelons must be well thought out, to cope with the fluid operational situation. Relying on archaic procedures and time-consuming as also uneconomical processes will surely not be able to deliver results in the future battlefield. Broad contours of future logistics are appended in the succeeding paragraphs.

Apex Level Organisation. In order to expedite decisions related to procurement of weapon and equipment, there is an urgent need to have an organisation which is accountable to both the services and the national leadership. To enable this organisation to perform this task, it must include all elements which are involved in functions related to procurement of equipment and stores for the armed forces. Further, the person heading this organisation must be one who can understand the pain of being ill equipped. It would be appropriate to nominate a senior military dignitary with DRDO, DGQA, OFB and other DPSUs being part of this organisation and accountable to the head of this set up. He should be directly accountable to the Raksha Mantri. This is important because a person who has been at the receiving end of this process will be best suited to make this organisation function. We need to adopt a similar system to make our logistics efficient and effective. It is recommended to set up Defence Logistics Agency (DLA) and an Army Logistics Corps (ALC).

The Defence Logistics Agency in coordination with the National Security Council should lay down the policies for encouraging defence industry within the national industrial policy. It should also synergise development of strategic infrastructure and logistics industry policies which facilitate mobilisation of military and national resources during conflict. DLA must have close coordination with newly set up Department of Logistics in the Ministry of Commerce. This will ensure seamless integration of military with the national logistics grid which will not only result in better defence preparedness but also industrialisation and job creation.

Organisational Changes. Based on the proposed establishment of DLA and the ALC, corresponding organisations at formation level moving towards single point logistics support and accountability should be established. As a start, merger of services with duplication of tasks must be achieved. Echelons of maintenance must be reduced where infrastructure is well developed, and response time is less. Reorientation of organisation to merge outsourced services with the integral structures in the combat zone will need to be factored in.

Indigenisation and Make in India. The following aspects need to be emphasised:

- **Self-Reliance**. To meet India's aspirations of becoming an important strategic player regionally if not globally, there is a need to give a major push to indigenisation through initiatives such as

'Make in India'. Having missed the industrial revolution, India needs to work in a smart manner towards transfer of technology and standardisation so that there is long term strategic capability building. A culture of encouraging self-reliance and indigenisation amongst all stakeholders needs to be embedded from the beginning so that we have a long-term cohesive policy formulation and implementation across all sections of the security apparatus. Defence technology related disciplines should be introduced in IITs and other leading technology universities to give research and development in defence industry the required importance and momentum. A culture of exercising economy and encouraging indigenisation must be inculcated even amongst the defence services officers so that the temptation to import is discouraged which will help the country becomes self-reliant in defence production in the long run.

- **Innovation**. Innovation in defence industry can always be dual use, thereby making our country a developed industrial nation and a self-reliant military power as well. Armed forces took the lead for several inventions in some Western countries which were later made available to civil industry of those countries thus economising and synergising evolution of a nation as a developed country. Export of defence equipment must to be encouraged so that industry can produce the required quantities in a sustained manner to make it economically viable. Private industry must be incentivised by reducing duties on raw material required for defence industry and helped even in reverse engineering existing products through product improvement route. There should be incentive for efficiency both in innovation and defence production by providing a level playing field to both public and private sector. Emphasis must be on output especially for research and development as well as production than just creating unwieldy, inefficient public sector structures. A time has come to dispassionately hold these organisations accountable.
- **Strategic Infrastructure**. Another idea of synergising national security and economy can be by creation of strategic infrastructure to include construction of elaborate highways along which smart cities are constructed along the border. This alignment must include parallel railway lines and airports at important places

along the way and ports or water ways where feasible. Implementation of such projects would be much easier, due to minimum land acquisition problems. These smart cities should have self-contained education cum industrial hubs oriented to defence production which will not only facilitate defence production but also kick start the economy in those remote areas, generate jobs and prevent migration of population to existing metros. Several logistic functions can be outsourced in such an environment since infrastructure has been created to meet the strategic and commercial needs. Locals must be encouraged to have stakes in such centres. One issue that will need attention is to integrate the necessary security aspect to prevent potential sabotage, etc., which can be easily, handled using technology.

- **Transportation**. A National Transport Company which can transport both commercial containers as also military tanks when required can be designed to operate along these highways. This will not only give a major boost to speed of mobilisation but will be economical to transport cargo to the ports on our West coast. Such an asset adds to the defence preparedness and acts as a deterrent when an adversary evaluates our capabilities. At the same time, it reduces the need for standing units of tank transporters. This will need Over Dimensional Clearance (ODC) since the width of such trailers will be more than normally permitted for commercial trailers. We can plan to operate them only along the Western highways connecting Jammu with Kutch fitted with GPS so that the vehicles can be located when required for the Army. This highway can be created/upgraded to such dimensions which facilitate movement of ODC trailers with ease. This can surely be a game changer for speeding up mobilisation as also kick starting economic activity in the border areas in J&K, Punjab, Haryana, Rajasthan and Gujarat.

Integration of Logistics. This is essential for the future to ensure optimised use of logistics. Details are elucidated below:

- **At the National Level**. In order to achieve economy and optimise meagre resources available to any country, it is best to optimally utilise the dual use assets and infrastructure to get the best output for the national security. We need institutionalised interaction between the National Security Council (NSC) and the proposed

DLA at the national level which can coordinate the strategic and development needs and prioritise them in an optimal manner. Military logistics must take full advantage of the national logistics grid which should be aligned to strategic needs to the extent possible. A well-developed defence industry both public and private must be integrated into the military logistics system for economy and quicker response.

- **Services**. There is a crying need to achieve integration of inter-service communication and logistics assets to avoid duplication and achieve economy. This would entail central control of logistics planning, standardised procedures, equipment and nomenclatures. The documentation related to basic functions such as demand and issue need to be standardised as a first step. There should be combined provisioning liability to achieve economy of scales; however, there must be a caution not to make the process too time consuming and bureaucratic thus affecting efficiency. Integration must not be confused with over centralisation. Integration must result in savings without compromising efficiency and quality of service. Integration within the Army to avoid two arms or services doing the same job needs to be addressed. To avoid duplication and achieve optimisation there have been proposals in the past at the highest level to merge ASC, RVC and Mil Farms as also AOC and EME. Such proposals must be revisited with urgency, decisions taken quickly and implemented with urgency so that precious national resources are optimally utilised.
- **Army Logistics Corps**. It is recommended to establish an Army Logistics Corps which should accept logistics appointments including PSOs at the service headquarters thus infusing specialisation and a degree of continuity. Cadre management and related issues can be resolved by appropriate branches.[5]
- **Outsourcing.** At a time when industry was not well developed, there was a need to have in-house facilities for the military so that the troops were not deprived of basic amenities at any stage during peace or war. Over the years, civil industry has grown exponentially in respect of items required for day to day consumption by the population which can be utilised for the defence forces as well there by relieving the combatants for other

operational duties. Automobile industry in India is very well developed and yet PSUs such as Vehicle Factory Jabalpur are involved in manufacturing vehicles. Established motor vehicle companies who have an elaborate distribution and service network must be contracted to deliver vehicles directly to the field formations and the Original Equipment Manufacturer (OEM) should at least provide spares for the vehicles if not comprehensive repair cover in military workshops supervised by the EME personnel. The original contract should also include disposal of condemned vehicles. This will free a lot of manpower and resources by shortening the supply chain and warehousing which are currently employed for this purpose. Similarly, reserves of common dual use inventory like vehicles can be held by the trade under their arrangement dispersed in the designated areas instead of the military vehicle depots. The warranty of the vehicle must commence from the day it is issued to a unit by the distributor of the OEM. Cost of back loading and disposal of condemned vehicles is at times more than what it is auctioned for. An arrangement with the OEM for in situ disposal of condemned vehicles must be provisioned for in the original contract which will streamline the supply chain and warehousing in a major way. Further Army needs to outsource procurement of equines from the civil industry so that massive resources involved in breeding and raring of these animals are made available for other operational tasks. Catering services in peace establishments need to be outsourced and so should bulk of transportation needs except sensitive cargo such as ammunition in the combat zone. Medical facilities for both serving and veterans can be optimised to facilitate better medical facilities and treatment in the border areas. Such facilities, incase integrated will not only facilitate forward treatment of casualties during war but provide state of the art medical treatment to citizens of the border areas. Private investment in such infrastructure must be encouraged.

Reserves. Level of reserves to be held in the base installations and in the Combat Zone need to be reviewed periodically to minimise wastage and dead inventory. The quantum and echelons must be 'need based' and tailor made for each theatre and equipment to ensure preparedness as also facilitate turnover especially of ammunition. Inventory of non-warlike stores must be trimmed, and procurement decentralised to avoid cost of warehousing and transportation. Similarly, establishment of industry related to food items of the army must be encouraged in the forward areas to reduce lead time in procurement and movement of these stores and reduce their levels of reserves. To counter the long-range precision weapons the reserves will need to be held dispersed and if possible, in a composite manner.

Adoption of Best Practices and Technology. Armed forces must adopt software and systems which help asset visibility and consignment tracking. Upgradation to the latest technology must be inbuilt in the contract or alternate provision made so that the projects do not become redundant and outdated even before implementation. We have attempted to develop these systems for each service within the army and haven't had any tangible success primarily due to hurdles of security clearances and technology getting outdated before being adopted at the formation level. We need to balance the security and efficiency needs, to put in place an efficient automated logistics system.

Operational Research. It is recommended to adopt Operational Research techniques, mathematical and statistical methods to arrive at requirements, most economical methods of warehousing and movement of logistics requirement for our operational formations especially those in the pivot role. By utilising techniques such as transportation model, most economical method of moving logistics requirements to multiple destinations can be arrived at. Since the requirement of most defensive formations is predictable, forecasting is much easier and resultantly execution of the logistics will be smooth and economical using the transportation model. The equipment must be maintained on life cycle concept to achieve specialisation, economy and efficiency.

Artificial Intelligence technologies can understand reason, learn and interact and do so at a very fast speed and scale. Since these systems continue to learn from the available data and processes, they become much more efficient and effective. Other technologies such as Internet of things and Three Dimension Printing will change the way logistic support is provided. It will usher in economy and efficiency localising manufacturing thus shortening the supply chain to a great extent. The manpower saved as a result of infusion of technology can be re-deployed for providing better services or for operational tasks. Employment of drones for delivery of critical stores especially across the valleys in mountainous terrain can be a force multiplier at critical stage of the battle.

Operational Logistics in the Combat Zone. Issues which merit importance are elucidated below:

- While the logistics system in the hinterland needs to work on the concept of economy of scales, the Operational logistics in the combat zone must provide highest assurance levels in terms of punctuality of delivery and the quantities even if it is sometimes uneconomical, hence the concept of 'Just in case' against the 'Just in time' for central procurement. However, with economic development even in the forward areas outsourcing in terms of civil hired transport and other services must be enhanced. Stocks need to be held dispersed due to long-range precision weapons and ammunition must be stored in tunnels or underground stores depending on the terrain.
- Fuel, oil and lubricants must be stored in dispersed tankages for which a lot of work has already been undertaken. Feasibility of a fuel pipeline for both civil and military purposes must be explored where feasible. Availability of fuel from the trade operated outlets even in operational areas as a backup must be catered for. Loads must be standardised in containers nationwide including the armed forces so that mechanical handling is facilitated to undertake logistic operations at a faster pace thus minimising employment of manpower. There is a requirement to develop foodstuff which is lighter in weight to facilitate carriage and has higher calorific value to give troops longer self-containment capability to undertake special operations.
- Repair of vehicles by the OEM as far forward as possible under the supervision of EME personnel will enhance efficiency and reduce downtime. Vehicles and equipment provided by the OEM must be maintained based on 'life cycle concept' using management techniques such as operational research to calculate requirement of spares for lifetime of the vehicle or the equipment. Civil medical facilities available in the forward areas must be surveyed and integrated with the military medical infrastructure so that they are optimally utilised during the operations. Treatment of causalities well forward is now possible because of better infrastructure. Hospitals both military and civil must be

equipped and prepared to perform urgent treatment including surgeries to ensure proper and timely treatment of casualties.

- A concerted effort must be put in to conserve the environment in the sensitive Himalayas and other glaciated regions which is being adversely affected due to increased human and vehicular / machine presence. Danger in future may be more from environmental disasters than enemy action. One way to give impetus to local economy would be to make it part of the military economy. The civil administration must encourage production of such agricultural and industrial products which can be utilised by the armed forces, so that not only are the requirements of the armed forces met in a shorter time frame, but such actions help the local economy in a big way.

Disaster Management. With climate change now being a reality, the incidence of disasters is likely to be more frequent than in the past. The Armed Forces are likely to be called in aid to civil authorities for which they need to be prepared. There will be added requirement of transport to move relief supplies as also need to utilise specialist equipment for immediate relief of people from a catastrophe be it floods or an earthquake. An integrated logistics support in synchronisation with the civil administration will ensure quicker and appropriate response during an unfortunate disaster situation.

Conclusion

Logistics for the future battlefield in the Indian subcontinent needs to evolve to match the fast-changing operational landscape. While the emphasis will be on protection from ambush of daily administrative convoys in an insurgency area, the need to carry sophisticated missiles in a temperature-controlled logistics vehicle will be the requirement in a conventional conflict. Switching forces within the theatre and inter theatre will be decided probably by the logistics ability to execute it in the desired time frame. This will need all means and modes of transport in a very quick time frame and recycled at even faster pace to meet the operational needs. This will have to be a national effort because no economy can afford such dedicated resources for their armed forces.

Logistics structures and processes will need to undergo transformation and not an incremental change as has been happening over the years without much outcome. A transformed logistics organisation both at the national and military level will facilitate adoption of focussed logistics system reducing the multi-echelon supply chain to need based tailor made system. While at the national level a mass-based approach to achieve economy may be viable but in the combat zone, the system must be lean and velocity based. Ultimately, a system which is lean and based on the concept of 'Sense and Respond' with no duplication and high level of accountability both during peace and war, is the need for the future battlefield in the subcontinent. The road map for the same has also been laid out in various studies over the years. Above recommendations sincerely implemented will go a long way in ensuring a versatile, agile and responsive logistics system to meet the challenges of future battlefield in the Indian subcontinent.

"Behind every great leader there was an even greater logistician."

– M. Cox[6]

NOTES

1 Sun Tzu, "The Art of Logistics", www.sun tzu on logistics. Accessed on August 24, 2019.

2 Adrian Willings," 28 incredible futuristic weapons and modern vehicles", www.pocket-lint.com, June 17, 2019. Accessed on August 24, 2019.

3 Col C Brandon Cholek and Chief Warrant Officer Matthew A Anderson, "Distribution Based Logistics in Operation Iraqi Freedom", Army Logistician, www.alu.army.mil, March-April 2007. Accessed on August 25, 2019.

4 Henry Kenyon, "Army readies major overhaul of logistics support", September 22, 2011, www.gcn.com. Accessed on August 25, 2019.

5 Colonel Sushil Chander, "Seminar Report, Revolution in Military Logistics", CLAWS, New Delhi, 17-18 March 2018, www.claws.in. Accessed on August 25, 2019.

6 "M Cox Logistics Quotes", www.mcoxlogisticsquotes Accessed on August 25, 2019.

Epilogue

Lieutenant General (Dr.) V K Ahluwalia and
Major General (Dr.) P K Chakravorty

"The character of war in the 21st century has changed, and if we fail to keep pace with the speed of war, we will lose the ability to compete."

– Gen. Joe Dunford, 19th Chairman of the US Joint Chiefs of Staff, 2017 [1]

Introduction

In a seminar held recently, the Chief of Army Staff of the Indian Army stated that, "Major Armed Forces must be prepared for future warfare with the changed characteristics as future wars would be more violent and unpredictable". He emphasised that despite this change, the soldiers would remain the primary assets. He also said one of the key battle zones would be the Information Domain with the constant battle of these narratives attempting to share perceptions across the World. Cyberspace was likely to be fiercely contested with threats of cyber-attacks on critical infrastructure. Further, conventional conflicts were likely to have large asymmetric components as technologies become the key drivers of the future wars. The contents of the book lucidly bring out these issues.

Michael E. O'Hanlon in his book, *The Future of Landwarfare*, unequivocally brings out the importance of ground operations and their importance. In his book he focuses on South Asia and the India–Pakistan scenario where a conventional war is possible and could be escalated to the nuclear level. He does mention the Kargil conflict and how nuclear restraint was observed and issues were settled at the conventional level.[2]

Need For Air Power and Maritime Power

In future conflicts would be short, intense, non linear, multi dimensional and hybrid. They would straddle land, sea, air, space , cyber and information domains. There would be need for integration and Jointness at all levels while undertaking operations on Land. Air power has a significant role to play in the land battle . First and foremost is surveillance, reconnaissance and selection of targets from the Air and Outer Space. The next is the destruction or degradation of these targets including Post Strike Damage Assessment. Finally protect Ground Forces from enemy aircraft , Unmanned Combat Aerial Vehicles and Missiles. Accordingly Air power would play an important role in future land operations.

Maritime forces are important in Out Of Area Contingency tasks as also undertaking operations to defend our own islands. India has 1195 islands and there is a need for integration and Jointness between the three services to protect these islands.

Navies have the capability of transporting troops, equipment and providing naval gun fire on targets. Navies today have the capability of firing missiles, launching aircraft and drones from War ships for land operations. They also assist in combine Operations like Operation Kayla Mueller launched by Team Delta of United States Central Command. Apart from Team Delta, there were CH 47 Chinook helicopters, fighters and naval ships with their electronics and fire support. The joint operation led to the elimination of leader of ISIS Abu Bakr Baghdadi on 27 October 2019. Accordingly Air and Maritime Forces have an important role in the future of Land Warfare.

Issues that Merit Importance

Despite geographical, historical, cultural, ethnic and linguistic linkages and similarities, South Asia is one of the most violent and unstable regions of the world. It is beset with interstate disputes, and, more importantly, intrastate conflicts are predominant due to a host of factors. India has unsettled territorial disputes with two of its neighbours—Pakistan and China. Most of our earlier wars/conflicts were fought in the disputed territorial areas.

The book visualises three types of wars to be fought in future. These are Overt, Covert and Outsourced. As days progress, all three would gain prominence due to conflicts moving to the Gray Zone and Hybrid Arena – these are discussed briefly as they would also have an impact on the land warfare. These two terms have been added to the glossary of terms of International Relations (IR) in the recent past. Hybrid warfare, also known as ambiguous warfare or fifth generation warfare is a blend of regular and irregular warfare. It is a blend of economy, military, information, psychology and cyber, with a view to achieve political objectives, and to achieve economic advantage. Although the Indian sub-continent continues to face sub-conventional war in the form of proxy war, it has not experienced the full dimension of hybrid war so far. Grey zone conflicts are conflicts which oscillate between war and peace and are generally waged by nations, who do not want to cross the threshold of an outright war to prevent large-scale casualties, collateral damage, and catastrophic disaster due to the nuclear threat, and yet aim to achieve their political and territorial objectives.

There could be seven triggers that would possibly initiate the three types of conflicts, discussed above. They would be Economic, Territorial, Nationalism, Religion, Revenge, Civil disturbances and Revolutionary. The point is how we narrow these issues to an Indian perspective. Limited to a 15 years' window, the book highlights the perceivable scenarios/triggers/irritants which may manifest into a conflict in the Indian subcontinent in context of India, focusing primarily on China and Pakistan, with some of the possible broad conflict/crisis scenarios in the future being:

(a) Hybrid Conflict and/or conventional war with China in a nuclear backdrop.
(b) Limited or Conventional Conflict with Pakistan with a nuclear overhang.
(c) Assistance to Indian Ocean Littoral States (pre-emptive or on request).
(d) Terrorism/Insurgency oriented threats in Kashmir, North East and the hinterland, aided and abetted by inimical regional player/s.
(e) Internal unrest due to growth of religious fundamentalism, socio and political inequalities and Naxal activities.
(f) Terrorist groups acquiring weapons of mass destruction (WMD).
(g) Population/refugee pressures and its impact on security.
(h) The problem of porous skies and waters.

4th Industrial Revolution (IR) and Technology

The next aspect is technology. The 4th IR is the fourth major industrial revolution that has built itself on 'electronics and IT' of the third revolution.

It has been built on the fusion of technologies, which has resulted in blurring the lines between the physical, digital and biological spheres, collectively referred to as 'cyber-physical systems'.[3] We must take a note of the new technologies like: internet of things (IoT), cyber security, simulation, lethal autonomous weapon systems (LAWS), artificial intelligence (AI) and big data, augmented reality, cloud computing, addictive manufacturing, 3D printing, etc. These technologies would have a great effect on the emerging security environment and its application on warfare of the future. These technologies would perhaps provide the architectural support for hybrid threats and challenges to security, which should be exploited by us to our advantage in a pro-active manner. In addition, AI, information warfare and cyber threats should form part of the national security strategy, as these are the new weapons of the future.

Technology and modern weapons are force multipliers for enhancing combat potential. The process of Modernisation primarily results in infusion of Technology to Doctrine. An example of this would be the Chinese developing the DF-21 D Anti-Ship Ballistic Missile which has a range of 1800 km and is capable of accurately targeting warships on a Carrier Battle Group. Improvement of capabilities by this method would also enhance Deterrence which is a mind game to avoid conflicts. The future battlefield as discussed will have the following features:

- Practically no warning with periods of high tempo and density.
- Non-linearity of operations. Operations linked to Artificial Intelligence could commence with destruction of Satellites on Outer Space, Cyber Warfare, Operations by Special Forces, covert actions in depth areas followed by multiple intrusions and an offensive in one of the weaker spots of the enemy.
- Combat Zones for land warfare would be deeper and wider. The entire combat zone would be Net Centric and would be to a large extent fed by Autonomous Systems.
- Future warfare would be asymmetric in nature and to a large extent depend on flexibility of mind and equipment to deal with these conditions. Special Forces would play an important role. The killing of ISIS leader Abu Bakr al-Baghdagi by US Central Command Army Rangers and Team Delta in Syria on October 27, 2019 bears testimony to the need for special operations in depth areas.
- Operations in the Indian subcontinent would be against a nuclear backdrop.

It would be interesting to note the critical technologies that would be important for the Indian Army. Development of these would lead to enhanced capabilities of the Indian Army. Critical technologies for futuristic requirement of the land forces which would be needed by the Indian Army are: Nano Technology, Big Data, Quantum Technology, Artificial Intelligence and Robotics, Bio Technology, Micro-Optronics/ Electronics, Cyber and Information Security, Radar and Microwave, Laser and Directed Energy systems, Avionics, Rockets and Missiles, Material Science, Manufacturing and Nuclear.

There is a need to comprehensively look at these technologies to understand their nuances, applicability to the Army and process of indigenisation. Undoubtedly, the future wars would have all these technologies especially Artificial Intelligence and Robotics playing a major role. Surveillance by Satellites, Drones and other resources would enable Real Time Intelligence with a Common Operational Picture. Information Warfare would play a critical role as described by the Chief of the Army Staff during the seminar on 13 April 2019. Houthi Drones have played a major role in destruction of Saudi Arabian oil fields on September 14, 2019 destroying 50 percent of the country's global supply of crude.

Manoeuvre Warfare and Firepower

Linked to Technology is Manoeuvre Warfare and Firepower. History is replete with examples where military commanders have used 'manoeuvre', to move with speed, position their forces at a position of advantage, disrupt and dislocate the enemy, defeat him in detail and /or break his will to fight. Genghis Khan, who lived about 800 years ago, is an acknowledged legend as a practitioner of manoeuvre. More often, his forces were outnumbered by his enemies; he still attained unmatched degree of operational and tactical mobility, to achieve speed, surprise, shock, disruption and dislocation of enemy forces. Manoeuvre Warfare emerged after the Vietnam War and it was conceptually different as one attacked enemy's weakness instead of strength. The martial art of judo is often used to illustrate the theory of manoeuvre. In a judo match, the skilful competitor exploits opportunities presented by the opponent's shift in balance or commitment.[4]

Manoeuvre Warfare intelligently synergises, Sun Tzu's 'Art of War' to Basil Liddell Hart's 'Indirect Approach'. Brigadier Richard Simpkin's book *Race to the Swift* provides a good theoretical analysis of Manoeuvre

Warfare. He analyses the Soviet Deep battle which includes Airborne and Mechanised Forces. Manoeuvre Warfare definitely lays down a technique but has to be applied in conjunction with all elements of Attrition Warfare. Often in areas where there are limited gaps and constraints for space, penetration by forces to create gaps is necessary prior to break out by forces using Manoeuvre Warfare. Accordingly, Manoeuvre Warfare takes into consideration the strengths and weaknesses of the enemy. The United States in the Gulf Wars intelligently applied Manoeuvre Warfare with Colonel Warden's theory of targeting by concentric circles which ensured that the enemy was defeated psychologically. In the future, manoeuvre will be characterised by more simultaneous actions than sequential and widespread over larger areas. Therefore, faster, lighter, and lethal forces with relatively lesser logistics would be more successful.

As we have territorial and boundary disputes with two of our neighbours, there is a great emphasis on not losing even an inch of one's territory. Our doctrine should factor this important aspect in formulating our strategy. The aim should be to have light, agile formations and units, which can operate in joint services environment, and be capable of rapid insertions at short notice. With an agile command and control structure, and quick decision being taken, the force should be capable of delivering a mass effect at the point of decision. Concurrently, the aim of border management strategy should be to effectively maintain the territorial integrity of the borders, and to take care of the multi-faceted threats and challenges along each border. Therefore, effective management of borders assumes huge significance, as it has a direct impact on our national security.

A brief look at the various major armies in the world clearly brings out the strategic importance associated with the Airborne Forces and in the future being considered a force multiplier and an essential component of the Armed Forces. The Airborne Forces are being structurally altered/ modified to generate a faster response and are modernising their equipment to meet the emerging challenges and be prepared to react to future operational requirements. Better and more protected battlefield mobility, stronger maneuverings capability, flatter and more responsive command structures, leveraging technology for achieving better battlefield transparency, command, control and communication and increased use of helicopters are some of the common aspects being implemented for enhancement of the combat potential of the airborne forces. They would be forces who would be assets for reaching objectives in depth and Out of Area Contingencies.

Given the increasing trend of urbanisation, particularly in Asia and Africa in the 21st century, the urban centres are the hub of political, governance, economic, communication, social and cultural importance. While insurgencies continue to sustain in the least developed and developing countries due to several reasons, they are likely to further enhance their spread to urban areas in the future. Therefore, the armed forces should be prepared to fight in the built up areas (BUAs), in a conventional and low intensity conflict (LIC) environment, or in a combination of both in the future.

Next we move on to the field of Logistics to support future conflicts in the subcontinent. It needs to be dynamic, versatile, agile and tailor-made for different types of terrain, nature of operations and the type of formations taking part in the operations. The conflicts will range from insurgency in hinterland or Border States to conventional or a hybrid war with a nuclear backdrop. The future logistics system must be agile to integrate and deploy at short notice independently in a theatre. It must have the physical agility to integrate information and distribution resources besides the material handling assets. The logistic support providers must have the mental agility to forecast and provide round the clock logistic support in a fluid and fast changing operational scenario. Deployment and relocation of logistic echelons must be well thought out to cope with the fluid operational situation.

The frequency and intensity of natural disasters and complex humanitarian-cum-relief related activities on the Indian subcontinent, and beyond, suggests continued predominant role of land forces in the foreseeable future.

Way Ahead For India

The security challenges for India are both External and Internal. India has to strain every sinew to maintain peace and harmony on land. Chanakya stated, "In trans-border relations, there are no permanent friends or permanent enemies or even permanent borders. There are only permanent interests and everything should be done to secure these interests." [5] It takes a lot of pain to stabilise Land Borders.

Considering the global geo-strategic environment and 'the mutually destructive power of nuclear weapons, international legal constraints and the declining appetite for violence of relatively prosperous societies', the probability of all-out wars between the global powers is low.[6] However, the probability of sub-conventional conflicts or limited conflicts in different regions, have the potential to spill over into a major conflict with hybrid contents.

In order to be prepared for the envisaged conflicts, we must improve our Integration and Jointness. Any operation on land will be joint and this becomes more important for the future. In future, the conflicts would be short, intense and multi-domain. There would be a need for joint application of forces in real-time based on intelligence inputs. India must have a real time Command, Control, Communications, Computer, Information, Intelligence, Surveillance and Reconnaissance (C4I2SR) which would lead to optimised use of forces based on Intelligence inputs. Further focus must be on Artificial intelligence, Cyber Warfare and Outer Space, which would directly impact operations on land. The decision to raise Cyber, Space and Special Forces has been a step in the right direction.

The critical issues for the future would be as under:

- Formation of a National Security Strategy. This must be formed and approved by the Cabinet Committee on Security as also reviewed periodically. The next aspect is Hard Power. Success and failure of a nation's foreign policy is largely a function of its power and the manner in which that power is wielded. While India's economic and military capabilities have no doubt increased substantially in recent times, with its GDP being third in the world in Purchasing Power Parity (PPP) and its military the second largest in the world. However, India is yet to master the ability 'to integrate the creation, deployment and use of military instruments in support of national objectives'.
- Military deterrence can only be achieved by improving our military capabilities in both conventional and non-conventional war-fighting mechanisms, soft power and demonstrated power.
- Limited war situation relevant to Pakistan is now equally relevant to China as well. The doctrine must lay down means to inflict max punishment within the domain of limited war which may be limited in dimensions of time-frame, area and damage caused to the military and economic potential of the adversary. The existing escalation ladders in the sub-conventional domain are largely adhoc. There is a definitive need to legislate rungs that will provide just, focused and proportionate response options to various scenarios and place the onus of any further escalation

entirely upon the adversary. These decision matrices must provide the political leadership with clear options to escalate/de-escalate and facilitate assertion of escalation dominance/escalation control.

- Emphasis on increased Indian aerospace power in a manner that provides a visible asymmetric edge over its likely adversaries. Proposal for creation of an Aerospace Command is a step in this direction. Further we must build asymmetric capabilities against China with three broad prongs. First of all would be to leverage existing terrain and trigger an effective insurgency in the areas occupied by Chinese forces. The second prong would be to build our communications on the Chinese Border and the third would be domination of the Indian Ocean and also portions of Western Pacific in conjunction with other countries.
- Both from the threat and capability point of view, we require a force-structure that would not only combat conventional forces with AI, cyber and space-based assets, but also to tackle the intrastate conflicts involving insurgents, terrorists and Violent Non State Actors (VNSAs), whenever required to do so.
- Last of all to be victorious in Land Warfare in the future, we have to keep abreast with the technology and its applications. We need a vibrant and strong economy, robust armed forces, and the Comprehensive National Power of the nation to grow exponentially. India will have many challenges on land in future and tackling these would need skill and dexterity.

NOTES

1 Robert Kozloski, Commentary 'War on the Rocks, The Path To Prototype Warfare', 17 July 2017. Accessed on 31 March 2019, https://warontherocks.com/2017/07/the-path-to-prototype-warfare/

2 Michael E O' Hanlon, "Order from Chaos-The Future of Land Warfare", www.brookings.edu. 31 August 2015. Accessed on August 3, 2019

3 World Economic Forum, Fourth Industrial Revolution, Accessed on September 5, 2019 https://www.weforum.org/focus/fourth-industrial-revolution . Accessed in September 2019.

4 Colonel Pat Stogran, "Manoeuvre Warfare: Using Clever and Unexpected Tactics to Defeat an Enemy by attacking their Weakness", The Arm Chair Colonel, espiritcorps.ca, 09 February 2017

5 Chanakya Quote, "In trans-border relations", Quote fancy, www.quotefancy.com, Accessed on 09 August 2019.

LIST OF CONTRIBUTORS

Lieutenant General (Dr.) VK Ahluwalia, PVSM, AVSM, YSM, VSM (Retd),** superannuated as Army Commander, Central Command in March 2012. Thereafter, he served as a Member, Armed Forces Tribunal (AFT), Jaipur Bench. He has served and commanded his units and formations in high altitude and in intense insurgency and terrorism-affected areas of Jammu and Kashmir, North East India and in the states critically affected by the Maoist insurgency in India. He has authored a book titled *Red Revolution 2020 and beyond*. Presently, he is the Director, CLAWS.

Lieutenant General (Dr.) Rakesh Sharma, PVSM, UYSM, AVSM, VSM (Retd), of 11 GR was superannuated as Adjutant General after forty years. He commanded Fire and Fury Corps in Ladakh responsible for Kargil, Siachen Glacier and Eastern Ladakh. He is currently Distinguished Fellow, CLAWS.

Lieutenant General RC Chadha, PVSM, AVSM, VSM (Retd), was former Director General of Operational Logistics and Strategic Movements and holds MPhil in Defence and Management Studies and Defence and Strategic Studies. He has been actively involved in strategic level planning process and takes interest in international relations and strategic issues.

Lieutenant General Balbir Singh Sandhu (Retd), has held appointments of the Director General of Supplies and Transport (DGST) and DGIT. He has attended NDC, Higher command and DSSC courses and was posted as instructor at NDA and a Directing Staff at DSSC Wellington. He has been Brigadier Administration of Corps, DAQMG of a Rashtriya Rifles Sector and commanded his Battalion deployed in CI ops.

Major General Bhupesh Kumar Jain, VSM (Retd), served in the Indian Army for over 37 years. He spent his initial years in the elite Parachute Regiment which forms a part of the Special Forces. The Veteran Officer has been commenting on national security, international defence relations and military issues, post retirement.

Colonel Rajeev Kapoor, commissioned into the JAK RIF has varied operational experience in CI Ops in J&K as well as in Manipur besides having done a stint with Rashtriya Rifles. The Officer actively participated in 'Op Vijay' and has also been in the UN environment. A regular contributor to CLAWS, he has co-authored a chapter in the book titled "Surprise, Strategy and *Vijay:* 20 Years of Kargil and Beyond", released by the COAS.

Colonel Puneet Doval, SM, has served with the United Nations (UNMEE) and done Courses in Israel and USA. Decorated thrice for Gallantry and once for devotion to duty, he was recently awarded ARTRAC Army Commander's Scholar Warrior Badge. As a Senior Fellow at CLAWS he undertook research on the topic of Flexible Response Options.

Colonel Anuraag Singh Rawat, SM, is currently a Senior Fellow at CLAWS. He is an alumnus of National Defence Academy, Indian Military Academy, Defence Services Staff College, and Wellington and was commissioned into the Mechanised Infantry in 1994.

Colonel Ranjan Prabhu, was commissioned into the Regiment of Artillery. An alumnus of National Defence Academy, Khadakvasla and DIAT, Pune, the officer has tenanted a number of important assignments including that of UN Military Observer in MUNSUCO. After commanding his unit on the Line of Control he is presently serving as Colonel Instructor in School of Artillery Devlali. Recipient of GOC-in-C Commendation for research work, the officer has contributed regularly on topics of concepts and technologies in Artillery publications and CLAWS journals.

Dr. Amrita Jash is a Research Fellow at the Centre for Land Warfare Studies (CLAWS), New Delhi. She has been a Visiting Fellow at the Department of Politics and International Studies, University of Cambridge. She holds a Ph.D. in Chinese Studies from Jawaharlal Nehru University (JNU). Her research interests are China's foreign policy, Chinese military, strategic and security issues.

Ms. Kritika Punia is currently pursuing Masters in History from Delhi University. Her area of interest includes Indian History, specifically Socio-economic History and Subaltern History. She is interested in gaining in-depth field knowledge of how different communities co-exist and how conflict can be managed at the micro level. She is dedicated to work towards inclusion of people living at margins.

Index